The Native Pottery of
Roman Dacia

Mircea Negru

BAR International Series 1097
2003

Published in 2016 by
BAR Publishing, Oxford

BAR International Series 1097

The Native Pottery of Roman Dacia

ISBN 978 1 84171 475 2

© M Negru and the Publisher 2003

Typesetting & layout: Darko Jerko

BAR Publishing is the trading name of British Archaeological Reports (Oxford) Ltd.
British Archaeological Reports was first incorporated in 1974 to publish the BAR
Series, International and British. In 1992 Hadrian Books Ltd became part of the BAR
group. This volume was originally published by Archaeopress in conjunction with
British Archaeological Reports (Oxford) Ltd / Hadrian Books Ltd, the Series principal
publisher, in 2003. This present volume is published by BAR Publishing, 2016.

Printed in England

BAR
PUBLISHING

BAR titles are available from:

BAR Publishing
122 Banbury Rd, Oxford, OX2 7BP, UK
EMAIL   info@barpublishing.com
PHONE   +44 (0)1865 310431
FAX   +44 (0)1865 316916
www.barpublishing.com

To my wife

FOREWORD

The present book is a Doctoral thesis, enriched and improved, undertaken by the author at the Romanian Institute of Thracology, at the end of 1998. The author was mindful of the suggestions of the scientific coordinator, Dr Gheorghe Popilian, those of the Committee formed by Professor Dr Alexandru Suceveanu, Professor Dr Dumitru Protase, Professor Dr Alexandru Barnea, as well as the latest evolutions in the field.

The subject was treated from different standpoints in a series of articles, studies, and sections of monographs. A general, detailed approach was deemed necessary as the discoveries of 'local tradition' pottery increased significantly over recent decades from the former territory of the Dacia province.

The development of this study required the study of archaeological material from several museums, including Muzeul Olteniei, Muzeul Judeţean Olt, Muzeul Oraşului Caracal, Muzeul Judeţean Vâlcea, Muzeul Govora, Muzeul "Ţării Secuilor" - Sfântu Gheorghe, Muzeul Naţional de Istorie a Transilvaniei – Cluj-Napoca and Muzeul Banatului - Timişoara. In these collections I was able to study the local tradition, as well as the provincial hand-made and wheel-made pottery discovered at Locusteni, Soporu de Câmpie, Govora-Sat, Enoşeşti-Acidava, Stolniceni-Buridava, Râşnov, Olteni, Breţcu, Noşlac, Tibiscum, Napoca, Buza, etc.

I would like to take this opportunity of thanking colleagues from these institutions for helping me access the above-mentioned material. Thanks also go to: Dr Florea Costea, Professor Dr Doina Benea, Professor Dr Dumitru Protase, Dr Gheorghe Popilian, Dr Constantin Preda, Dr Sorin Cociş, Dr Ioan Mitrofan, Dr Bartok Botond, Maria Iosifaru, Aurelia Grosu, and Gheorghe Petre-Govora.

I express my special gratitude to Dr Gheorghe Popilian for so willingly granting me access to the archaeological material discovered within the Locusteni cemetery, and for his general support of this monograph.

I am also grateful to Archaeopress for their interest in publishing this book in the BAR series.

The Author

CONTENTS

Chapter I
INTRODUCTION

1. The organization of Dacia province and the question of native pottery

In the summer of 106 AD, a part of Dacia became a Roman province (Macrea 1968, 29; IDR, I, 18). As a result of the 101-102 AD war between the Romans and the Dacians, the southern part of Dacia - including the Banat area and southern Transylvania - had already been annexed to Moesia Inferior (Macrea 1968, 37; Petolescu 1971, 411; Petolescu 1982, 67-68; Petolescu 1985, 45-46). Pressed by Roxolan Sarmatians, at the start of his rule Emperor Hadrianus abandoned Wallachia and southern Moldavia, which belonged to Moesia Inferior (Piso 1973, 1001-1002; Petolescu 1983, 242).

Latest research has raised the idea that Dacia was divided into three provinces (Petolescu 1986a, 159-160) after the Emperor's rule. According to its position in terms of the Danube River, southern Carpathian Dacia (including south-eastern Transylvania) was called Dacia Inferior, while that area of Dacia within the Carpathians Mountains, the regions of Banat and Drobeta, and the southern and central parts of Transylvania all constituted Dacia Superior. Dacia Porolissensis was established in northern Transylvania, and was named after the Roman camp (then Municipium) of Porolissum, which held a special strategic position for the province. The geographical anomalies – such as the fact that Drobeta belonged to Dacia Superior (then Apulensis), and south-eastern Transylvania to Dacia Inferior (then Malvensis) – were due to the strategic importance of the Roman roads that followed the courses of the great rivers.

The administrative organization of the three Dacian provinces probably best solved the problem of the region's security. Later, Dacia Inferior and Dacia Superior were named after their capitals – Malvensis and Apulensis. The northern Dacian province was created especially for the defense of the Someş River valley, considered the most important gateway to the Barbarian world, the North, and to the North-West. Dacia Inferior had a well-defended eastern border (limes Alutanus and limes transalutanus).

Since the 18th century, the problem of the presence of the indigenous population in Dacia has been the subject of intense debate among Austrian, Hungarian and Romanian historians and archaeologists. The obvious political aspect of the problem has had a harmful effect on medium- and long-term scientific research.

This book intends to make an objective analysis of "local tradition" pottery from Dacia province, i.e. only the pottery clearly deriving from the classic Dacian Late Iron Age. I consider the term "local pottery" similar to "local tradition pottery", "native pottery", and "indigenous pottery". Although descendents of the colonists lived in the province at a certain moment, I consider it exaggerated to call them "native" in the sense of a human community while the indigenous people continued to live there. Therefore, the pottery produced by the descendents of the first Roman colonists cannot be considered as "native". It is usually defined as "Roman provincial pottery", "Roman pottery" or "Celtic tradition pottery". At the same time, I consider the fact that in the European specialty literature, the term "native pottery" was only applied to pre-Roman tradition pottery.

I emphasize that this study only concerns pottery; I have little information regarding other fired clay objects (weights of fired clay, etc.).

In the present book I thought it appropriate rigorously to respect the borders of the province and the chronology of the discoveries. Therefore my study does not refer directly to material discovered in the Drajna de Sus Roman camp, Rucăr Castle (for a short time these were inside Moesia Inferior), the Chilia cemetery, or the settlements of Coloneşti-Mărunţei and Scorniceşti No. 2 (they belong to the post-Roman Dacian period).

2. The history of research

2.1. The 17th-19th centuries

The first archaeologist in Romania is considered as being Count Luigi Fernando Marsigli, a friend of Contantin Brâncoveanu, the Prince of Wallachia. Between 1689-1692 he made some archaeological expeditions within and around the Carpathian Mountains. (He later published two accounts of these travels – Marsigli, 1726; Marsigli, 1740). He identified the Roman ruins of Drobeta and also made a topographical map of Reşca-Romula and Jidava.

The first pottery discoveries - considered for a long while as being Dacian - come from the tumbler incineration cemetery at Caşolţ. As a result of excavations undertaken between 1843-1861, Carl Goos considered that there was a Dacian layer from the pre-Roman period, and another from the Roman period; the coin and pottery finds were his proof (Goos 1876, 85). Further investigations showed that the cemetery in fact belonged to a population originating from Noricum and Pannonia (Protase 1980, 45).

Between 1845-1851, several "Celtic urn" fragments associated with imperial Roman coins coming from Hadrianus to Philip Arabs (as well as fragments of terra sigillata) were discovered at Gusterita-Hammerdorf (Kenner 1860, 401; Ackner 1858, 83-85). Carl Goos thought that the discoveries were datable to a pre-Roman period, but that "some of the vessels are similar to those from Caşolţ", and were discovered with Roman lamps and coins issued during the rule of Philip Arabs (Goos 1876, 78). Unfortunately, we have no clear, or more precise, information concerning this question.

Between 1851-1855, Friedrich Müller researched the Roman camp of Sighişoara (Schässburg), where he found a great amount of pottery and coins issued between the times of Marcus Aurelius to Gordianus III (Müller 1857, 194; Müller 1859, 69-74; see and Kenner 1860, 402). The excavator noticed wheel-made vessels and "Dacian dishes discovered in the Roman settlement" (Müller, 1859, 194), from within the archaeological material exhibited at the local Gymnasium. Karl Fabritius asserted that they might have belonged to "the colonists that were, perhaps, mixed among the inhabitants of the Dacian province", considering, at the same, that there was also some pre-Roman archaeological material (Fabritius 1862, 303). The same author mentioned the presence of "rough, hand-made pottery scattered with the wheel-made ware", and attributed to the Celts, who would have been colonized there during the Roman period (Fabritius 1862, 311-312). In turn, Carl Goos noticed the discovery (within the same Roman camp) - of several "rough, hand-made urns filled with earth", dated by coins from the time of the Emperors Traianus, Hadrianus and Antoninus Pius (Goos 1876, 106-107). The research - continued between 1964-1967 - brought to light a pre-Roman Dacian settlement, a Roman camp dating from the 2nd century AD, and a settlement raised over the Roman camp in the 3rd century AD (Lazăr 1995, 235-236).

The research undertaken in 1856 by M. J. Ackner at Şeica Mică (Kleinschelcken) found "Roman stones, bricks and tiles, mortaria, fragments of wheel-made pottery, and hand-made fragments" (Ackner 1857, 95). Carl Goos thought that the strange shape of the settlement showed a Dacian fort, rather than a Roman camp (Goos 1876, 108). Between 1884-1887, twenty-six pits were uncovered which contained Dacian and Roman pottery, bones, and other archaeological material (Protase 1980, 64).

Important contributions to the questions of the continuity of Dacian habitation and the Roman period were made by the research and work of Johann Neigebauer (Neigebaur 1894, 156), Carl Goos (Goos 1876, 64-130), Johann Aschbach (Aschbach 1858, 197-220), Friedrich Müller (Müller 1858, 257-263), Julius Jung (Jung 1894, 156), Cichorius (Cichorius 1896-1900), and others.

Archaeological research outside the Carpathians comprised observations, the collection of archaeological material, and so-called archaeological excavations.

In 1845, August Treboniu Laurian made the first archaeological trips along the Danube, Olt and Jiu Rivers, describing Roman forts and settlements and also several objects he considered important (Laurian 1846, 73-119).

The scholar Cezar Bolliac was remarkably active. He undertook a series of "archaeological travels" following the above-mentioned route. Unlike Laurian, Bolliac dug at nearly all the settlements he visited (1858-1869), using an impressive number of workers - rarely less than 100 and sometimes as many as 200. His inscriptions, fragments of statuettes, metal objects, coins and, exceptionally, complete pottery finds are generally mentioned in terms of his research at Turnu Măgurele, Băneasa, Celei, Reşca, Drobeta, and other sites (Bolliac 1861, 5-80; Bolliac 1869, 11-67). Of special note is his assertion that "Roman and Dacian vestiges" were discovered at Băneasa Castle, i.e. "many iron objects, violet-blue and red pottery fragments, and a few bronze and silver coins from Antoninus Pius to Antoninus Caracalla" (Bolliac 1869, 14). The nature of his information, however, remains questionable.

In spite of great interest in the remains discovered, the removal of antiquities in a rush to provide sensational material for publications such as "The Carpathians Trumpet", the chaotic digging and destruction that went on under Cezar Bolliac's very eyes, all conspired to set Romanian archaeology off on the wrong tack.

The first to notice this was Alexandru Odobescu, who wrote: "A few hours' stroll with a group of hastily-gathered, tip-chasing, hard-drinking men, or some summer's excursion, are not the best ways to explore a hillside and make its findings available to science" (Odobescu 1958, 95).

From Cezar Bolliac's imaginings on the tomb of a woman discovered at Celei, and from an article entitled "Smoking in Prehistoric Times", Alexandru Odobescu asserted that an archaeologist "should think seven times before stating an eccentric opinion" (Odobescu 1958, 115). Odobescu's remarks tempered somewhat Bolliac's zeal and imagination, but prompted Dumitru Tudor to say of him: "He opened the way towards a school of critical archaeology that was to remove the "antiquarian" dilettantism from this field of science" (Tudor 1961, 46).

A further contribution by Alexandru Odobescu was the drafting of a bibliography of Dacia (Odobescu 1872a). The lack of well-trained collaborators made it impossible for him to reach the targets he outlined in the "1872 Archaeological Questionnaire".

The diggings undertaken by Grigore Tocilescu, and then by Pamfil Polonic (in the last decade of the 19th century and the beginning of the 20th) at archaeological sites along the Danube, Olt and Jiu rivers, resulted in numerous finds of bricks, statuettes, coins, pottery fragments, and some complete vessels (G. Tocilescu, P. Polonic, manuscripts nos. 5133, 5134, 5135, 5137 and 5139, The Library of Romanian Academy, Bucharest). The written reports have no drawings, or they have sketches that cannot be used. Relatively correct topographical plans were drawn, but usually the drawn profiles refered only to the elements of Roman entrenchment. A more detailed profile is the one drawn in 1896, at the foot of the Drobeta Bridge (P. Polonic, manuscript no. 5135, 72, The Library of Romanian Academy, Bucharest). In this, one may detect the more systematic style of the architects Johann Fakler and Otto Richter, collaborators of Pamfil Polonic.

It is hard to know whether any Dacian pottery was discovered during these researches as Polonic's weekly or general reports (found in the manuscripts preserved at the Romanian Academy Library) refer mostly to just: "many bricks and pottery fragments".

The serious discrepancy between researches carried out in Transylvania and the area of Romania outside the Carpathians Mountains remains a problem in our understanding of Romanian archaeology at that time.

2.2. Archaeological research during the first half of 20th century

During the 1912 research undertaken at the villa rustica of Mãnerãu-Magyarosd, Arpad Buday discovered a rough-paste, hand-made pottery (Buday 1913, 128, fig. 13:1). Also, at the villa rustica of Cluj (Kistarcsa quarter), another fragment was found, wheel-made and decorated with incised zigzag lines (Buday 1913, 164, fig. 19:1). Both discoveries were made within archaeological complexes dated by coins that were issued from Geta to Elagabalus and Caracalla.

The inter-war period saw the start of systematic research into the indigenous pottery of Roman Dacia. Substantial progress was made (beyond the obvious and, in fact, inherently political real cause that often led to errors, or exaggerations) by highlighting the problem of the persistence of the native population in Roman Dacia, as a series of 19th century discoveries had already suggested.

Systematic archaeological research into the Roman period in Dacia was continued into the early 1930s and increased over the next decade and throughout the Second World War. There was a continual increase in the number of settlements where Dacian pottery was discovered.

According to the information I hold, the first discoveries were the results of the work (1925) of Dorin Popescu at the Lechinţa de Mureş settlement. The excavator noticed that: "Late Iron Age shapes keep repeating during the Roman period" and "Late Iron Age shapes are being transposed in Roman clay". A "small Late Iron Age vessel" was also found (Popescu 1925, 332-333, 344, pl. 15:8).

Unfortunately, the extremely wide dating of the archaeological site - between the 2nd-4th centuries AD - does not allow us to use the published Dacian material in our study on native pottery in Roman Dacia.

Dacian hand-made, or wheel-made, pottery was uncovered by Constantin Daicoviciu (1926-1927) in the Roman camp at Breţcu (Protase 1966, 19-20). Excavations also took place in 1926 on the plateau of Chilia at Vãrãdia; as well as fragments of Roman provincial pottery, sherds of hand-made pottery were also found (Nica 1928, 153). Recent research undertaken by Octavian Bozu in the same area has illustrated the existence of a Roman period building, inside which a "Dacian pot" was found. The vessel was associated with a series of Roman archaeological material, including a coin issued during the rule of the Emperor Traianus (Bozu 1999, 127-128).

Surveys at the Cristeşti settlement (1928) allowed Alexandru Ferenczi to report that: "even at the end of the Roman conquest, the pottery retained - in both technique and ornamentation - its old, local elements" (Ferenczi 1926-1928, 217).

Starting from the great quantity of fine, grey paste wheel-made pottery, present within the research undertaken between 1928-1930 in the Roman camp of Rãcari, Grigore Florescu wondered if "this might be a local tradition" (Florescu 1930, 395; Florescu 1931, 23).

In 1929, in the civilian settlement of the Roman camp of Micia, Constantin Daicoviciu and Ioan Malasz discovered a hand-made pot decorated with an alveolar cordon (Daicoviciu, Malasz 1930-1931, 10, fig. 5).

Consequent to the diggings undertaken (1932) at the Roman camp of Vãrãdia, Grigore Florescu found "local barbarian pottery, the same as the style found at Chilia (the Chilia plateau) in the pre-Roman settlement" (Florescu 1937, 71-72).

South of the Carpathians, in Moesia Inferior, Professor Gheorghe Ştefan discovered a few "hand-made vessel fragments adorned with finger imprinted buttons, cells, and a few black or grey wheel-made pottery fragments", with incised lines decoration, similar to the Late Iron Age. The author of the research also underlined the fact that these vestiges do not form a special level separate from the Roman origin archaeological material (Ştefan 1934-1935, 344).

During excavations undertaken in the Roman camp at Drajna de Sus by the same archaeologist, two hand-made Dacian cups were found, near the western gate, along with Roman-type vessels, in a level dated with coins issued during the reign of the Emperors Traianus and Hadrianus (Ştefan 1945-1947, 133-134, fig. 15:1,2).

During the research of Octavian Floca at the Caşolţ settlement (1939, 1941), Dacian-type pottery was found associated with Roman provincial products (Floca 1938, 98-100, fig. 44).

Mihail Macrea also recorded the presence of Dacian pottery during the digs of 1939 at the Râşnov Roman camp (Macrea 1941-1943, 234-235; Daicoviciu 1937-1940, 316).

During the Second World War, Dacian hand-made pottery appeared in the excavations undertaken by Mihail Macrea in the Mehadia (Macrea 1951, 293, note 9) and Porolissum (Gudea 1989, 501-502) Roman camps, and also in the finds of Zoltan Székely at the civilian settlement of the Comalău Roman camp (see Protase 1980, 141).

All these discoveries, together with those dating before the Second World War, resulted in the first publications that pointed out the maintenance of the local traditional pottery during the Roman Period in the wider context of Dacian continuity in the Roman Dacia.

From 1926, Vasile Pârvan suggested that Dacian pottery of the Late Iron Age continued to be produced throughout the Roman period and the 4th century AD. The observation could have been a contribution to the theory of Romanian continuity within the Carpathian-Danubian space; the rise of the problem was premature, as the archaeological material available at the time was "incompletely studied and then locked away in Museum stores, or still buried" (Pârvan 1926, 570). Vasile Pârvan reasserted his idea in his posthumous "Dacia", in which he doubted that there was a "local industry of Late Iron Age vessels, made by the local people who continued to inhabit the territory of Roman post-Roman Dacia" (Pârvan 1928, 107).

The data accumulated after the archaeological research undertaken during the inter-war period allowed Constantin Daicoviciu to elaborate his first studies regarding the Dacian continuity in Roman Dacia, according to archaeological evidence. These studies contained important references to Dacian-type pottery (Daicoviciu 1936-1940, 231; Daicoviciu 1940, 24-33). The permanent reference to the Dacian Late Iron Age, the re-evaluation of some research carried out from the 19th century up until to the First World War, and the presentation of several photographs, outlined a coherent persuasive style that was maintained by Romanian archaeologists throughout the first decades after the Second World War. The problem was taken up again by the paper "La Transylvanie dans l'antiquité" (Daicoviciu 1945, 122-124).

In 1940, in the Romanian edition of the paper "O enigmã şi un miracol istoric: popoporul român" (An Enigma and a Historic Miracle: the Romanian People), George Brătianu introduced a chapter concerning proof of the continuity of the local population throughout the Roman period, up to the 6th century AD. Besides his presentation of some discoveries attesting the continuity of the Dacian traditional pottery in Romanian territory, the author also committed some errors and exaggerations. In this context, I recall the assertion that: "the Cucuteni or Vidra (Neolithic – note of author) primitive

shapes were influenced, over the centuries, by Roman pottery, and, later on, by Byzantine pottery that introduced the varnishing technique" (Brătianu 1988, 138).

In 1944, the paper "Dacian keleti hotarvonala iz az ugynevezetk dak ezustkinesck Kerdese", written by Istvàn Paulovics, was published in Cluj. Beyond its incontrovertible content (presenting the history of research in the Roman camps along the eastern border of Dacia, with bibliography, as well as detailing the topography and elements of military architecture), I draw attention to the lack of description of an archaeological inventory, suggesting that some of the conclusions in the publication are invalid. Launching himself into the polemics of the continuity/discontinuity of the local people in Roman Dacia, Istvàn Paulovics held that research had lost its initial reality of "sine ira et studio" because Romanian archaeologists opted for "casual proof for propaganda regarding the Romanian continuity" (Paulovics 1944, 115). Although supportable in several cases, the assertion did not solve the essence of the matter. The paper is still significant as it was the first synthesis of the research of the eastern "limes" of the Roman Dacia.

2.3. Archaeological research and studies from the second half of the 20th century

2.3.1. The sixth decade

Archaeological research almost ceased during the first years that followed the Second World War. After this caesura, Dacian-type pottery continued to appear during the research in Roman camps and in the provincial rural settlements and cemeteries as well.

Significant quantities of hand-made or wheel-made Dacian pottery resulted from the excavations undertaken in 1949 and 1951 by Mircea Rusu (Rusu 1953, 699, fig. 8; Protase 1980, 142-143). Further examples turned up (1950) for Mihail Macrea and his collaborators at the Breţcu (Macrea, Buzdugan, Ferenczi, Horedt, Popescu, Russu 1951, 292-293, figs. 3-4; Protase 1980, 139) and Gilău (Macrea, Rusu, Winkler 1959, 453, fig. 1:11, 15; Rusu 1979, 153-192) Roman camps and also for Grigore Florescu (1960) at the civilian settlement of the Bumbeşti Roman camp (Protase 1980, 141), for Dumitru Protase at the Orheiul Bistriţei Roman camp (Protase 1960, 189-194, figs. 1-2), and for Zoltan Székely (1960) at the Sărăţeni Roman camp (Székely 1962, 35, fig. 7:6-7).

Within the pottery material discovered at Gilău during the 1960 campaign, the Dacian types represented 25%, including post-Roman discoveries. The local pottery was discovered in all parts and habitation layers of this Roman camp.

The most important progress was the extension and intensification of research in rural areas. Dacian pottery was discovered in 1950 by Dorin Popescu and his collaborators at the settlement of Criteşti (Popescu, Covaciu, Puşcaş 1951, 282; Protase 1966, 32; Protase 1980, 49-50), by Dumitru Berciu and his collaborators at the Verbicioara settlement

(Berciu et al. 1952, 174-176), in 1953-1954 by Mircea Rusu at the Gligoreşti (see Protase 1980, 51) and Sângeorgiu de Mureş (see Protase 1980, 71) settlements, and, in 1956-1961, by Dumitru Protase and Ioan Ţigăra at the Soporu de Câmpie cemetery (Protase, Ţigăra 1959, 430, fig. 6:2; Protase, Ţigăra 1960, 383-396; Protase 1966, 52-58; Protase 1980, 122-123), in 1957 by B. Blaga at Obreja settlement (see Protase 1966, 43-44), in 1958 by Zoltan Székely at the Medieşorul Mare (see Protase 1980, 54) and Matei (Protase 1980, 54) settlements, in 1958-1959 by Sebastian Morintz at the Chilia settlement and cemetery (Morintz 1961, 443-444; Morintz 1961a, 397-398; Morintz 1963, 513-518), in 1958 by Nicolae Lupu at the Roşia settlement (Lupu 1968, 447; Protase 1980, 66) and in 1960 by Mircea Rusu at the Sfântu Gheorghe-Iernut settlement (Vlassa, Rusu, Protase, Horedt 1966, 403, fig. 5:16, 21-22, 24). In all these settlements and cemeteries, a continuation of the traditional Late Iron Age shapes, ornamentation and techniques was observed within the local pottery.

The research at Caşolţ brought to light a settlement of local population, the cemetery of which has not yet been identified, the one known from the literature belonging to some colonists who had come from Noricum and Pannonia - although some traditional Dacian pottery shapes were manifest within it (Protase 1980, 46). At the same time, systematic research of the Soporu de Câmpie cemetery showed the constant presence of Dacian pottery within the funerary inventory of the local population of the Roman Dacia.

In his study: "Les Daces à l'époque romaine à la lumière des recentes fouilles archéologiques", Mihail Macrea noticed the almost unchanged presence of hand-made Dacian cups in the Roman camps of Mehadia, Breţcu, Micia, Drajna de Sus, in the civilian settlement of the Comalău Roman camp, in the rural settlements of Lechinţa de Mureş and Cristeşti, and also in the cemeteries of Potaissa and Caşolţ. He further underlined the local contribution to the apparition of the "dollia" (large provision jars), typical of the Roman period in the Lower Danube area (Macrea 1957, 205-206, fig. 8:2, 19).

2.3.2. The seventh decade

The research undertaken during the seventh decade in the Roman camps (but mainly in the local population settlements and cemeteries, and, more seldom, in the villae rusticae) continued to bring to light Late Iron Age tradition Dacian pottery.

Such discoveries were made in 1963 by Nicolae Gudea at the Buciumi Roman camp (Gudea 1970, 299-311), in 1964 by Dumitru Tudor at the civilian settlement of the Slăveni Roman camp (Protase 1980, 147), in 1965 by Dumitru Tudor (Tudor 1967, 655-656, fig. 2:1-7; Tudor 1968, 22) and then by Gheorhe Petre-Govora at the civilian settlement of the Roman camp of Stolniceni-Buridava (Petre-Govora 1968, 147, fig. 2:4), in 1966 by Dumitru Tudor at Castra Traiana settlement (Tudor 1970, 249), by Octavian Floca at the civilian settlement of the Micia Roman camp (Floca 1968, 52-53, fig. 1), by Octavian Floca and Liviu Mărghitan at the Micia Roman camp (Floca 1970, 53, fig. 11), by Mihail Macrea and his

collaborators at the Orheiul Bistriţei Roman camp (Macrea, Protase, Dănilă 1967, 116, fig. 6), in 1969-1970 by Nicolae Gudea at the Bologa Roman camp (Gudea 1969, 503-505; Gudea 1973a, 123-124, pls. 16:1, 3-5; 17:4-10; Gudea 1973b, 48-56, fig. 23:1-29), in 1967-1968 by Nicolae Gudea and Eugen Chirilă at the same Roman camp (Chirilă, Gudea 1973, 120), in 1967-1968 by Dumitru Tudor, Gheorghe Poenaru-Bordea and Cristian M. Vlădescu at the Bivolari Roman camp (Tudor, Poenaru, Vlădescu 1969, 1970, 26, fig. 23:4), by Expectatus Bujor at the civilian settlement of Bumbeşti Roman camp (Bujor 1970, 108), between 1968-1971 by Zoltan Székely at the Olteni Roman camp (Székely 1980, 60, 62, fig. 6), in 1969 by Nicolae Gudea at the Râşnov Roman camp (Gudea 1973c, 20-22), in 1970 by Nicolae Gudea and Ioan Uzum at the Pojejena Roman camp (Gudea, Uzum 1973, 89, fig. 6:7).

According to the statistics of Mihail Macrea, hand-made Dacian pottery represented about 5% of the total pottery discovered at Orheiul Bistriţei Roman camp. This percentage is more realistic than the 25% recorded at Gilău during the 1956 archaeological campaign, bearing in mind that, unlike Gilău, where a post-Roman level is also present, at Orheiul Bistriţei the only discovered level belongs to the Roman Period.

Dacian style pottery was discovered in rural areas during the digs undertaken during 1961-1963 and 1969-1970 by Dumitru Protase at the Obreja settlement and cemetery (Protase 1971, 137, 139, 151-154; Protase 1980, 57-61), in 1961-1962 by Octavian Floca and Mihai Valea at the cemetery having belonged to the villa rustica of Cinciş (Floca, Valea 1965, 190, figs. 19-20), by Zoltan Székely at the Cernatu de Jos settlement (see Protase 1980, 47), in 1963 by Geza Ferencz at the Sic (see Protase 1966, 49) and Sava (Protase 1980, 67) settlements, in 1963 by Ioan Mitrofan at the Ciunga (Mitrofan 1972, 145-146; Protase 1966, 31; Protase 1980, 48) and 1963-1966 at the Noşlac (Mitrofan 1971, 443-444, fig. 3:1-15; 4:1-5; Protase 1966, 42, fig. 16:2-3, 6; Protase 1980, 55) settlements, in 1963 by Gheorghe Popilian at the Castranova settlement (Protase 1980, 45), in 1964 by Gheorghe I. Petre-Govora at the Ocnele Mari settlement (Petre-Govora 1966, 172, fig. 1:1-3), in 1964 by Dumitru Protase at the Ocna Sibiului settlement (Protase 1968, 230-233, figs. 3-5), in 1967 by Emil Moscalu at the Govora settlement (Moscalu 1970, 655, figs. 4-5), by Gheorghe Bichir at the settlement no. 1 Scorniceşti and its cemetery (Bichir 1986, 117-120), in 1968 by Zoe Voivozeanu and Petre Voivozeanu at the Socetu settlement (Voievozeanu, Voievozeanu 1970, 530), in 1969 by Iudita Winkler and her collaborators at the Cicău settlement (Winkler, Takacs, Păiuş 1979, 145-148) and at the villa rustica of Aiud (Winkler, Vasiliev, Chiţu, Borda 1968, 72, fig. 7:1-3). In this context, I have observed the presence of Dacian pottery within settlements that continue the classic Late Iron Age – at Cernatul de Sus, Ocna Sibiului or Roşia Sibiului – and also within Roman farms – at Cinciş and Aiud.

The 1960s saw an improvement in the conditions of presentation of local pottery by increased attention to descriptions and also by the illustration of the archaeological material discovered. Numerous studies and papers were published concerning the continuity of the local population in Roman Dacia, among which I especially mention the writings of Dumitru Protase and Nicolae Gudea.

In his study "La permanence des Daces en Dacie romaine telle quelle resulte de l'archéologie", Dumitru Protase wrote a brief history of the discoveries attributed to the local population (Protase 1964, 193-212). Within the hand-made local pottery, he remarked a simplification of the adornment, and also the Dacian influence upon Roman provincial pottery (Protase 1964, 199).

Nicolae Gudea's studies concerning the Dacian pottery discovered in the Roman camps of Buciumi (Gudea 1970, 299-311, figs. 2-8) and Bologa (Gudea 1969, 503-508, figs. 1-3) are especially significant. These studies sprang from Dumitru Protase's precedent created by his research at the Orheiul Bistriței Roman camp (Protase 1960, 189-194). The catalogue-based presentation of all the pottery items discovered at the Buciumi (1963) and Bologa (1967-1968) camps, accompanied by a minute description of the clay, shape and adornments, allowed the scientist to observe the frequent presence of "hand-made pots", the simplification of adornments, changes in the profile of several vessels, and a certain influence upon Roman provincial pottery. The Dacian pottery presented by the author is exclusively hand-made (at the Bologa and Buciumi Roman camps). The discovery of such pottery within the whole area of the Roman camp of Bologa, and its frequency in the military huts of the Buciumeni Roman camp strengthens the idea of the presence of several natives among the Roman army. I would like to mention that a part of this pottery imitates Roman shapes, so it cannot be considered as Dacian.

In a paper studying the persistence of the Dacian population in south-eastern Transylvania, Zoltan Székely referred to the discovery of some pottery fragments in terms of the excavations undertaken at the Brețcu and Olteni Roman camps (Székely 1970, 53).

In another paper, Dumitru Protase presented a part of the native pottery discovered at the Soporu de Câmpie cemetery (Protase 1969, 301-302, fig. 9:1-6). The same researcher is the author of two reference books concerning the continuity of the native population in Roman Dacia. In a first, entitled "Problema continuității în Dacia în lumina descoperirilor arheologice și numismatice" (The problem of continuity in Dacia according to archaeology and numismatics), he presents a catalogue of the discoveries attesting the persistence of the native population in Roman Dacia. Dacian pottery is a constant presence within these discoveries (Protase 1966, 19-107). The second book, "Rituri și ritualuri funerare la daci și daco-romani" (Rites and funerary rituals at Dacians and Daco-Romans), was written in the same spirit, with the proviso, of course, that it only refers to cemeteries (Protase 1968a, 15-121).

Finally, in his book "Viața în Dacia romană" (Life in Roman Dacia), Mihail Macrea recalls the Dacian tradition pottery discovered within the Roman camps, settlements and cemeteries in the rural areas of the Roman Dacia (Macrea 1968, 256-269).

2.3.3. The eighth decade

In the 1970s, research continued unceasingly at the Roman camps, their civilian settlements, and in the rural area settlements and cemeteries.

Dacian pottery discoveries continued to be made during the research undertaken (1970-1975) by Dumitru Protase and Andrei Zrinuy at the Brâncovenești Roman camp (Protase, Zrinyi 1975, 57-69), in 1971 by Nicolae Gudea at the Bologa Roman camp (Gudea 1977, 183-185), in 1973-1974 by Nicolae Gudea and Ioan I. Pop at the Râșnov Roman camp (Gudea, Pop1973, 20-22, figs. 19:1-15; 20:1-17; Gudea, Pop 1974-1975, 57, fig. 2:5; Gudea, Pop 1974-1975a, 71, figs. 10:1-10; 11:1-14), during 1976-1985 by Dan Isac and his collaborators at the Gilău Roman camp (Isac, Diaconescu, Opreanu 1980, 45; Isac 1980, 297, fig. 5:1-7; Isac, Diaconescu, Opreanu 1981, 295-296; see and Marcu, Țentea 1997, 221-268), during 1976-1979 by Petru Bona and his collaborators at Tibiscum Roman camp (Bona, Petrovszky, Petrovzsky 1982, 410, pls. 2:1-2, 4, 6; 3:7), during 1978-1980 by Doina Benea and her collaborators, at the Tibiscum civilian settlement and Roman camp (Benea 1981, 306-311, figs. 20:1; 27:1-4; Benea 1982, 29-35; Benea 1985, 12-13, fig. 4:1-6), in 1978 by Dumitru Protase, Corneliu Gaiu and George Marinescu at the Ilișua Roman camp (Protase, Marinescu, Gaiu 1981, 289-291, fig. 4), in 1978-1983 by Cristian M. Vlădescu at the Bumbești Roman camp (Vlădescu 1986, 133-137; see and Marinoiu, Camui 1986, 154), in 1980 by Ioan Piso and his collaborators at the Cășei Roman camp (Piso, Isac, Diaconescu, Opreanu 1981, 298), by Liviu Mărghitan at the Micia civilian settlement and Roman camp (Mărghitan 1976, 133; Mărghitan 1979, 134-135), and by Gheorghe Popilian at the civilian settlement of the Slăveni Roman camp (Popilian 1981, 30, pl. 8).

The native pottery discovered in 1971 by Gheorghe Poenaru-Bordea and Cristian M. Vlădescu at the Rădăcinești Roman camp, was attributed to the Dacian layer disturbed during the Roman Period (Poenaru-Bordea, Vlădescu 1972, 482, fig. 5:8). Instead, Dacian pottery was discovered in the civilian settlement of the Tibiscum Roman camp, within closed complexes dated from the first decades of the Roman ruling.

The discoveries of Dacian pottery went on in the rural areas of Roman Dacia. Such discoveries made by Gheorghe Popilian and Marin Nica at the Cârcea settlement (see Popilian 1976, 132, 134), in 1970 by Florea Costea at the Feldioara settlement (Costea 1971, 30-31), in 1971 by Gheorghe Bichir at the Vulturești settlement (Bichir 1984, 7), in 1971-1973 by Ioan Glodariu at the Slimnic settlement (Glodariu 1972, 119-129; Glodariu 1981), in 1973-1974 by Gheorghe Popilian at the Dobrun settlement (Popilian 1976, 134), in 1973 by Florea Costea at the Râșnov-Blocuri settlement (Costea 1974-1975, 66-70), in 1974 by Mihai Blăjan and his collaborators at the Micăsasa settlement (Blăjan, Stoicovici, Georoceanu, Păcurariu 1978, 61), in 1974 by Iudita Winkler and Mihai Blăjan at the Copșa Mică settlement (Winkler, Blăjan 1979, 460-462), Vasile Moga at the Blandiana settlement (Moga 1976, 95-96, pl. 33:1-5), in 1976 and 1983-1984 by Petre Gherghe at the Săcelu settlement (Gherghe 1985, 52, pl. 3:4-

6), in 1976-1977 and 1979 by Gheorghe Popilian and his collaborators at the Locusteni settlement and cemetery (Popilian, Nica, Mărgăţit-Tătulea 1980, 254-255), during 1976-1979 by Ioan Glodariu at the Şura Mică settlement (see Protase 1980, 75), bz Nicolae Gudea at the Gornea settlement (Gudea 1977, 25, 30, figs. 14:7-8; 15:3-4; 17:6-7), in 1978 by Mihai Petică at the Voivozeni settlement (Petică 1979, 130), in 1978-1979 by Gheorghe Bichir at the Coloneşti-Gueşti settlement (Bichir 1984, 6), in 1979 by Adrian Bejan and Doina Benea at the Hodoni-Pustă settlement (Bejan, Benea 1981, 388-389), in 1979 by Gheorghe Popilian and Teodor Niţă at the Leu settlement and cemetery (Popilian, Niţă 1982, 132-133), in 1980 by Adrian Bejan, Doina Benea and Mircea Mare at the Timişoara-Cioreni settlement (Bejan, Benea 1981a, 381-382).

The Dacian type of pottery was also signaled by a series of studies and papers published in the field. The native pottery was found at the Amărăşti (Popilian 1976, 132), Apele Vii (Popilian 1976, 132), Cluj (see Protase 1980, 48-49), Laslea (see Protase 1980, 52), Leu (Popilian 1976, 132, 134), Vulcan (Protase 1980, 76), Feldioara (Glodariu, 1975, 229, fig. 3:1-3), Dedrad (Protase 1980, 50), Chinteni (Matei 1974-1975, 299-300) settlements and at the Daneţi cemetery (Popilian 1982, 48, 50).

In Ioan Mitrofan's paper concerning the rural settlements and the villae rusticae from Dacia Superior, native pottery has a modest place (Mitrofan 1972, 141-162; Mitrofan 1973, 127-150). Instead, in his articles regarding the research at the Bologa (Gudea 1977, 183-185, figs. 15:1-15; 16:1-9), Râşnov (Gudea 1973c, 20-22), Inlanceni (Gudea 1979, 188, pl. 10:6-8) and Breţcu (Gudea 1980, 303-305) Roman camps, Nicolae Gudea continues his typical systematic and minute research of native pottery, adding a few observations showing its evolution compared to the Dacian Late Iron Age period. Dacian pottery is also present in the monographs on the Roman camps at Râşnov (Gudea, Pop 1971) and Gornea (Gudea 1977), written by the same author (alone, or with some collaborators).

During 1976 and 1980, the archaeological monographs of the Daco-Roman cemeteries of Soporu de Câmpie (Protase 1976) and Locusteni (Popilian 1980) were published by Dumitru Protase and Gheorghe Popilian respectively. Thanks to good drawing presentations, these books allowed the initiation of research work into the typology of Roman period Dacian pottery, starting from the discoveries made at the two above-mentioned archaeological sites. In fact, as early as 1976, in his book "Ceramica romană din Oltenia" (The Roman pottery in Oltenia), Gheorghe Popilian made a first attempt to establish a typology of the local tradition pottery in Roman Dacia from south of Carpatians Mountains (Popilian 1976, 131-138). In the study entitled "Traditions autocthones dans la ceramique provinciale romaine de la Dacie meridionale", the same author analyzed the shapes, adornments and specific techniques of native pottery from Dacia Inferior (Malvensis), and underlines its influence on Roman pottery south the Carpathians (Popilian 1976a, 279-286).

In 1980, Dumitru Protase's book: "Autohtonii în Dacia" (The natives in Dacia), presented a true repertoire of the most important archaeological discoveries that attests to the presence of the local element in the Roman Dacia, a fact reflected by the Dacian-type pottery as a constant presence at the sites (Protase 1980, 32-170).

2.3.4. The ninth and tenth decades of the 20th century

It is difficult to sketch a history of archaeological research during the 1980s and 90s, as many of the results are still unpublished.

Excavations continued to trace native pottery from the researches made during 1981-1983 by Gheorghe Bichir at the civilian settlement of the Stolniceni-Buridava Roman camp (Bichir, Bardaşu 1980, 339; Bichir 1983, 12), by Vasile Marinoiu and Ion Camui at the Bumbeşti Roman camp (Marinoiu, Camui 1986, 154), in 1987 by Zoltan Székely at the Olteni Roman camp (Székely 1990-1994, 18-20), during 1998-1991 by Vasile Marinoiu, Gheorghe Calotoiu and Dan Ionescu at the Bumbeşti camp and civilian settlement (Marinoiu, Camui 1986, 154; Marinoiu 1992, 27), in 1985 and 1996 Doina Benea and her collaborators at the Tibiscum Roman camp (Petrescu, Rogozea 1990, 115, pl. 5:2; Ardeţ, Ardeţ 1997, 67-68), in 1998 by Octavian Bozu at the civilian settlement of the Vărădia Roman camp (Bozu 1999, 128), during 1990-1995 by Constantin Preda and Aurelia Grosu at the civilian settlement of the Enoşeşti-Acidava Roman camp (Preda, Grosu 1993, 56, pl. 8:1-3; Preda, Grosu1996, 41-42), Dumitru Protase, George Marinescu and Corneliu Gaiu at the Ilişua Roman camp (Protase, Marinescu, Gaiu 1981, 291-292; Protase, Gaiu 1995, 29), in 1995 by Mihai Moga, Mihai Drîmbocianu at the legionary camp at Apulum (Moga, Drîmboceanu 1996, 3), between 1982-1984 by Constantin C. Petolescu at the Roman camp of Cătunele (Petolescu 1986, 162).

In rural areas Dacian pottery was discovered by Petre Roman and his collaborators at the Ostrovul Corbului settlement (Roman, Dodd, Dogaru, Simon 1992, 104), between 1994-1998 by Vasile Stîngă at the Gârla Mare villa rustica (Stîngă 1998, 40-41, pl. 61:6; Stîngă 1999, 43; Stîngă 1999a, 36), between 1982-1984 by Doina Benea and her collaborators at the Timişoara-Cioreni settlement (thanks to Professor Dr Doina Benea for these informations) and between 1984-1992 and 1998 at Timişoara-Freidorf settlement (Benea 1985, 24-25; Benea 1996, 147-148; 153-156; 176-178; Benea 1997, 55-76; Mare 1999, 122-123), in 1998 by Adrian Bejan and Marius Grec at the Sânnicolau Mare settlement (Bejan, Grec 1999, 103), in 1983-1984 by Petre Gherghe at the Săcelu settlement (Gherghe 1985, 47-52), in 1985-1986 by Octavian Bozu at the Moldova Veche (Bozu 1990, 151) and Grădinari (Bozu, Sousi 1987, 244) settlements, by Mihai Bădău-Wiettenberg at the Buza settlement (Bădău-Wittenberger 1994, 369), in 1994-1995 and 1998 by Marin Nica at the Cârcea settlement (Nica 1995, 31; Nica 1996, 30; Nica 1999, 28), in 1989-1990 by Ioan Mitrofan at the Noşlac (Mitrofan 1999, 71) and in 1996 at Micăsasa (Mitrofan 1996, 78) settlements.

Special importance is attributed to the hand-made Dacian pottery found in 1992-1994 and 1996 at the Roman City of

Napoca (Cociş, Voişian, Paki, Rotea 1996, 636; Alicu, Voişian, Bota 1997, 14). I add a series of native hand-made pottery fragments discovered in the civilian settlement of the Enoşeşti-Acidava Roman camp, preserved in the collection of the School of Piatra-Sat (Negru, Ciucă 1997, 23-29, pls. 1, 2).

The local archaeological repertories elaborated by Gheorghe Calotoiu (Calotoiu 1982, 49, 59), Mihai Blăjan (Blăjan 1989, 317-330), George Marinescu (Marinescu 1989, 5-66), Mircea Negru (Negru 1994, 61-80), Valeriu Lazăr (Lazăr 1995) and others made important contributions to the research of the native pottery of the Roman Dacia.

During the 1980s, Ioana Bogdan-Cataniciu published her discoveries made at the Rucăr Roman castle (Bogdan-Cătăniciu 1985-1986, 201-209). Petru Rogozea also published his findings from the civilian settlement of the Tibiscum Roman camp (Rogozea 1988).

Of special significance is Nicolae Gudea's and Ion Moţu's study of the hand-made Dacian pottery discovered in Dacian Roman camps. The authors started from several observations concerning the less rigorous way previous research was undertaken, and the lack of publications on native pottery found in Roman camps, and go on to suggest some available criteria for scientific analysis, and investigation methods for the archaeological material, offering a possible model for future research (Gudea, Moţu 1988, 229-236).

In addition, the book "Aşezări dacice şi daco-romane la Slimnic" (Dacian and Daco-Roman settlements at Slimnic) written by Ioan Glodariu (Glodariu 1981), and also "Geto-dacii din Muntenia în epoca romană" (The Geto-Dacians from Muntenia in the Roman period) by Gheorghe Bichir, present many pottery fragments that can be attributed to the native population in Roman Dacia (Bichir 1984).

In one of his books, Nicolae Branga showed that numerous hand-made or wheel-made pottery Dacian vessels were discovered in the villae rusticae of Apoldu de Sus and Apoldu de Jos (Branga 1986, 163, 180).

In 1993, a monograph was issued entitled "Castrul roman de la Mehadia" (The Roman camp of Mehadia), written by Mihai Macrea, Nicolae Gudea and Ion Moţu. The book illustrates the native pottery discovered in this camp over its many periods of excavation (Macrea, Gudea, Moţu 1993, 84-85).

The following year, Dumitru Protase and Andrei Zrinuy published the results of research undertaken (1970-1987) at the Brâncoveneşti Roman camp (Protase, Zrinyi 1994, 64, pl. 78:1).

In 1995, Nicolae Gudea published the first volume dedicated to the military complex of Porolissum, also showing the Dacian-type material discovered during the archaeological campaign of 1943 and 1958 (Gudea 1989, 501-502). The author published the second volume the following year, presenting the results of the Porolissum custom research (Gudea 1996).

In 1997, "Dacia sud-vestică în secolele III-IV" (South-Western Dacia in the 3rd-4th centuries AD) was published by Doina Benea (Benea 1997).

Eight volumes were issued on the occasion of the 17th International Congress of Research Concerning the Roman Empire Borders (held in Zalău, in September 1997), concentrating on several Roman camps on the northern limes of Roman Dacia, and one in the Meseşului Mountains. References to local tradition pottery were made in the volumes of the Gilău (Isac 1997, 56-57), Romiţa (Matei, Istvan 1997, 57, 124) and Buciumi (Gudea 1997b, 34-36) camps, also to the Roman camp of Bologa and its civilian settlement (Gudea 1997a, 29, 49).

Finally, in 1998, a study was published by Sorin Cociş and Coriolan Opreanu who tried to date more precisely a series of graves from the Locusteni cemetery which they considered as belonging to a Daco-Sarmatian Moldavian group that settled there after 118 AD (Cociş, Opreanu 1998). As evidence, the authors hypothesize that, of the 27 brooches discovered, 24 have close analogies from eastern Carpathia, and their association is made with objects created in the filigree technique, attributed exclusively as Carpian (Cociş, Opreanu 1998, 201-202). Interesting in that it presents a restrained chronology of the brooches, the study picks up, with new evidence, the obsessive thesis of the Carpian origin of some cemeteries – referring to the most important one studied so far – within Dacia province.

Without going into detail, I must add that there is some evidence against the theories presented in that article. First, there is no single tomb in this cemetery that can be certain attributed to a Roxolan Sarmatian. No "Sarmatian mirror type" was discovered, nor any other typical object. Concerning the pottery, one notices the presence of biconical shaped vessels with umbo, obviously of Celtic type. Their presence might be connected to some Celtic potter, but one cannot exclude the presence of such of population or of that of some Dacians from the contact area with the Celtic World. Yet, one can certainly speak of a clear predominance of Roman products (pottery, metal objects) that would hardly belong to a newly colonized population from the space where these products were rare – such as the eastern Carpathian territory. In conclusion, I consider that the metal objects (brooches, fittings, and pearls made in the filigree technique) are not evidence enough for an exclusive attribution of the Locusteni cemetery to a Daco-Sarmatian group; the rites, the funerary rituals and the pottery do not explicitly sustain this hypothesis. How did the above-mentioned brooches reach the location? By exchange, or with some group that might have joined the local population, assuming that the cemetery belongs to a majority Dacian population that was becoming Romanized.

The problem raised by this cemetery shows how difficult it is to re-make the geographical frame of a small rural settlement and, in a wider context, how complex this situation must have been at the level of the whole Dacia province – and that of other Roman provinces as well. In this discussion, I think there were settlements that we can attribute to one single, ethnic group, and others inhabited by different ethnic groups together, in various proportions and from case to case. Further detailed research and excavation is required to clarify the issue.

Research into Roman Dacia native pottery went through the same stages as that of archaeological research in Romania. Clear advances can be seen in terms of both excavation techniques and also the way finds are assessed and conserved. Thus, from work aimed exclusively at finding sensational remains there was a shift towards exploratory investigations and then to systematic excavations that were often exhaustive. These new results are providing better evaluation. Thus, the presentation of native pottery has progressed from simple references of "hand-made pottery", "Barbarian pottery", or "Late Iron Age tradition pottery", to minute descriptions - in a series of books, and even special studies (Popilian 1976a; Bogdan-Cătăniciu 1985-1986; Gudea, Uzum 1988; Gudea 1989; Negru 1997; Negru 1998a).

Yet, the problem raised by the local tradition pottery in Roman Dacia is far from being solved. There still is no typology of Dacian pottery from the Roman period, a fact that still makes it difficult to differentiate it from the Geto-Dacian classic Late Iron Age pottery (Tudor, Purcărescu 1976, 41), or from post-Roman pottery (Berciu 1965, 597-610; Marcu 1968, 43-45; Marcu 1973, 39-41; Costea 1974-1975, 280; Ferenczi, Ferenczi 1976, 242). At the same time, I draw attention to the fact that a series of hand-made vessels considered (in various publications) as Dacian just because they were hand-made, are in fact Celtic or even Roman, or belong to some anterior or ulterior period than the Roman one. Therefore, the considerations made concerning the Locusteni cemetery are also applicable in this situation.

Future research will have to focus mainly upon a more accurate chronology of Dacian pottery during the Roman period. This will only be possible after an exhaustive research of the several archaeological sites and by the integral and comparative analysis of the Dacian, Roman and Celtic archaeological material, or of that of other possible origin, predominantly from closed complexes.

Chapter II
THE NATIVE HAND-MADE POTTERY

Compiling a typology of hand-made Dacian pottery from the classic Dacian period of Late Iron Age and the 2nd-4th centuries AD is a difficult task because of the great diversity of the vessel shapes. The fact can be partly explained by the great number of pottery workshops producing these vessels, and also by the impossibility of moulding by hand a series of identical vessels, as was the case with those molded in patterns, or like the very similar ones that were wheel-made. In spite of all this variety of shapes, which sometimes makes us believe that each hand-made vessel is unique, scientists have tried to determine several categories and types of such vessel: jars of ovoid, biconical, pear, cylindrical shape, pots, Dacian cups, conical vessels, lids (Crişan 1969; Bichir 1973, 63-69; Popilian 1976, 220-221; Popilian 1976a, 285; Bichir 1984, 30-34).

For my typology, I have determined a set of criteria which, when correlated, can offer a more balanced image of the various shapes of vessels, especially the similar ones.

The typology I suggest combines functionality with shape. Firstly, I considered that, according to their destination, the local traditional hand-made Dacian forms are vessels for food storage, table ware, and kitchen ware. In establishing a typology within these categories, I have assumed – and this is not new (Preda 1986, 55) – that the profile of the vessel body has priority compared to the secondary characteristics such as rim profile, or the number of handles, or to tertiary important attributes such as paste, firing, or decorative elements.

The local tradition of Dacian pottery categories comprises vessels used for storage (provision vessels, some of the medium-sized vessels and pots), kitchen vessels and table ware. Most of the cups or conical vessels were used for illumination, it seems, although there are signs that some were not used for this purpose (the lack of a secondary burning). At the present state of research, with incomplete information on technical data, it is hard to distinguish between a medium-sized vessel used for the temporary storage of food and another used in the kitchen – and there must have been, indeed, kitchen vessels used for food storage – therefore, I have considered it necessary to make a global presentation of the medium-sized vessels, among which I include jars.

The types of hand-made vessels identified resulting from the analysis of the discoveries published to date are as follows:

provision jar, tall jar, Dacian cups, conical vessels, dishes and lids. The presentation order of these categories is based upon their utility – obvious or supposed – and also upon the relationship between heights, maximum diameters, the rim diameters and the base diameters.

While archaeological opinion is in agreement as regards the denomination of hand-made vessel categories, it differs regarding the presentation of the types or versions of jars (starting with etymological problems), a fact that shows the difficulties inherent in describing profiles of similar vessels. Because the specialized literature has used various terms for vessels of the same shape (for instance either biconical jar or biconical pot), I have considered the term "jar" is the most appropriate in this case.

Due to a convergent evolution of the tall vessels – an evolution that started during the pre-Roman Period – when the more or less obvious changes in the vessels' bodies, and especially the rounding or the turning up of their rims, resulted in the fusion of several shapes under the name of jar-pots or pots. (Their classification was made cautiously and, in general, no satisfactory solution was found.) These are the most numerous vessels within the hand-made pottery discovered in the local settlements and cemeteries that were attributed to the native population (as well as in the Roman camps, their civilian settlements, the villae rusticae and, more seldom, in the Roman cities of Dacia).

Their frequency is due to their multiple uses in everyday life, from food preparation to urns. The various uses must have generated the numerous categories and types of hand-made jars in circulation during the Roman Period. In fact, each type responded to a certain necessity. This can be deduced from the presence of the main types of jars over the entire territory inhabited by the Dacians during the 2nd-3rd centuries AD.

According to their shape, the discussed jars can be oval, biconical, bell-shaped, with curved body (pots), globular, pear shaped, or cylindrical. I have arrived at this order according to the biconical coefficient, or to that of the curve – to the minimum or to the maximum – of the vessel body according to which the categories were divided.

The typology I suggest confirms the perpetuation of the most important shapes of the jars that had appeared and evolved during the first and Late Iron Ages on the Dacian inhabited territory, and presents a range of jars whose bodies vary from curved to cylindrical (straight), and by so doing eliminating or attenuating a series of confusions and ambiguities in the analysis of the Dacian hand-made jars shapes dating to the Roman Period.

The present study only includes references to vessels that were certified as belonging to the local tradition pottery of the Dacia province. The jars that did not agree with this criterion might be dealt with in another study.

A first category comprises the vessels that were not precisely dated to the Roman Period. Among them, I mention first the "Dacian handle-less cups", with cells decorating the base and discovered in a series of Roman camps from the inter-Carpathian area of Dacia province (Opreanu 1993).

In other cases, the profiles of some jars were entirely re-made, starting only from some upper part fragments or from the rim alone – a fact that makes us wary with regard to their re-shaping (Gudea 1996).

Finally, because of reasons related to the chosen subject, I could not include in my research those vessels discovered in some Roman fortifications situated on the territory of the former kingdom of Dacia (Bogdan-Cătăniciu 1985-1986; Ştefan 1935-1936, 344; Ştefan 1945-1947, 132-134), which, from a juridical point of view, were for a short time part of Moesia Inferior. This separation was absolutely necessary, bearing in mind the fact that only a part of pre-Roman Dacia was transformed into a Roman province, and also considering the existence of this kind of pottery all over Dacia province.

Storage ware

I. Provision jars (1-4)

Outsize jars do not show signs of secondary burning. This observation, correlated to the great size of the bodies, leads me to believe that they were used to preserve provisions. Their bodies are tall, with the rim diameter usually larger than that of the base.

I.1. Great ovoid jars with maximum diameter in the upper part of the body (1-2)

I.1.1. Ovoid jars with everted rim

The maximum diameter is in the upper half, in the shoulder area (1). The walls are slightly curved.

The jar was made in a paste mixed with sand and gravel, and is brick-coloured. The maximum diameter area was decorated with a celled cordon, from which start several hook-shaped segments. The jar was discovered in the Râşnov settlement, where it was dated from the 2nd-3rd century AD.

This kind of jar was found in some Dacian archaeological sites from the Late Iron Age (Turia: Crişan 1969, 161-162, pl. 57:9; Pecica-Ziridava: Crişan 1979, 115-116, pl. 59:1; Brad-Zargidava: Ursachi 1995, 161, pl. 61:4).

I.1.2. Ovoid jars with enlarged rim. The maximum diameter is in the upper half (2).

The body is slightly curved. The maximum diameter is formed slightly in the upper section. The mouth is almost as wide as the large base. The base is flat. It was made in a paste containing sand and gravel.

A jar of this shape was found in the civilian settlement of the Stolniceni-Buridava Roman camp. It was dated from the 2nd century AD and the beginning of the 3rd century AD. The jar has a parallel at Brad, a Dacian fort of the Late Iron Age (Ursachi 1995, 161, pl. 61:5). In the 2nd-3rd centuries AD, a similar jar was found in the free Dacian territory in the east Carpathian Mountains (Poiana-Dulceşti: Bichir 1973, 67, pl. 43:3).

I.2. Ovoid jars with the maximum diameter located at the middle of the body (3, 4)

The diameter of the mouth is larger than that of the base. The rim is everted. The base is flat and narrow.

The jars were made of a sandy paste (3), or a paste of sand and gravel (4). They are brick red and large in size.

A cordon with cells, applied above the maximum diameter (4), represents the decoration.

These jars were discovered at the Locusteni cemetery, where they dated from the 2nd century AD (3), and the first half of the 3rd century AD (4).

In everyday life they must have been used to store provisions.

Similar jars were found in some Dacian sites dated from the 3rd-2nd centuries BC (Ciumeşti: Crişan 1969, 110, pl. 29:10), and from the 1st century BC to the 1st century AD (Brad-Zargidava Căpitanu 1995, pl. 64:10; Bâtca Doamnei: Buzilă 1970, 239-240, figs. 2:6-7; 3:8, 10; 12:5; Bâzdâna: Mărgărit-Tătulea 1984, 104, fig. 10:2-3; Pecica-Ziridava: Crişan 1978, 234, fig. 49:2; Doboz-Hajduirtas: Visy 1970, pl. 3:4; Budapest-Tabán: Hunyady 1942, 81, 101:1). Such jars were also produced in Dacian territories outside Roman Dacia - during the 2nd-3rd centuries AD (Poiana-Dulceşti: Bichir 1973, 67, pl. 49:1; Bucureşti-Militari "Câmpul Boja": Negru 2000, 70, 72, pls. 79:6; 92:3).

Storage and kitchen ware

While big or medium-sized ovoid jars were used to preserve provisions, numerous other categories of jars could have been used both for preserving food, and as kitchen ware to prepare, or heat, food. The differences can only be ascertained by careful examination of the individual items, and by complete information concerning any secondary burning and where it is to be found on each jar. At the same time, it was possible to observe signs of both functions on each vessel, and this made it at times impossible to distinguish clearly between these two kinds of vessels.

II. Biconical jars (5-16)

According to body profile and the relevant dimensions, the biconical jars may be classified in three types and in several versions.

II.1. Short biconical jars (5-10)

II.1.1. Short biconical jars with slightly everted rim. The maximum diameter is located at the middle of the body (5). The mouth diameter is larger than that of the base. The rim has a horizontal margin. The base is flat and narrow.

II.1.2. Short biconical jars with much-everted rim. The maximum diameter is slightly displaced towards the lower part of the body (6, 7). The upper part is more slender. The mouth diameter is almost equal, or slightly smaller than that of the base. The base is flat.

II.1.3. Short biconical jars with everted rim. The maximum diameter is located towards the middle of the vessel (8-10). The mouth diameter is slightly smaller than that of the base. The base is flat and large (8, 9).

Type 1 comprises, for the moment, only six jars that can be completely restored. The biconical shape of these jars is obvious. The maximum diameter is at the middle of body, or at its lower part. The mouth diameter is larger, or almost equal to that of the base. The rim is more or less everted. The base is flat.

The present vessels were made of a paste containing sand and gravel (8), sand and mica (10), or just sand (6, 7). These jars are brick-coloured (5), brown-red (8), grey (7), ash-coloured (10) or grey-black (6). Two of them are miniatures (height = 100 mm), and the other three belong to a small- or medium-sized category of jars (8-10).

The decoration is present on the upper part of the jars. The relief decoration technique was used exclusively. A simple relief cordon (7), one (5, 10) or two (6) cordons with cells. One of the jars was decorated with a cordon with cells on the exterior edge of the rim (5).

These jars were discovered in the cemeteries of Locusteni (5), and Daneți (7), in the Feldioara settlement (6), in the Roman camps of Buciumi (8) and Ilişua, as well as in the civilian settlement of the Stolniceni-Buridava Roman camp (10). The jar found at Feldioara was dated to the beginning of the 2nd century AD. The samples from Locusteni and Daneți were dated

from the 2nd century AD, the one from Stolniceni-Buridava to the beginning of the 3rd century AD, and those from Buciumi and Ilişua to the 2nd-3rd centuries AD.

From a chronological and typological point of view, these jars have their closest analogies in Dacian sites from the Late Iron Age (Răcătău: Căpitanu 1976, 63, figs. 14:8; 21:6; Sf. Gheorghe: Crişan 1969, 163, pl. 77:8; Hărman: Crişan 1969, 111, pl. 32:2; Brad-Zargidava Căpitanu 1996, pl. 51:6; Upper Tisa area: Kotigoroško 1996, 235, fig. 116:30-31). I should also emphasize the fact that, as far as we know, this type of jars vanished from the 2nd-3rd centuries AD outside Roman Dacia, except for the area of the upper course of the Tisa River (Stanciu 1995, fig. 37:27; Kotigoroško 1996, 136, fig. 113:6).

II.2. Short slightly biconical jars (11-14)

The maximum diameter is located at the upper part, or at the middle of the jar. The mouth is slightly larger than the base.

The jars were made in a rough paste containing sand (11, 14), and sand and gravel (12, 13). Two of the jars are brown-coloured (12, 13), one is yellowish (14), and another is brick (11). The decoration was placed on the upper part of the jars, and consists of a cordon with cells applied above the maximum diameter (11-13), round bosses applied on the shoulder (12) or neck, (11) or rectangular bosses applied on the middle area (14). Two of them were also decorated with stripes or incised waved lines (11, 13).

Such jars were found in the Roman camps of Buciumi (11, 12), and Brețcu (13), as well as in the Locusteni cemetery (14). In the cemetery of Locusteni, they were dated to the 2nd century and the first half of the 3rd century AD, and from the 2nd-3rd centuries AD in the above-mentioned Roman camps.

These jars have analogies in Dacian archaeological sites from Late Iron Age (Poiana Tecuci: Moscalu 1983, 30, pl. 26:3; Moigrad-Porolissum: Macrea, Rusu 1960, 23, fig. 11:7; □idovar: Gavela 1952, 66, fig. 20:4-5). For the moment, they have not been discovered in other archaeological sites from 2nd-3rd centuries AD.

II.3. Slender biconical jars

II.3.1. Slender biconical jars with the slightly flaring rim. The maximum diameter is located at the middle of the jar (15). The mouth diameter is almost equal to that of the base. The flat base is shaped.

The only jar of this kind was discovered in the Soporu de Câmpie cemetery. It was made in rough, crumbly, blackish-coloured paste. The jar is medium-sized. It has a delimitating line slightly above the maximum diameter. It was part of the inventory of a 3rd century AD grave.

This kind of jar was also produced during Dacian settlements and forts from the Late Iron Age (Dezmir: Crişan 1969, 110, pl. 32:5; Cristeşti: Crişan 1969, 163, pl. 78:11; Brad-Zargidava: Ursachi 1968, 117, fig. 55:4; Răcătău: Căpitanu

1976, 57, figs. 13:3; 15:2; Deva: Crişan 1969, 163, pl. 100:4; Ţemplin: Budinsky-Krička 1968, 219, pl. 4:7). A similar jar was discovered in the free Dacian area in the east of the Carpathian Mountains, dating to the 2nd-3rd centuries AD (Poiana-Dulceşti: Bichir 1973, 67, pl. 48:1).

II.3.2. Slender biconical jars with the everted rim. The maximum diameter is located at the middle of the jar (15). The base is flat.

A vessel of this kind was found in the Obreja rural settlement. It was decorated with a celled cordon at the area of the maximum diameter. The jar was dated to the 2nd-3rd centuries AD.

III. Bell-shaped jars (17-22)

The bell-shaped jars have their mouth diameter larger than that of the base, and the maximum diameter situated in the upper part of the body. The rim is bent outwards, and the base is flat. To me they appear set almost upside down.

III.1. Slender body bell-shaped jars with the mouth wider than the shaped base (17-22)

The maximum diameter is at the upper part of the jar. The mouth diameter is larger than that of the base. The rim is bent outwards. The base is flat. The jars are medium-sized.

Such jars were discovered in the cemeteries of Locusteni (17), and Soporu de Câmpie (22), in the rural settlements of Filiaşi (19) and Buza (20), also in the Roman camps of Ilişua (18) and Bologa (21). They dated to the first decades of the 2nd century AD (20), 2nd century AD and the first half of the 3rd century AD (17), in the 2nd-3rd centuries AD (19, 21, 22), and in the middle of the 3rd century AD (18).

This shape of jar was also discovered in a series of Dacian archaeological sites, dating from the 1st century BC to the 1st century AD (Pecica-Ziridava: Crişan 1978, 234, pl. 49:1-2; Crişan 1969, 163, pl. 72:3; Upper Tisa River area: Kotigoroško 1996, 83, fig. 43:15). Similar jars, dated to the 2nd-4th centuries AD were found in some sites from Moesia Inferior, Moesia Superior and the territories inhabited by the Dacians not comprised within the borders of the Roman Empires (Biharkèresztez: Nepper-Ibolya 1969-1970, 86-87, 80, figs. 2, 4; Puchov culture: Kolnik 1972, 530, fig. 32:1-10; Mâtâsaru: Bichir 1984, pl. 12:8, 10; Văleni: Ioniţă, Ursachi 1988, 68, fig. 33:29; Upper Tisa River area: Kotigoroško 1996, figs. 113:2-3; 114:5). I might mention that similar jars, of Celtic origin and decorated with the "broom" design, were discovered in Dacia (Benea 1981, fig. 16; Bona, Petrovzky, Petrovzky 1982, 410, pl. 2:2; Rogozea 1988, 166, figs. 3:1; 12:1) and Pannonia (Bónis 1942, 36, pls. 2:3; 3:1) provinces.

IV. Pear-shaped jars (23-37)

Pears shaped jars are more slender than the bell-shaped examples.

IV.1. Pear-shaped jars with everted rim (23-33)

IV.1.1. The maximum diameter is located towards the upper half of the body (23-27). The mouth diameter is larger than that of the base. The rim is everted. The base is flat and narrow.

The jars were made in crumbly paste containing sand (24) or sand and gravel (24, 25). They are brick-coloured (24, 27) or blackish (25).

Three small, round bosses were applied on the shoulder of one of the jars. Others were decorated with a celled prominent fragment (23), irregular grooves (25) and incised horizontal stripes framing a stripe of waved incised lines (27).

These jars were discovered in the Soporu de Câmpie cemetery (24, 25), and in the Buciumi (23), Ilişua (26) and Olteni (27) Roman camps. Except for the jar discovered at Olteni, which was dated to the middle of the 3rd century AD, all the others were dated to the 2nd-3rd centuries AD.

A similar jar was found in the Dacian Late Iron Age settlement of Slimnic, where it was dated from the 1st century BC to the 1st century AD (Crişan 1969, 163, pl. 72:1). Jars of this type were discovered in the free Dacian area in the east of the Carpathian Mountains, dating from the 2nd-3rd centuries AD (Poiana-Dulceşti: Bichir 1973, 67, pl. 43:3), and in the upper course of the Tisa River, where they were dated to the 2nd-4th centuries AD (Kotigoroško 1996, 135, fig. 114:10).

IV.1.2. Short-bodied pear-shaped jars. The maximum diameter is at the shoulder or the middle of the body (28-33). The mouth diameter is larger than that of the base. The rim is everted. The base is flat.

The jars were made in a paste containing sand (28) or sand and gravel (31). They are brick-coloured (28, 33), or brown-reddish (31).

One of the jars has a cordon with cells applied at the maximum diameter area (28).

These jars were discovered in the Locusteni (28, 33) and Soporu de Câmpie (30) cemeteries, and in the Roman camps at Ilişua (29, 32) and Buciumi (31). They were dated to the 2nd century AD and the first half of the 3rd century AD (28, 33), and in the 2nd-3rd centuries AD (29-32).

A jar of the same shape was discovered in the Dacian pre-Roman settlement of Pecica-Ziridava, where it was dated from the 1st century BC to the 1st century AD (Crişan 1969, 163, pl. 76:12). Similar jars were found in the upper course of the Tisa River, where were dated to the 2nd-4th centuries AD (Kotigoroško 1996, 136, fig. 114:9).

IV. 2. Slender pear-shaped jars with outward bent rim (34-37)

IV.2.1. Slender pear-shaped jar with large mouth (34)

The maximum diameter is at the upper part of the body. The mouth diameter is much larger than that of the base. The rim is bent outwards. The base is flat and narrow.

The jar was made in sandy paste and are brick-coloured. It is medium-sized. A waved line incised on the shoulder represents the decoration. It was dated to the 2nd century AD and the first half of the 3rd century AD.

Similar jars were found in Dacian sites from the Late Iron Age, where they were dated from 1st century BC to the 1st century AD (Bicsad: Crişan 1969, 163, pl. 78:9; Bâtca Doamnei: Buzilă 1970, 241, fig. 6:1)

IV.2.2. Slender-bodied, pear-shaped jars with slightly flaring rim (35-37)

The maximum diameter is towards the shoulder. The mouth diameter is much larger than that of the base. The rim is flared. The base is flat and narrow.

The jars were made in a paste that contained much sand (35), or sand and gravel (36-37). They are brick-coloured and medium-sized.

In the maximum diameter area they were decorated with a simple relief cordon (35), two half-moon buttons (36), or round bosses with four cells (37).

This shape of jar was found in the Locusteni cemetery (35-36), and in the one belonging to the Aiud villa rustica (37). They were dated to the 2nd century AD and the first of the 3rd century AD (35-36), and to the 2nd-3rd centuries AD (37).

Similar jars dated to the Late Iron Age (Murighiol: Moscalu 1983, 34, pl. 24:8; Bâtca Doamnei: Buzilă 1970, 245, fig. 14:3; Gorno Gradiste: Georgieva 1952, 269, fig. 255) were discovered in that area of the Lower Danube that was inhabited by Dacians. Vessels of this shape were also found in the upper course area of the Tisa River, where they dated to the 2nd-4th centuries AD (Kotigoroško 1996, 136, fig. 114:4, 10).

V. Globular jars (38)

The globular jars have strongly curved walls, giving them a globular, rounded aspect.

V.1. Globular-shaped jar (38)

The maximum diameter is slightly displaced towards the upper half. The base is flat. The mouth is missing.

One single example was found in the Obreja cemetery, where it was dated from the middle of the 2nd century AD to the end of the 3rd century AD. In the maximum diameter area, the jar was decorated with a celled belt on which flat, round buttons were applied.

A few similar jars were discovered in the Locusteni cemetery (Popilian 1980, 24, pl. 12, M 78, 1; 25; pl. 12, M 83, 1).

Unfortunately, these were preserved to a lesser degree than the example from Obreja.

VI. Pots

The pots are curved-bodied jars, with the neck diameter almost equal to that of the base. The maximum diameter is usually located at the middle, or lower part of the body and only in exceptional cases at the upper part. The rim is everted or turned outwards.

VI.1. Short curved jars (39-40)

The maximum diameter is located at the middle of the jar (39-40). The mouth diameter is larger than the base. The base is slightly concave (39) or flat (40).

One of the jars was made of a paste containing only sand, and is brick-coloured (39). Both jars are medium-sized.

The decoration was set on the upper part of the jars. On the maximum diameter (40), or above it (39), a celled belt was applied.

These jars were discovered in the Locusteni cemetery (39) and in that of Soporu de Câmpie (40). The pot discovered at Locusteni was dated from the 2nd century AD to the first half of the 3rd century AD, and the one found at Soporu de Câmpie to the 2nd-3rd centuries AD.

This shape of pots was frequent in the Dacian levels of the Late Iron Age (Costeşti: Crişan 1969, 163, pl. 77:7; Slimnic: Glodariu 1981, 35, fig. 36:5; Răcătău: Căpitanu 1976, 62, fig. 16:6; Pecica-Ziridava: Crişan 1978, 130, pl. 7:3). During the 2nd-3rd centuries AD, this kind of jar was also produced in Moesia Inferior (Enisala: Babeş 1971, 30, fig. 7:2; Teliţa-Amza: Baumann 1995, 97, pl. 54:9).

VI.2. Tall curved pots (41-42)

The maximum diameter is at the upper part of the jar (41-42). The mouth diameter is larger than that of the base. The rim is turned outwards. The base is flat or slightly concave.

One of the jars was made in a paste containing much sand (42). The pots are blackish (41) or brick-coloured (42) and are medium-sized.

One of them was decorated with a cordon applied on the maximum diameter and with four bosses set symmetrically on it, and with a horizontal strip of parallel incised lines (42). The other pot has two incised lines on the shoulder, in a horizontal wave (41).

The mentioned pots were discovered in the Soporu de Câmpie (41) and Locusteni (42) cemeteries. They were dated from the 2nd century AD to the first half of the 3rd century AD (42), and to the 2nd-3rd centuries AD (41).

Pots of this kind were found in the classic Dacian period from the Late Iron Age (Răcătău: Căpitanu 1969, 62, figs. 16:3;

17:5). For the time being, we know only one similar jar at Sarichioi-Sărătură (Baumann 1995, 188-189, pl. 11:10), in Moesia Inferior.

VI.3. Wide dished pots (43-65)

VI.3.1. Wide dished pots with the flaring rim (43-52)

The maximum diameter is slightly displaced towards the lower half of the body. The mouth diameter is larger than that of the base. The base is flat.

The pots were made of a sandy paste (46, 49) or of a paste containing sand and gravel (43, 48, 51), sand, mica and gravel (47). They are brick-coloured (43-49, 51) and are medium-sized.

The relief decoration is concentrated on the upper part of the body. A simple relief cordon was applied above the maximum diameter (45, 52), in other cases decorated with cells (43-44, 46), or notched (47). One of them was decorated with four bosses applied to the maximum diameter area (51), another one has the maximum diameter marked by a caesura (48). Two further pots were decorated with a horizontal row of cells on the shoulders and with vertical cells set between the shoulders and rims (47, 50).

These pots were discovered at the Locusteni cemetery (44, 46, 48, 51), in the Roman camp of Râşnov (45, 49), Olteni (47), and Ilişua (50), in the civilian settlement of Enoşeşti-Acidava Roman camp (43) and in the rural settlement no. 1 from Scorniceşti (52).

They were dated to the 2nd century AD (45), from the 2nd century AD to the first half of the 3rd century AD (44, 46, 48, 51), from the second half of the 2nd century AD to the first half of the 3rd century AD (52), in the middle of the 3rd century AD (47), and in the 2nd-3rd centuries AD (43, 45, 50).

Such pots were also found on the Ocniţa-Buridava site (Berciu 1981, figs. 84:3; 104:1-3) and Gropşani (Popilian 1999, 79, pl. 55:14), where they were dated to the classic Dacian period of the Late Iron Age. A pot with this shape was discovered in the rural settlement of Sarichioi-Sărătură (Baumann 1995, 188-189, pl. 11:11) from Moesia Inferior, and dated to the 2nd-3rd centuries AD.

VI.3.2. Wide dished pots with everted rim (53-55)

The maximum diameter is slightly displaced towards the lower part of the body. The mouth diameter is slightly larger than that of the pot base. The rim is short and much everted. The base is large and slightly concave.

The pots were made in a paste containing chaff and gravel (53), or sand (54-55). Two are brick-coloured (53-54), and one is blackish (55). They are of small dimensions (53-54) or medium-sized (55).

Celled cordons applied on the pot shoulder (53-55) represent the decoration.

The present pots were discovered in the Locusteni cemetery (54-55), and in the civilian settlement of the Enoşeşti-Acidava Roman camp (53). They were dated from the 2nd century AD to the first half of the 3rd century AD (54-55), and in the 2nd-3rd centuries AD (53).

Pots of this kind were discovered in the classic Dacian period of the Late Iron Age (Pecica-Ziridava: Crişan 1969, 163, pl. 78:8; Brad-Zargidava: Ursachi, pl. 63:4; Malaja Kopanija: Kotigoroško 1996, figs. 31:8, 12; 42:2; 116:20).

VI.3.3. Slender curved pots (56-63)

The maximum diameter is slightly displaced towards the lower part of the body (56-63). The mouth diameter is slightly larger than that of the base. The rim is everted (56, 60, 61) or turned outwards (58-59). Some of them have a well-marked neck (60-61). The base is flat or slightly concave.

The pots were made in paste containing sand (56, 60-61, 63), or sand and gravel (57, 59). They are brick-coloured (56, 57, 59, 61, 63), or grey-blackish (60).

Many of these pots were decorated with a celled cordon applied above the maximum diameter (56-58, 61), one being decorated with bosses applied over the maximum diameter and incised line (59), and with two rows of alveoli (60).

The pots were discovered in the Locusteni cemetery (56-57, 59, 61) in the Roman camp of Olteni (63), in the civilian settlements of the Enoşeşti-Acidava Roman camp (58, 60), and Stolniceni-Buridava (62). In the Locusteni cemetery they were dated to the 2nd century AD (59), from the 2nd century AD to the first half of the 3rd century AD (56-57, 61), at Stolniceni-Buridava to the beginning of the 3rd century AD (62), in the Roman camp of Olteni to the middle of the 3rd century AD (63), and in the civilian settlement of the Roman camp of Enoşeşti-Acidava to the 2nd-3rd centuries AD (58, 60).

The pots of this shape have analogies in the classic Dacian period of the Late Iron Age (Răcătău: Căpitanu 1976, 62, fig. 15:3; Ocniţa-Buridava: Berciu 1981, 110-111, pl. 84:5; Pecica-Ziridava: Crişan 1978, 130, fig. 7:3; Széremie: Visy 1970, pl. 1:1). During the 2nd-3rd centuries AD, such pots were also produced in the free Dacian area from the east of the Carpathians (Poiana-Dulceşti: Bichir 1973, 67, pl. 47:4; Văleni: Ioniţă, Ursachi 1988, 68, fig. 37:55), and in Moesia Inferior (Enisala: Babeş 1971, 30, fig. 6:1, 3).

VI.3.4. Tall curved pots with outward turned rim (64-65)

The maximum diameter is located at the middle of the body. The mouth is larger than that of the base. The rim is turned outward. The base is flat and slightly shaped.

The pots were made of sandy brick-coloured paste and are medium-sized.

The decoration is represented by the cordon with alveoli applied above the maximum diameter (64), or by round buttons applied on the shoulder and incised lines on the maximum diameter, or on the shoulder (65).

These pots were discovered in the Locusteni cemetery, where they were dated to the 2nd century AD (65), and from the 2nd century AD to the 3rd century AD (64).

The origin of these pots can be also placed in the classic Dacian period from the Late Iron Age (Ocniţa-Buridava: Berciu 1981, fig. 7:3; Széntendre: Visy 1970, pl. 5:9). A similar shaped pot was found in the rural settlement of Teliţa-Amza, in Moesia Inferior, dated to the 1st-2nd century AD (Baumann 1995, 95, pl. 54:7).

VII. Ovoid jars (66-74)

VII.1. Short ovoid jars (66-67)

The maximum diameter is located at the middle of the body. The mouth diameter is larger than that of the base. The rim is everted. The base is flat and narrow.

These jars were made from brick-colored paste (66) or from grey-blackish paste (67). They are large vessels.

One of the jars was decorated with a cordon with alveoli from which small sticks with alveoli hang. The neck was adorned with two incised lines (66). The other example has a horizontal incised line on the shoulder (67).

The jars were discovered in the Locusteni (66) and Soporu de Câmpie (67) cemeteries. They were dated from the 2nd century AD to the first half of the 3rd century AD (66), and to the 3rd century AD (67).

Similar jars were discovered in the Dacian levels of the Late Iron Age (Dezmir: Crişan 1969, 110, pl. 31:1-2; Răcătău: Căpitanu 1976, 62, fig. 15:2). During the 2nd-3rd centuries AD, these jars were also being produced in the territories inhabited by the free Dacians (Mătăsaru: Bichir 1984, pls. 11:6; 12:4; Poiana-Dulceşti: Bichir 1973, 67, pl. 44:3).

VII.2. Ovoid jars with vertical or outward turned rim (68-70)

The maximum diameter is at the middle of the body (68-70). The mouth diameter is almost equal to that of the base. The rim is vertical, turned outward or flaring. The base is flat and narrow.

The jars were made from brick-coloured sandy paste (70), or grey-reddish paste (68), or grey-blackish paste (69) and are medium-sized.

The decoration is represented by small round buttons applied on the jar shoulder (69) or by a cordon with alveoli applied over the maximum diameter (70).

These jars were discovered in the Soporu de Câmpie (69) and Locusteni (70) cemeteries, and also in the civilian settlement of the Tibiscum Roman camp (68). They were dated from the 2nd century AD to the first half of the 3rd century AD (70), to the 3rd century AD (69), and to the 2nd-3rd centuries AD (68).

Jars of the same shape were discovered in Dacian sites from the Late Iron Age (Răcătău: Căpitanu 1976, 57, fig. 13:2; Brad-Zargidava: Ursachi 1968, 177, pl. 55:3; Gorno Gradişte: Georgieva 1952, 269, fig. 252). Similar jars, dated to the 2nd-3rd centuries AD, were discovered within the Roman camp at Barboşi from Moesia Inferior (Sanie, Dragomir 1980, 343, fig. 6:6), and in the area of the upper Tisa River (Kotigoroško 1996, 135, fig. 113:7).

VII.3. Slender ovoid jars (71-74)

VII.3.1. Slender ovoid jar with the maximum diameter located at the shoulder (71)

The mouth diameter is larger than that of the base. The rim is very slightly turned outward. The base is concave.

The jar is brown-yellowish. Four bosses were applied on the shoulder, from which hangs an oblique segment adorned with alveoli.

This jar was discovered in the rural settlement of Slimnic, and dated to the 2nd-3rd centuries AD.

Similar jars were found in some Dacian sites dated from the 2nd BC to the 1st century AD (Sf. Gheorghe: Crişan 1969, 163, pl. 75:4-5; Costeşti: Crişan 1969, 163, pl. 75:9; Moigrad-Porolissum: Macrea, Rusu 1960, 213, fig. 11:6, 14; Pecica-Ziridava: Crişan 1978, 217, pl. 15:2).

VII.3.2. Tall ovoid jars with the maximum diameter located at the middle of the jar (72-74). The base is flat. The rim is everted.

The jars were made from a paste containing sand (72-73), and are brick-coloured (72, 74), or grey (73). They were decorated with two incised stripes or horizontal lines separated by two other stripes of incised waved lines (72), by a relief segment (73), and a cordon with alveoli applied over the maximum diameter (74).

The present jars were discovered in the civilian settlements of the Roman camps of Enoşeşti-Acidava (72) and Stolniceni-Buridava (73), and also in the Locusteni cemetery (74). They were dated from the 2nd century AD to the 3rd century AD (74), to the beginning of the 3rd century AD (73), and to the 2nd-3rd centuries AD (72).

A similar jar was found in the Dacian site of Moigrad-Porolissum, where it was dated from the 1st century BC to the 1st century AD (Crişan 1969, 163, pl. 74:4).

VIII. Tall cylindrical jars (75-88)

The tall cylindrical jars have slightly curved walls, sometimes shaped at a particular part of their body. Their maximum diameter is usually located at the middle of the body.

VIII.1. Tall cylindrical jars with slightly curved walls (75-78)

VIII.1.1. Tall cylindrical jars with slightly curved walls at the third section of the body (75)

The maximum diameter is situated at the upper part of the body. The mouth diameter is larger than that of the base. The rim is turned outward. The base is flat.

The jar was made from rough, very friable grey paste. It is medium-sized.

In the maximum diameter area a cordon with cells was applied, and a waved line was incised on the neck.

The jar was discovered in the Soporu de Câmpie cemetery, and dated to the 2nd-3rd centuries AD.

VIII. 1.2. Tall cylindrical jars with slightly curved walls (76-78)

The maximum diameter is located in the middle part of the body. The mouth diameter is larger than that of the base. The rim is flared. The base is flat.

The jars were made from a very sandy (76, 78), friable paste (77). They are brick-coloured (76, 78), or brown-blackish (77), and of middle-sized.

The decoration is represented by two cordons with cells, applied under the rim (76) and a cordon with cells applied at the maximum diameter area (77-78).

These jars were discovered in the Locusteni (76) and Soporu de Câmpie (77) cemeteries and in the rural settlement of Filiași (78). They were dated from the 2nd century AD to the first half of the 3rd century AD (76), and to the 2nd-3rd centuries AD (77-78).

Jars like these were found in several Dacian archaeological sites from the Late Iron Age (Pecica-Ziridava: Crișan 1969, 163, pl. 78:1; Martfü: Visy 1970, 8, pl. 2:6; Răcătău: Căpitanu 1976, 62, fig. 19:3). They were also produced in the 2nd-3rd centuries AD in the territories inhabited by the Dacians outside the Dacia province borders (Ruptura: Bichir 1973, 67, pl. 47:1).

VIII. 2. Tall cylindrical jars with slightly shaped walls (79-86)

The maximum diameter is located at the middle of the body. The mouth diameter is larger than that of the base. The rim is everted. The base is flat (79, 81-83) or slightly concave (80).

These jars were made from a paste containing sand (80, 86), or sand and gravel (83, 85). They are brick-coloured (80, 83, 85), blackish (79), grey (86) and grey-yellowish (84).

Decoration is by way of a threshold (84-85), an oblique segment (86), a cordon with alveoli (80, 82-83), and by cells on the rim (83).

The jars were discovered in the Săcelu (79) and Scornicești (82) settlements, in the Locusteni (80) and Soporu de Câmpie (83-84) cemeteries, in the Roman camps of Ilișua (81), Olteni (85), and also in the civilian settlement of the Stolniceni-Buridava Roman camp (86). They were dated to the second half of the 2nd century AD (83), from the 2nd century AD to the first half of the 3rd century AD (82), and to the 2nd-3rd centuries AD (79, 81, 84). This kind of jar was also found in many Dacian sites from the Late Iron Age (Răcătău: Căpitanu 1976, 62, pl. 16:4; Gorno Gradiște: Georgieva 1952, 269, fig. 253; Căpâlna: Glodariu, Moga 1989, 184, fig. 47:4; Arpașu de Sus: Macrea, Glodariu 1976, fig. 26:29; Moigrad-Porolissum: Crițan 1969, 163, pl. 74:7; Budapest-Tabán: Hunyady 1942, 81, 101:6; Zemplin: Kolnik 1972, 524-525, fig. 27:1). During 2nd-4th centuries AD, such jars were also produced within the territories inhabited by the free Dacians (Butnărești: Bichir 1973, 67, pl. 44:4; Văleni: Ioniță, Ursachi 1988, 68, figs. 33:1; 39: 47).

VIII.3. Tall cylindrical jars with straight walls (87-88)

The mouth diameter is almost equal to that of the base. The rim is everted. The base is flat. They are small-sized jars.

A cordon represents the decoration, with cells applied on the lower part of the body (88).

These jars were discovered in the rural settlement no. 1 of Scornicești (87) and in the civilian settlement of the Roman camp of Enoșești-Acidava (88). They were dated from the second half of the 2nd century AD to the first half of the 3rd century AD (87), and in the 2nd-3rd centuries AD (88).

The present jars have analogies with some discovered in Dacian sites dated to the 3rd-2nd centuries BC (Cetea: Crișan 1969, 163, pl. 79:1; Pecica-Ziridava: Crișan 1969, 163, pl. 39:2-6). Such jars were discovered in Moesia Inferior at the Rucăr Roman castellum (Bogdan-Cătăniciu 1985-1986, 205, fig. 2:5-7), where they were dated to the first two decades of the 2nd century AD, and also within the territories of the free Dacians (Poiana-Dulcești: Bichir 1973, 67, pl. 48:3; Mătăsaru: Bichir 1984, pl. 12:2; Janoszàllàs: Pàrducz 1956, 27, fig. 2:10).

IX. Large cylindrical jars (89-97)

The large cylindrical jars have slightly curved walls. Their maximum diameter is located at the middle or lower part of the body. The rim is short and everted. The generally accepted traditional denomination should be that of "sack-type" jars.

IX.1. Large almost cylindrical jars (89-96)

The maximum diameter is at the middle of the body. The mouth diameter is larger than that of the base. The rim is more (90, 92, 96) or less (89, 94-95) everted. The base is flat and sometimes shaped.

The jars were made from sandy paste (89, 91, 95), or from a paste with sand and gravel (93, 96). They are grey (89), brick-coloured (90, 93), blackish (91) or brown-reddish (95). All of them are medium-sized.

This type of jar was discovered in the cemeteries of Leu (89) and Locusteni (90, 93), in the rural settlement of Obreja 991), and in the Roman camps of Gilău (92), Ilişua (94) and Buciumi (95-96). They were dated from the 2nd century AD to the first half of the 3rd century AD (89-90, 93), and to the 2nd-3rd centuries AD (91-92, 94-96).

Similar jars were found in some Dacian archaeological sites dated from the 1st century BC to the 1st century AD (Gropşani: Popilian 1999, 85, 86, pl. 57:3; Pecica-Ziridava: Crişan 1978, 130, fig. 7:2; Tilişca: Lupu 1989, 110, fig. 9:8; Sighişoara: Crişan 1969, 163, pl. 79:11). During the 2nd-4th centuries AD, such jars were also produced in Moesia Inferior (Enisala: Babeş 1971, 30, fig. 7:3), and in the territories inhabited by the free Dacians (Upper Tisa River area: Kotigoroško 1996, 136, fig. 113:9, 11; Poiana-Dulceşti: Bichir 1973, 65, pl. 44:1; Teliţa-Amza: Baumann 1995, 96; Janoszàllàs: Pàrducz 1956, 29, fig. 3:10).

IX.2. Large cylindrical jar with narrow base (97)

The maximum diameter is located at the upper part of the body. The mouth diameter is much larger than that of the base. The rim is flaring. The base is flat, narrow and shaped.

The jar was made from a paste containing sand and gravel. It is brick-coloured and of medium size.

Four wavy segments with cells were applied on the shoulder, in "W" character shape.

The jar was discovered in the Locusteni cemetery, where it was dated from the 2nd century AD to the first half of the 3rd century AD.

A similar jar was found in the Dacian site at Pecica-Ziridava, dated from the 1st century BC to the 1st century AD (Crişan 1969, 163, pl. 73:2).

Kitchen ware

X. Lids (98-109)

X.1. Curved shaped lids (98-103)

X.1.1. Hemispheric lids with button (98-100)

The rim is rounded. The upper part with the button is missing. All these lids come from the rural settlement at Timişoara-Freidorf, where they were dated to the 2nd-3rd centuries AD.

Similar wheel-made lids were discovered in the classic Dacian Late Iron Age settlements (Crişan 1969, 182-183, pl. 83:6, 10-11). Some hand-made lids dating from the 2nd-4th

centuries AD were found in the upper course area of the Tisa River (Kotigoroško 1996, 137, fig. 115:16, 20).

X.1.2. Calotte-shaped lids with button (101-103)

The rim is horizontally cut. The button is short and flat (101, 103), or celled (102). They are brick-coloured (102), or brownish-red (101).

This kind of lid was found in the civilian settlement of the Roman camp of Tibiscum (101-102) and in the rural settlement no. 1 of Scorniceşti (103). The lid from Scorniceşti was dated from the second half of the 2nd century AD to the first half of the 3rd century AD, and those at Tibiscum to the 2nd-3rd centuries AD.

This kind of lid was discovered in some Dacian sites from the Late Iron Age (Sprâncenata: Preda 1986, 91, fig. 26:5; Căpâlna: Glodariu, Moga 1989, fig. 62:13-14; Upper Tisa River area: Kotigoroško 1996, 85, fig. 43:31). Similar discoveries were made in the free Dacian settlement of Bucureşti-Militari "Câmpul Boja", where they were dated to the middle and the third quarter of the 3rd century AD (Negru 2000, 72, pl. 92:9). In the 2nd-4th centuries they were also made in Moesia Inferior (Barboşi: Sanie, Dragomir 1980, 343, fig. 6:4) and in the area of the upper course of the Tisa River (Kotigoroško 1996, 137, fig. 115:12, 15, 17).

X.2. Conical lids (104-109)

X.2.1. Conical lids with outward bent walls (104-107)

The button is short, and the rim is flaring. This type of lid was discovered in the rural settlements of Timişoara-Freidorf (104) and Dedrad (107), within the Roman camp of Ilişua (106), and in the civilian settlement of the Roman camp of Tibiscum (105). They were dated to the 2nd-3rd centuries AD (104-105), from the 2nd century AD to the middle of the 3rd century AD (107), and to the middle of the 3rd century AD.

Similar lids were discovered in Dacian sites from the Late Iron Age (Malaja Kopanja: Kotigoroško 1996, 84, fig. 35:11; Brad-Zargidava Ursachi 1995, 162, pl. 68:31; Pecica-Ziridava: Crişan 1978, 183, pl. 98:3).

X.2.2. Tall conical lids with tall body and short button (108-109)

The button is celled and the rim is narrow. Two such lids (that could be pieced together) were discovered in the Roman camp of Gilău, where they were dated to the 3rd century AD. They are imitations of a wheel-made lid type found in some Dacian archaeological sites from the Late Iron Age (Brad-Zargidava Ursachi 1995, 182-183, pl. 112:6; Piatra Neamţ: Crişan 1969, 183, fig. 97:5; Poiana-Tecuci: Crişan 1969, 183, fig. 97:7; Meleia: Crişan 1969, 183, pl. 187:6-8; Guşteriţa: Crişan 1969, 183, pl. 187:9; Pecica-Ziridava: Crişan 1979, 131, pl. 98:1-2). From the middle and the third quarter of the 3rd century AD, similar lids were also produced in the free Dacian settlement of Bucureşti-Militari ("Câmpul Boja") (Negru 2000, 70-72, pls. 82:4; 88:1; 92:10).

Table ware

XI. Dish (110)

XI.1. Conical dish with rounded rim (110)

Such a vessel was discovered in the rural settlement no. 1 of Scorniceşti. It was dated from the second half of the 2nd century AD to the first half of the 3rd century AD.

Illuminating vessels

XII. Dacian cups (111-150)

According to the number of handles, the Dacian cups can be divided into one-, two-, and three-handled cups. Those with two handles are rare and the example of the cup with three was exceptional.

XII.1. Single handle Dacian cups (111-144)

XII.1.1. Cups with short conical body (111-124)

XII.1.1.1. Cups with short conical body and flat bottom (111-120)

The rim is a prolongation of the walls (98-107), or slightly flaring (119-120). The bottom is flat. The cups were made from a paste containing sand and gravel (111, 113, 115). They are blackish (111), brown-reddish (115) or brick-coloured (119). They are small-sized (114, 117) or middle-sized (98-102, 115-116, 118-120).

The present cups were discovered in the Scorniceşti settlement no. 1 (114), the Obreja settlement (116-118), the Locusteni cemetery (113, 119), the Roman camps of Porolissum (115), Olteni (112) and Orheiul Bistriţei (120), and also in the civilian settlement of the Roman camp of Enoşeşti-Acidava (111).

The above-mentioned cups dated from the 2nd century AD, the first half of the 3rd century AD (113, 119), the second half of the 2nd century AD, the first half of the 3rd century AD (114), the middle of the 3rd century AD (112), and the 2nd-3rd centuries AD (111, 115-118, 120).

XII.1.1.2. Short conical cups with shaped bottom (121-124)

The rim is a continuation of the walls (123-124). The flat bottom is shaped. All the examples have a single handle.

The vessels were made from rough paste (121-122), with sand and gravel (123). They are brick-coloured (121-122) or brown-reddish (123).

These vessels were discovered in the Leu-Albota settlement (122), and in the Roman camps of Drobeta (121), Breţcu (123) and Gilãu (124). All the present cups were dated to the 2nd-3rd centuries AD.

The short, conical-bodied Dacian cups had appeared by the beginning of the 2nd century BC (Boroneanţ, Davidescu 1968, 259; Moscalu 1983, 85) and continued to be produced during the whole of the classic Dacian period of the Late Iron Age (Rãcãtãu: Cãpitanu 1976, 57, fig. 23; Poiana-Tecuci: Crişan 1969, 156, fig. 66:2, 4; Zimnicea: Alexandrescu 1980, 47, 77, fig. 23:31; Ghizdaru: Turcu 1979, 118, fig. 15:5; Cozia Veche: Moscalu 1968, 636, fig. 5:5; Sprâncenata: Preda 1986, 87, 88, pls. 15:6, 7; 17:2; Ocniţa-Buridava: Berciu 1981, figs. 8:2; 50:7; Devetaki: Mikov, Djambakov 1960, 155, figs. 117-118; Cãpâlna: Glodariu, Moga 1989, 67, pls. 28:10, 14; 29:3, 7; Tilişca: Lupu 1989, 66, pls. 6:9; 7:7; Pecica-Ziridava: Crişan 1978, 128, pl. 32:12; Crişan 1969, 155, fig. 65:4; pl. 47:1; Gomolava: Brukner 1990, 26, 34, pl. 20:144; Sandor 1960, 128, pl. 10:6; Jovanović 1971, 144, pl. 5:1; Židovar: Todorović 1962, 145-146, fig. 2; Doboz-Hajduirtas: Visy 1970, pl. 1:4; Chotin: Točik 1959, 855, fig. 322:8; Altimir: Nikolov 1965, 175, fig. 16v; Staroe Selo: Angelov 1952, 376, fig. 381a). During the 2nd-3rd centuries AD, this type of cups was being produced in Moesia Inferior (Tãrgovište: Ohcearov 1965, 35, fig. 3) and in the territories inhabited by the free Dacians (Bucureşti-Strãuleşti: Tzony 1980, 312, fig. 2:2; Bucureşti-Militari "Câmpul Boja": Negru 2000, pl. 58:4; Mãtãsaru: Bichir 1984, pl. 10:1; Poiana-Dulceşti: Bichir 1973, 64, pl. 39:6). The Dacian cup stopped evolving in the 4th century AD (Crişan 1955, 133).

XII.1.2. Slender conical cups (125-144)

XII.1.2.1. Tall conical cups (125-128)

The rim is a continuation of the walls and is rounded, turned down inwards, or flaring. The bottom is narrow and flat.

The vessels are medium to large in size, except for one miniature example (126).

Cups of this shape were found in the rural settlement of Obreja (125, 128), in the Locusteni cemetery (127), and in the Roman camp of Porolissum (126).

The present cups were dated from the 2nd century AD to the first half of the 3rd century AD (127), also from the 2nd-3rd centuries AD (125-126, 128).

The origin of the tall, conical Dacian cup can be placed during the period of the classic Dacian sites from the 1st century BC to the 1st century AD (Rãcãtãu: Cãpitanu 1976, 57, pl. 23:5; Lukaşevka: Crişan 1969, 162, fig. 71:5; Bâtca Doamnei: Buzilã 1970, 242, 246, fig. 23:4, 8; Piscu Crãsani: Andrieşescu 1924, 25-26, figs. 62, 64-65; Sprâncenata: Preda 1986, 87, pl. 15:8; Bucureşti - Lacul Tei: Turcu 1979, 119, fig. 15:6; Ocniţa-Buridava: Berciu 1981, fig. 50:1-3; Altimir: Nikolov 1966, 175, fig. 16b; Costeşti: Crişan 1969, 155, pl. 46:25; Chotin: Točik 1959, 861, pl. 325:1-2). They continued to be produced (1st-2nd centuries AD) in the rural settlement of Revãrsarea-Cotul Tichileşti (Baumann 1995, 236-237, pl. 14:15), in Moesia Inferior, and in Bucureşti-Militari ("Câmpul Boja") settlement from the middle and the third quarter of the 3rd century AD (Negru 2000, 71, pl. 88:3).

XII.1.2.2. Slender conical cups with flaring upper section (129-137)

The rim is narrow and flaring. The bottom is flat. All the examples that could be pieced together had a single handle.

The vessels were made from a paste containing much sand (129, 133), or with sand and gravel (131, 136-137). They are brick-coloured (129-132), grey (133), or brown-reddish (136-137). All the present cups are medium-sized. Only one was decorated with a cordon with alveoli applied at its base (132). One cup was decorated with a fir-tree branch and with oblique notches on the rim (131).

These vessels were discovered in the rural settlement of Obreja (131), Scorniceşti (135), the Locusteni cemetery (129-130, 132), in the civilian settlement of the Stolniceni-Buridava Roman camp (133), and in the Roman camps of Olteni (136), Micia (134) and Breţcu (137).

They were dated from the 2nd century AD to the first half of the 3rd century AD (129-130, 132), from the second half of the 2nd century AD to the first half of the 3rd century AD (135), at the end of the 2nd century AD and the beginning of the 3rd century AD (133), and in the 2nd and 3rd centuries AD (131, 134, 136-137).

XII.1.2.3. Conical-shaped cups with everted upper half (138-140)

The rim is everted. The bottom is flat. All these cups are medium-large sized.

One of the discovered items was decorated with cordon alveoli under the rim and on the base (138).

The present Dacian vessels were discovered in the rural settlement no. 1 of Scorniceşti (138), abd in the Roman camps of Olteni (139) and Ilişua (140). They were dated from the second half of the 2nd century AD to the first half of the 3rd century AD (138), and also to the 2nd-3rd centuries AD (139-140).

XII.1.2.4. Tall conical-shaped cups with upper part much-everted (141-144)

The rim is narrowed. The bottom is flat and narrow. Sometimes the cups have a full handle (143), or a button at the base (144).

These cups were made from a paste containing sand (143), or sand and gravel (142). They are brick-coloured (143), or brown-reddish (142).

The present vessels were discovered in the rural settlement no. 1 of Scorniceşti (141, 144), and in the Roman camps of Porolissum (142) and Olteni (143). They were dated from the second half of the 2nd century AD to the first half of the 3rd century AD (141, 144), to the 3rd century AD (142), and to the 2nd-3rd centuries AD (143).

A miniature cup, similar to that of Porolissum (142), was found in the Dacian fortress of Brad-Zargidava, where it was dated to the classic Dacian period of the Late Iron Age (Ursachi 1995, 163, pl. 72:16-29).

The origin of the Dacian cup type 1.2 may be placed in the classic Dacian period of the Late Iron Age (Brad-Zargidava Ursachi 1968, 177, fig. 55:1, 8; Răcătău: Căpitanu 1976, 62, fig. 23:1-2; Orlovka: Babeş 1980, 13, fig. 1B, 5; Bâtca Doamnei: Buzilă 1970, 242, fig. 22:5, 7-8; Cozia Veche: Moscalu 1968, 636, fig. 5:4; Tinosu: Vulpe, Vulpe 1924, 203, fig. 32:2; Radovanu: Turcu 1979, 119, fig. 24:5; Bucureşti: Turcu 1979, 119, fig. 24:4; Căţelu Nou: Leahu 1962, 32, fig. 22:4; Sprâncenata: Preda 1986, 87-88, figs. 16:3, 5; 17:6; 18:3, 8; Zimnicea: Alexandrescu 1980, 47, fig. 23:32; Ocniţa-Buridava: Berciu 1981, figs. 10:5; 24:1, 3; 25:1; 105:4; Staro Selo: Angelov 1952, 376, fig. 381v; Slimnic: Glodariu 1981, 35, fig. 40:6; Căpâlna: Glodariu, Moga 1989, 67, fig. 28:1; Tilişca: Lupu 1989, 66, pl. 15:1; Moigrad-Porolissum: Crişan 1969, 157, fig. 67:11; Arpaşu de Sus: Macrea, Glodariu 1976, fig. 38:21; Pecica-Ziridava: Crişan 1969, 155, pls. 46:11, 13, 18, 22; Židovar: Gavela 1952, 66, figs. 16:1; 17:1, 3; 20:17; Todorović 1962, 145-146, fig. 32; Brestović: Todorović 1962, 145-146, fig. 4; Gomolava: Jovanović 1971, 144, pl. 5:3; Simanovči: Brukner 1987, fig. 16:3; Progar: Brukner 1987, fig. 19:4; Budapest-Tabàn: Hunyady 1942, 81, 101:3; Besa: Lamiovà-Schmiedlova 1969, 460, fig. 37:2; Srem: Brukner 1988, 96, pl. 1:4). During the 2nd-3rd centuries AD, cups with a flared upper section continued to be produced in Moesia Inferior (Barboşi: Sanie, Dragomir 1980, 343, fig. 6:3; Buceag: Scorpan 1969, 49, fig. 16, 17; Hotniţa: Sultov 1980, 384, fig. 11d [wheel-made]; Revărsarea-Cotul Tichileşti: Baumann 1995, 236-237, pl. 14:17) and in the free Dacians' territories (Bucureşti-Militari "Câmpul Boja": Negru 2000, 72, pl. 92:2; Poiana-Dulceşti: Bichir 1973, pls. 38:1; 39:4; Văleni: Ioniţă, Ursachi 1988, 68-69, fig. 53:47).

XII.2. Dacian cups with two handles (145-148)

XII.2.1.1. Dacian cups with short conical-shaped body (145-146)

The handles are attached under the rim and above the base line. This kind of cup was discovered in the Soporu de Câmpie cemetery (145), and in the rural settlement of Obreja (146), where they were dated to the 2nd-3rd centuries AD.

XII.2.1. Dacian cups with tall conical-shaped body (147)

The handles were fixed under the rim and above the base line. The vessel was made from a paste containing sand. It is brick-coloured.

The only item of this type found was discovered in the Locusteni cemetery, where it was dated from the 2nd century AD to the first half of the 3rd century AD.

Dacian cups with two handles, and tall (Pecica-Ziridava: Crişan 1978, 226, pl. 31:7; Moigrad: Crişan 1969, 155, pl. 47:11), or short (Pecica-Ziridava: Crişan 1969, 155, pl. 47:9; Crişan 1978, 226, pl. 31:5), conical-shaped bodies were discovered in the Dacian pre-Roman Period.

XII.2.2. Dacian cups with flaring upper part (148-149)

The rim is narrow and flaring. The base is flat. Two such cups were discovered in the Locusteni cemetery, where they were dated from the 2nd century AD to the first half of the 3rd century AD.

Cups of this shape were found in archaeological sites dating from the classic Dacian period of the Late Iron Age (Poiana: Crişan 1969, 156, fig. 66:10), and in the free Dacian area (Poiana-Dulceşti: Bichir 1973, 64, pl. 60:1).

XII.3. Dacian cup with three handles (150)

Upper, half-flaring body. The handles were fixed under the rim and on the base line.

The only example of this type found was discovered in the Obreja rural settlement, where it was dated to the 2nd-3rd centuries AD.

This cup is unique so far in 2nd-3rd-century AD contexts, and for the classic Dacian period of the Late Iron Age.

XIII. Conical-shaped vessels (151-175)

The Conical-shaped vessels were inappropriately called "handle-less Dacian cups". They are similar in profile to the Dacian cups, according to the principles used in the typology.

XIII.1. Conical-shaped vessels (151-164)

XIII.1.1. Conical-shaped vessels with inward turned rim or flaring rim (151-159).

The base is flat or often shaped (151-155). Such vessels were discovered in the Roman camps at Ilişua (151, 153) and Gilău (154, 156), in the civilian settlements of Tibiscum (152) and Enoşeşti-Acidava (155, 157), and also in the Scorniceşti (158) and Slimnic (159) rural settlements.

They were dated from the first half of the 2nd century AD (152) and second half of the 2nd century AD to the first half of the 3rd century AD (158), to the 3rd century AD (154, 156), and to the 2nd-3rd centuries AD (151, 153, 155, 157, 159).

The origin of these vessels may be placed in the early Dacian period of the Late Iron Age (Buceag: Moscalu 1983, 70, pl. 51:2). Numerous vessels of this shape were found in the Dacian fortifications from the Late Iron Age at Brad-Zargidava (Ursachi 1995, 162, pl. 66) and Ocniţa-Buridava (Berciu, Iosifaru, Diaconescu 1992, 115, figs. 2:2-3, 7-8; 5:2). One similar vessel was found at the Sarichioi-Sărătură Roman rural settlement from Moesia Inferior (Baumann 1995, 212, pl. 12:13), and another in the rural settlement of the free Dacians from Bucureşti-Militari ("Câmpul Boja") (Negru 2000, 65, 71, 74, pls. 66:1; 72:6; 85:8; 98:7). The vessel from Bucureşti was dated to the middle or the third quarter of the 3rd century AD, and the other to the 2nd-3rd centuries AD.

XIII.1.2. Conical-shaped vessels with flaring rim (160-163)

The conical-shaped body is tall. The base is flat. One such item was discovered in the Slimnic rural settlement (160), and others were found in the civilian settlement of the Enosesti-Acidava Roman camp (161) and in the Gilău Roman camp (162-163).

The vessels found at Gilău were dated to the 3rd century AD (162-163), the others were dated to the 2nd-3rd centuries AD.

Similar vessel were found in Moesia Inferior, in the Roman settlement of Sarichioi-Sărătură (Baumann 1995, 208, pl. 12:8), and in the Roman camp of Barboşi (Sanie, Dragomir 1980, 343, fig. 6:2). They were dated to the 2nd-3rd centuries AD.

XIII.1.3. Slender conical-shaped vessel (164)

The slender, conical-shaped body leads one to consider that it was used as a cup. The rim is narrowed. The base is shaped.

The only example of this form was discovered in the civilian settlement of the Enoşeşti-Acidava Roman camp, where it was dated to the 2nd-3rd century AD.

XIII.2. Conical-shaped vessels with flaring upper half (165-175)

XIII.2.1. Short conical-shaped with flat large base (165-166)

Two such vessels were discovered in the Ilişua Roman camp, where they were dated to the 2nd-3rd centuries AD.

XIII.2.2. Conical-shaped vessels with slightly flat base (167-170)

The base is flat (167), or slightly shaped (169). They are small to medium sized.

Such vessels were found in the Roman camps of Buciumi (167), and Gilău (168-170). They were dated to the 3rd century AD (168, 170) and the 2nd-3rd centuries AD (167, 169).

XIII.2.3. Slender conical-shaped vessels (171-173)

The base is flat. They were made from a paste containing sand (172-173), and are brick-coloured (173), or brown-reddish (172).

This kind of vessel was discovered in the rural settlement of Obreja (171, 173) and in the Roman camp of Pojejena (172). These vessels were dated to the 2nd-3rd centuries AD.

XIII.2.4. Conical-shaped vessels with very flared upper part (174-175)

The rim is a continuation of the body. The base is shaped. Two such vessels were discovered in the Gilău Roman camp, where they were dated to the 3rd century AD.

Similar vessels were discovered in several Dacian sites of the Late Iron Age from Pannonia and Moesia Inferior, where they were dated from the 1st century BC to the 1st century AD (Gomolava: Brukner 1990, 34, pl. 20:143; □idovar: Gavela 1952, 66, fig. 19:2; Sirmium: Brukner 1981, 186, pl. 3:10; Pannonia: Bónis 1942, 36, pl. 2:3-4, 8). Vessels of the same shape were also found in the free Dacian settlement of Mãtãsaru, where they were dated from the 2nd century AD to the beginning of the 4th century AD (Mãtãsaru: Bichir 1984, pl. 10:9-11, 14).

Chapter III
THE WHEEL-MADE POTTERY

The examples of native tradition, wheel-made pottery discovered in Dacia province are not numerous, and there are only a few fully reconstructed vessels. In such circumstances, research depends exclusively on the state of the excavations that impose some limits to the approach to this subject.

Other problems concern the context of the discoveries, their chronological delimitation, and the matter of their belonging to the local tradition pottery from Dacia province.

Some vessels discovered at Reşca-Romula could not be used in the present study as they were not found in clear stratigraphic conditions that would allow clear dating to the Roman Period, and traces of 2nd-3rd centuries AD habitation were also found (Mãrgãrit-Tãtulea 1994, figs. 17:3; 22:4).

Other biconical jars considered to be local tradition pottery obviously imitate shapes from the Celtic pottery repertory (Popilian 1980, 84, pl. 76:5). It is possible for those vessels to have been produced in Dacia province, but for the time being they cannot be considered as ware of local tradition. My reticence is based mainly on the possibility that future research might observe signs of co-habitation between the Dacians and the Celts during the last decades of the first century AD. This situation was theoretically possible in south-eastern Dacia.

The main problem with local tradition pottery made on a potter's wheel seems to be its delimitation from Roman provincial pottery made of fine paste. This delimitation can be made particularly by comparative analysis with the Dacian pottery dating from the 1st century BC to the 1st century AD (Negru 2000a, 235-240). Nevertheless, there is a risk that a shape taken by Dacians before the Roman conquest might also appear in the repertory of Roman provincial pottery (cups, pots, lids). In such a case, an attentive study of the paste composition and colour is necessary, and the results should be compared to those typical of the classic Dacian period from the Late Iron Age and of Roman provincial samples. In the same way one can resolve the dilemma of the presence of supposed free Dacian pottery in the Dacia province, as far as this has its origins in the same Dacian, pre-Roman, pottery.

Storage ware

A. Provision jars (176-177)

Within the range of storage vessels, two ovoid jars can also be included (based on their shape and dimensions).

A.1. Jar of large dimensions with ovoid body (176)

The maximum diameter is slightly displaced towards the upper part. The rim is flared. The base is flat and narrow.

One single item of this kind was discovered in the rural settlement of Obreja, where it was dated from the middle of the 2nd century AD to the end of the 3rd century AD. In the maximum diameter area it was decorated with a cut cordon.

The above-mentioned jar is a wheel-made version of the very common hand-made shape from the classic Dacian period of the Late Iron Age, as well as the Roman Period (see the bibliography for jars nos. 1-4).

A.2. Jar with ovoid body (177)

The rim is everted. The vessel was made from a sandy, very friable paste. On the shoulder it was decorated with a cordon of waved incised lines, under which there is another cordon of horizontal incised lines.

The jar was discovered in the Locusteni cemetery, where it was dated from the 2nd century AD to the first half of the 3rd century AD.

This jar has parallels in the Ocniţa-Buridava archaeological site from the classic Dacian Late Iron Age period (Berciu 1981, 123, pl. 101:1). Similar hand-made jars were discovered in the Locusteni cemetery of the Roman Period (Popilian 1980, 83).

Kitchen ware

B. Pots with curved body (178)

B.1. Pot with slightly curved body (178)

The maximum diameter is at the middle of the body. The rim is everted. The base is flat.

The pot was made from a fine, grey paste containing sand as a degreasing substance. A strip of incised horizontal lines was traced on the shoulder, with another, of waves lines, above it.

It was discovered in the Locusteni cemetery, where it was dated to the 2nd century AD.

A further example was at found Ocniţa-Buridava, dated to the classic Dacian period of the Late Iron Age (Berciu 1981, 26, pl. 7:3). During the 2nd-3rd centuries AD at Locusteni such shapes were hand-made (see above jars nos. 55-59).

C. Strainers (179-180)

C.1. Strainers with biconical shape body (179-180))

C.1.1. Strainers with bitronconical shape body (179)

The rim is everted. The base is flat. There are no ears.

The only example was found in settlement no. 1 at Scorniceşti, where it was dated from the second half of the 2nd century AD to the first half of the 3rd century AD.

The strainer has a parallel at the Dacian Late Iron Age site of Sf. Gheorghe (Crişan 1969, 171, pl. 56:6).

C.1.2. Strainers with biconical shape body (180)

The rim is everted. The neck is short and cylindrical.

A fragment of such a strainer was discovered within the rural settlement no. 1 of Scorniceşti, where it was dated from the second half of the 2nd century AD to the first half of the 3rd century AD.

The above-mentioned strainer has numerous analogies in the classic Dacian period of the Late Iron Age (Răcătău: Căpitanu 1976, 63, fig. 30:3-6; Poiana-Tecuci: Vulpe, Vulpe 1957, 156, fig. 8:2; Piscu Crăsani: Andrieşescu 1924, 71, fig. 185; Ocniţa-Buridava: Berciu 1981, pls. 8:1; 12:17; 25:6; Tilişca: Lupu 1989, 66, pl. 9:6; Arpaşu de Sus: Macrea, Glodariu 1976, fig. 47:1; Bicsad: Crişan 1969, 171, pl. 56:1). Other such vessels were discovered in Pannonia (Sirmium: Brukner 1987, 31, fig. 24:12; Acuincum: Brukner 1981, 99, pl. 99:7), Moesia Inferior (Troesmis: Opaiţ 1980, 333, pl. 5:3), and also in the free Dacian territories of the 2nd-3rd centuries AD (Poiana-Dulceşti: Bichir 1973, 85, pl. 135:1-2; Mătăsaru: Bichir 1984, 36, pl. 13:4).

Fragments of strainers that could not be typologically classified were also discovered in the Dacia province at Ocna Sibiului (Protase 1968, 232, fig. 3:1) and also at Dedrad (Glodariu 1975, 239).

Table ware

D. Jugs (181-187)

D.1. Biconical jugs (181-186)

D.1.1. Short biconical jugs (181-182)

The maximum diameter is measured at the middle of the vessel or at its lower part. The rim is obliquely everted. The base is flat and shaped. The over-rising handle is fixed under the rim and above the maximum diameter.

The jugs were made from fine grey paste. They are medium-small in size. Two such jugs were found in the Daneţi cemetery (181) and in the rural settlement no. 1 of Scorniceşti (182). They were dated from the 2nd century AD to the first half of the 3rd century AD.

Similar vessels were found in some Dacian sites from the 3rd-2nd centuries BC (Moreşti: Crişan 1969, 118, pl. 38:1; Zimnicea: Alexandrescu 1980, 48, figs. 35:4; 36:10). The jugs have numerous analogies within the discoveries made at a series of archaeological sites dating from the 2nd century BC to the 1st century AD (Moigrad-Porolissum: Crişan 1969, 165, pl. 62:7; Macrea, Rusu 1960, 214, fig. 12:1; Brad-Zargidava Ursachi 1968, 181, fig. 54:1; Socu: Gherghe 1985, 55, fig. 11:6; Ocniţa-Buridava: Berciu 1981, 34, fig. 14:2; Sighişoara: Crişan 1969, 165, pl. 63:10; Pecica-Ziridava: Crişan 1978, 114, 118, fig. 34:10; Ungaria: Hunyady 1942, pls. 71:10; 73:9; Gropşani: Popilian 1998, 86-87, pl. 58:2).

This type of jug was frequently found in the 2nd-3rd centuries AD within free Dacians territories - outside the province of Dacia itself (Poiana-Dulceşti: Bichir 1973, 83, pl. 123:1-2, 5; Poieneşti: Bichir 1973, 83, pl. 125:2; Largu: Bichir 1984, pl. 61:7).

D.1.2. Slender biconical jugs (183-186)

D.1.2.1. Small slender biconical jugs (183-184)

The maximum diameter is located at the middle of the vessel. The rim is flared. The base is concave. The over-rising handle was fixed at the rim and shoulder.

One of the small jugs was made from grey, rough paste (184).

These small jugs were discovered in the Obreja rural settlement (183) and in the Locusteni cemetery (184).

They were dated from the 2nd century AD to the first half of the 3rd century AD (184), and to the 2nd-3rd centuries AD (183).

Similar jugs were found at some sites from the classic Dacian period of the Late Iron Age (Sprâncenata: Preda 1986, pl. 33:4; Brad-Zargidava Ursachi 1995, 174, pl. 97:2).

D.2. Jugs with curved body (185)

The handle is fixed to the rim and shoulder. The jug is made from fine, grey paste.

One sample of this shape was discovered in the civilian settlement of the Tibiscum Roman camp, where it was dated to the beginning of the 2nd century AD.

A similar jug was found at Piscul Crăsani where it was dated to the classic Dacian period of the Late Iron Age (Andrieşescu 1924, 71, fig, 182).

A similar jug of this type was found at a Late Iron Age Dacian site (Fotoş: Crişan 1969, 177, pl. 70:14). This type of jar was also produced in Moesia Inferior (Horia: Scorpan 1968, 351, fig. 8b) and within the free Dacian territories (Mişina: Smisko 1960, 29, pl. 12:9) throughout the 2nd-3rd centuries AD.

E. Fruit-bowls (186-188)

E.1. Fruit-bowl with biconical shaped body (186)

The rim is wide and almost horizontal. The leg is broken. The single example of this shape that could be fully pieced together was made from grey paste.

The vessel was discovered in the Locusteni cemetery and was dated to the 2nd century AD.

Emil Moscalu placed the origin of this shape of vessel in its hand-made form within the Basarabi culture (Moscalu 1983, 90), and its wheel-made version within the Greek milieu of the 7th century BC (Moscalu 1983, 98).

For the Dacians, the hand-made fruit-bowl is attested from the 6th century BC (Gruia: Moscalu 1983, pl. 66:9), while the wheel-made variant had begun its evolution by 188-150 BC (Poiana-Tecuci: Crişan 1969, 169, fig. 81:1; Sprâncenata: Preda 1986, 89-90, fig. 22:2; Slimnic: Glodariu 1981, 35, fig. 40:3; Moigrad-Porolissum: Macrea, Rusu 1960, 214, fig. 12:2; Pecica-Ziridava: Crişan 1978, 124, fig. 26:4). This type of fruit-bowl continued production into the 2nd-4th centuries AD in the Dacian territories outside the borders of the Roman Empire (Pererosli: Smisko 1960, 97, pl. 14:5).

E.2. Fruit-bowls with deep globular cup (187-188)

The rim is wide, horizontal (188) or short, and slightly curved (187). The vessels were made from fine, grey paste containing sand.

Two such vessels were discovered in the Obreja settlement (187) and in the Locusteni cemetery (188). They were dated from the 2nd century AD to the first half of the 3rd century AD (188), and to the 2nd-3rd centuries AD (187).

Fruit-bowl fragments were also discovered at the Roman camps of Sărăţeni (Székely 1962, 328, fig. 6:6-7) and Olteni (Székely 1980, 60, 72, fig. 6:2), in the Aiud villa rustica (Winkler, Vasiliev, Chiţu, Borda 1968, 72, fig. 7:1), and in the settlements of Săcelu (Gherghe 1985, 52), Govora-Sat (Moscalu 1970, 655, fig. 4:11; 5:3), Ocna Sibiului (Protase 1968, 233, fig. 3:5), Blandiana (Blăjan, Stoicovici, Georoceanu, Păcurariu 1978, 60, fig. 31:3) and Slimnic (Glodariu 1981, 79, fig. 79:5-6). However, because of their fragmentary condition they could not be classified to any particular type.

The origin of this fruit-bowl may be placed within the 4th-3rd centuries BC (Zimnicea: Moscalu 1983, fig. 66:19). It was produced throughout the entire classic Dacian Late Iron Age period (Răcătău: Căpitanu 1976, 63, fig. 30:2; Poiana-Tecuci: Crişan 1969, 169, figs. 81:2; 82:6; Slimnic: Glodariu 1981, 35, fig. 39:4; Arpaşu de Sus: Macrea, Glodariu 1976, figs. 33:25; 34:10; Pecica-Ziridava: Crişan 1978, 124, fig. 23:4; Crişan 1969, 168, pl. 48:1) and during the 2nd-3rd centuries AD in the territories inhabited by those Dacians who lived outside the Roman Empire borders (Bichir 1973, 76, pl. 103:6).

F. Dishes (189-193)

F.1. Tronconical shaped dishes (189-192)

F.1.1. Tronconical shaped dish (189-190)

The walls are slightly curved. The thickened rim has a rounded edge. The base is flat and more or less shaped.

Two of such dishes were discovered in settlement no. 1 at Scorniceşti, where they were dated from the second half of the 2nd century AD to the first half of the 3rd century AD.

Similar vessels were found at Dacian sites from the Late Iron Age (Ocniţa-Buridava: Berciu 1981, 28, pl. 4:12; Tilişca: Lupu 1989, 65, pl. 12:3, 5, 6). They continued in production in Moesia Inferior (Troesmis: Opaiţ 1980, 336, pl. 9:4) and in free Dacian territories (Bucureşti-Străuleşti: Tzony 1980, 312, fig. 2:3) throughout the 2nd-4th centuries AD.

F.1.2.1. Dish with tronconical-shaped body (191)

The walls are slightly curved. The rim is obliquely thickened.

The only example was discovered in the rural settlement of Timişoara-Freidorf, where it was dated to the 2nd-3rd centuries AD.

Similar pots were found at several Dacian Late Iron Age sites (Sprâncenata: Preda 1986, pl. 37:2; Ocniţa-Buridava: Berciu 1981, 34, pl. 14:4; 17:11).

F.1.2.2. Dish with tronconical-shaped body (192)

The walls are slightly curved. The base is horizontally everted. The shoulder is well marked.

The vessel was discovered in settlement no. 1 of Scorniceşti where it was dated from the second half of the 2nd century AD to the first half of the 3rd century AD.

Similar pots have occurred at a series of Dacian Late Iron Age sites (Vasieni: Crişan 1969, 159, fig. 71:2; Ocniţa-Buridava: Berciu 1981, 34, fig. 16:5).

F.2. Dish with tall conical-shaped body (193)

The vertical rim is thickened and rounded. The base is very narrow and has a support ring.

The only complete vessel was discovered at the Buza rural settlement, where it was dated to the beginning of the 2nd century AD.

The vessel has analogies in the Poiana Dacian fortress (Crişan 1969, 180-182, fig. 96:5, 6, 11, 12), and in the Gropşani Dacian rural settlement (Popilian 1998, 47, dwelling no. 4, pl. 38:1). According to the opinion of Ion Horatiu Crisan - in which I concur - this pot represents a local shape that appeared during the Early Iron Age and continued throughout all the classic Dacian Late Iron Age period (Crişan 1969, 180).

G. Lids (194-196)

G.1. Hemispheric lids (194)

G.1.1. Hemispheric lids with a narrow button and wide covering edge (194).

The edge is bent slightly inwards. The lid was discovered in the Locusteni cemetery, where it was dated from the 2nd century AD to the first half of the 3rd century AD.

Similar lids (or examples identical in shape) were discovered at numerous archaeological sites dating from the classic Dacian Late Iron Age period (Rudele: Crişan 1969, 183-184, pl. 83:2; Pecica-Ziridava: Crişan 1978, 131, pls. 97:6; 98:4-5; Arpaşu de Sus: Macrea, Glodariu 1976, fig. 37:13; Brad-Zargidava: Ursachi 1995, 182, pl. 111:1, 6, 9). In the free Dacian area from the East of the Carpathian Mountains, such a lid was found at Poienesti (Bichir 1973, 78-79, pl. 104:1), where it was dated to the 2nd-3rd centuries AD.

In fact, these lids had imitated a Roman pottery shape since the classic Dacian Late Iron Age (Crişan 1969, 183-184; Crişan 1978, 131).

G.2. Conical shaped lids (195-196)

G.2.1. Conical shaped lids (195)

The rim is vertical, and the covering edge is horizontal. The button is missing.

The lid was discovered in the Daneţi cemetery, where it was dated from the 2nd century AD to the first half of the 3rd century AD.

A similar lid was found in the Poiana Dacian site. Concerning its origins, Ion Horatiu Crisan considered that it imitated a Roman shape (Crişan 1969, 183, fig. 57:4).

G.2.2. Short, conical shaped lid with short button (196)

The horizontal covering margin is bent and curved. The edge bends very slightly inwards.

The only lid of this type was discovered in the Locusteni cemetery, where it was dated from the 2nd century AD to the first half of the 3rd century AD.

A similar lid was found in the Dacian fortification of Arpaşu de Sus, where it was considered an imitation of a Roman shape (Macrea, Glodariu 1976, 68, fig. 37:2).

Illuminating vessels

H. Dacian cups (197)

H.1. Slender conical-shaped cup (197)

The rim is a continuation of the body. Such a cup was discovered in the Locusteni cemetery, where it was dated from the 2nd century AD to the first half of the 3rd century AD. Another wheel-made cup, the shape of which we do not know, was found in the civilian settlement of the Roman camp of Stolniceni-Buridava (Bichir 1983, 12).

Wheel-made cups, with a different profile than those found at Locusteni, were discovered that dated from the classic Dacian Late Iron Age period (Crişan 1969, 155, pl. 47:4, 7; Ursachi 1995, 177, pl. 101:1-2), and to the 3rd-4th centuries AD (Sultov 1980, 384, fig. 11d).

Chapter IV
FINAL CONSIDERATIONS

The fact that a part of the Dacian territory was turned into a Roman province caused fundamental changes from the political, military, economical, and cultural points of view. From an ethnic perspective, the formation of a new province led to the extensive settling there of various populations brought in to create a base for the new administration, or those who were simply attracted by the predictable prosperity of this territory. Roman citizens or not, the newcomers were bearers of the Roman civilization and, however consciously, they planted its fundamental characteristics in Dacia.

The other ethnic and cultural component (known by the generic term "autochthonous") was the Dacian population. Too numerous to be exterminated or chased away by the conquerors, who might have been interested in de-populating the province, the Dacians lived side-by-side with the newcomers. This fact is confirmed by the frequent archaeological discoveries that bring to light more and more evidence.

Within the range of archaeological finds, pottery quantitatively reveals the richest and most credible evidence illustrating the persistence of the local population in Dacia.

Indigenous pottery continued to be made, by hand as well as wheel, within Roman Dacian territory.

IV.1. Considerations on native hand-made pottery

IV.1.1. The typology of hand-made pottery

Compiling a typology implies, first of all, establishing a structure that is based upon the constant use of a set of criteria relevant to the study of pottery.

The logical scheme I suggest to delimit the categories is a simple one, and it remains open to subsequent addition. Thus, I delimit pottery vessels according to manufacturing technique and geometrical body shape. As to technique, the vessels can be either hand-made or wheel made. Numbering the former with Roman numerals, and the latter with capital Latin letters differentiates the manufacturing process. In both cases, the

following Arabic numerals give the type, variant, and sub-variant.

As far as typologies should aim to delimit structure, the forms or shapes should be ordered by firm and constant criteria. For the time being, I do not know, or I have not access to, better-suited criteria than those of spatial geometry, and to more exact means than figures. The use of geometric elements in making a typology, especially for hand-made pottery vessels, is not a new approach (Teodor 1996).

Therefore, I see nothing wrong in providing such close scrutiny to those details that may be summarized into what we call a particular "shape". In this way we can use different languages to delimitate the same shape (Crişan 1969, 164), or we may describe the same shape in various ways (Crişan 1969, 161-163). The constant use of the above-mentioned criteria can help us appreciate errors, and reach a uniform language that best suits the specialized literature.

In this respect, I consider that the best way to distinguish the difference between types and variants is to use the denominations according to the geometric features of the respective vessels.

IV.1.2. Structure

Building up a structure of the categories, types, variants and sub-variants noticed within the native hand-made pottery of Roman Dacia, implies the correlation of shape and functionality. I considered that, however risky, at this state of the research classification is necessary to distinguish this pottery according to functional categories. Within the categories, shapes and types are delimited according to the basic profile of the various vessels.

The hand-made pottery may be classified in the following functional categories of vessels: storage vessels, kitchenware, tableware, and illumination vessels. These categories contain shapes of vessels that may be identified according to body profile, first of all by the position of the maximum diameter in relation to the vessel's height, and the ratio between the diameter of the mouth to that of the vessel's base. The types contain variants and sub-variants. In this last case the differences are minor and consist of the variety of the ways the rims are made, or of other insignificant details.

IV.1.3. Frequency

According to its frequency, the hand-made pottery is present first within the cemeteries and rural settlements, then within Roman camps and their civilian settlements, next within the villae rusticae, and more seldom in cities. Its rarity in urban areas should not be surprising. During the classic Dacian period from the Late Iron Age, the hand-made pottery that was discovered in the semi-urban settlement of Sarmisegetuza Regia, for instance, was also present only in modest quantities (Crişan 1969, 153).

The most frequent vessels found in the rural area of the Dacia province were pots, biconical-shaped vessels, pear-shaped, bell-shaped or cylindrical-shaped jars, followed by the Dacian cups. A similar situation was noticed in Roman camps and their civilian settlements.

IV.1.4. The geography of the discoveries

Native hand-made pottery is abundantly present in the rural areas of the province – that is in the settlements, cemeteries, and villae rusticae spread all over the Roman Dacia territory, and comprising the eastern border area that was considered as "terra deserta", meant to ensure the peace of the province (Bichir 1984, 105).

This uniform distribution of native hand-made pottery found in the territory of Roman Dacia, and of the free Dacians as well, is a cultural and ethnic reality for these territories during the 2nd-4th centuries AD.

The few examples of hand-made pottery that have been preserved complete (or which were discovered and subsequently restored) and have been published to date, are not sufficient for us to try to delimit clearly the various aspects of native pottery in Roman Dacia. However, a few considerations may be made – with a caution implied by the present state of research – that may become starting points for future investigations.

Without neglecting the numerous fragments of hand-made vessels discovered, I consider that their use in this study would generate a series of potential problems. The first is connected to a resultant wider chronological delimitation that would have altered the original typological structure of this pottery survey. A further problem could be the possibility of making errors due to the fragmentary state of the objects. Finally, I believe that an analysis of the more than 1000 pottery fragments would have given an exaggerated bias of information to this study, and added very little. (Not to mention the existence of hundreds of other fragments – recalled or not – that exist in the museums.)

Up to now, the specific categories of Dacian pottery have been discovered in the territories of Dacia province, Moesia

Superior, Pannonia Inferior, and those territories inhabited by free Dacians. Therefore, either in compact areas, or in island-like territories, this cultural and ethnic entity (which had defined itself in relations with its neighbours from the 1st century BC to the 1st century AD) continues to manifest itself throughout the 2nd-3rd centuries AD (Popilian 1997).

According to Emil Moscalu, the Sarmizegetusa culture appeared in the Carpathian-Danubian regions during the classic Dacian Late Iron Age period. The culture was named after the Capital of the Dacian State (Moscalu 1983, 187-208).

The study of hand-made autochthonous pottery in the Dacia province shows us, for the time being, the existence of some regional style of vessels in Dacia South, the Carpathians (56-63), and in the northern region of Roman Dacia (23-35). These differences may be due to the vicinity of the Northern Dacians, of their having been colonized in the province (Dio Cassius, LXXII, 3, 3), or mainly due to the perpetuation of some regional Late Iron Age characteristics. E. Moscalu considered the term of Sarmizegetusa-Popeşti-Bâtca Doamnei culture was not relevant and proposed the term of Sarmizegetusa culture (Moscalu 1983, 188, 198).

I consider that the material culture of Dacians had the same major components, but with some local diversity. For this reason it does not seem a good idea to give the name of the Dacian capital (Sarmizegetusa) – which was a very particular cultural phenomenon – to the entire Dacian culture.

Future research will certainly bring more information regarding the regional characteristics of the Dacian and Daco-Roman culture throughout the 2nd-3rd centuries AD.

IV.1.5. Technical details

IV.1.5.1. The paste

The paste from which the pottery was made has received no special attention from archaeologists. Unfortunately, with some exceptions, the authors of the archaeological findings failed to mention paste quality and composition. At the same time, one notices the lack of any clear terminology used in describing various categories of paste. In such a situation, I consider that the only available criteria relate to composition and some mechanically, or chemically, measurable features. Therefore, I shall only make reference to the cases in which I could directly study the native pottery of the Dacia province (Locusteni, Stolniceni-Buridava, Scorniceşti, Enoşeşti-Acidava, Olteni, Râşnov and others).

The paste used contained sand and mica as main degreasing agents. Sometimes, gravel or limestone was added.

Several categories were identified within the Locusteni cemetery, according to paste composition, primary firing, or the presence/absence of film. (I am most grateful to Dr Gheorghe Popilian who was so kind as to allow me to inspect the native pottery found by him in this cemetery).

A. The fine paste

The fine paste contains well-sifted sand as the main degreasing agent. Several types of fine paste can be distinguished according to the various combinations of degreasing substances.

1. Fine coarse paste containing much well-sifted sand and mica as digressing substances

2.1. Paste with well-sifted sand and mica. The primary firing is uniform. The paste is coarse to the touch. It was covered with a thin film on the outside. The paste was covered with a film.

2.2. Paste with sand and gravel. The primary firing is not complete. The paste was covered with a film on the outside.

3.1. Paste with sand, gravel, and fragments of rounded limestone. The primary firing is complete. The paste is relatively coarse to the touch.

3.2.1. Paste with sand, gravel, and fragments of pounded limestone. The primary fing is complete. On the outside, the paste was covered with a film. The paste is soft to the touch.

3.2.2. Paste with sand, gravel, and fragments of pounded limestone. The primary firing is not complete. On the outside, the paste was covered with a film. The paste is soft to the touch.

B. Rough paste

The rough paste contains sand and gravel, in small quantities. Its rough aspect is given by a preparation technique that makes it look carelessly manufactured.

1. Paste with sand and gravel. The primary firing is not complete. The paste is soft to touch. Vessels made of this paste have the appearance of being rather carelessly made, and are friable.

Of course, my analysis is very detailed, and it could even indicate references within the pottery production. Yet, I find it important to classify the Locusteni cemetery pottery in three wide categories – fine paste ceramics, semi-rough paste ceramics and rough paste ceramics. It is also observed that vessels made of semi-rough paste represent the overwhelming majority.

I mention the fact that the classification within the three above-mentioned categories was made according to the technology of the mineral production of the paste (excepting the clay, obviously present in every case). I also note the vessels' feel to the touch and to the presence/absence of the exterior film.

In the Locusteni cemetery, in almost all the cases, the native hand-made pottery was especially friable, frequently breaking when discovered (Popilian 1980, 78). And yet, more resistant pottery is also present.

The fact that, often, vessels with the same mineral composition, and the same kind of primary firing, have different degrees of resistance, leads me to suppose that there are differences in the technology of paste preparation. I do not exclude the importance of the paste composition and that of firing conditions, but I believe they take a secondary role in terms of paste resistance. This explains why, at Locusteni, identical vessels – from the point of view of paste composition and firing – differ in their resistance values.

Within the assemblage of vessels discovered in the civilian settlement of the Enoşeşti-Acidava Roman camp, two main categories of paste can be identified. I should also mention that, very seldom, chaff appears here instead of pounded limestone (Negru, Ciucã 1997, 23-28).

Concerning the vessels discovered in the Roman Dacia camps, N. Gudea and I. Uzum showed that some of the vessels have sand and gravel in their composition – a paste considered to be porous – while composition of other vases is similar to that of the Roman provincial pottery in common use (Gudea, Uzum 1988, 232-234). This last category comprises a series of Roman shapes (dishes, lids) that were wrongly considered as Dacian because they are hand-made. The same scientists observed that the firing was not generally complete, but that it was not prejudicial to the paste quality (Gudea, Uzum 1988, 232-234).

Within the Carpathian range, three paste categories were noticed. The first included those vessels made of a fine paste containing fine sand (Soporu de Câmpie, Obreja, Noşlac, Buza), or sand with medium-sized grains (Obreja, Napoca, Noşlac). In the second category I classify semi-rough paste vessels containing sand and gravel (Soporu de Câmpie, Obreja, Napoca), and third category comprises vessels made from rough, porous paste, containing sand, limestone or chaff (Soporu de Câmpie).

IV.1.5.2. Colour

Regarding colour, I observe that in the Locusteni cemetery the dominant colour is brick red (Popilian 1980, passim); grey vessels are very much rarer. At Stolniceni-Buridava, most of the vessels found were grey (Tudor 1967, 655-656; Petre-Govora 1968, 145-158). At the Dedrad settlement, the Dacian pottery is brown-blackish (Glodariu 1975, 229). The hand-made pottery discovered in the Roman camps is brown-reddish, reddish, grey, dark-grey or grey-reddish (Gudea, Uzum 1988, 232).

IV.1.5.3. The firing

Primary firing

The primary firing was of both kinds, complete and incomplete. Incomplete firing did not affect paste resistance in a decisive way.

In numerous cases, the vessels discovered in the Locusteni cemetery were clear-brick coloured, and blackish on the interior side of the wall. This shows an incomplete oxidant firing. Whether one can speak of a first stage – one of in-oxidant firing – and what would the aim be of such a primary stage, are questions I do not feel competent to discuss.

Secondary firing

I should emphasize that, in several cases, the vessels from the Locusteni cemetery underwent a strong secondary firing. Where this occurred the result is a brick-yellowish colour.

Of nearly all of the vessels used as urns (within the same cemetery), it is believed they had been ritually purified by fire, inside and out, or that they had only been exposed to kitchen use (Popilian 1980, 55). I do not exclude the possibility that they had been in contact with the hot ashes of the funeral pyre. These vessels usually present exterior areas where initial light-brick colour was covered by the blackish hue typical of weak secondary or in-oxidant burning (smoke colours/shades).

Based upon the results of the research undertaken at Bucureşti-Militari "Câmpul Boja" (Negru 2000, 92), I consider that most of the vessels with smoke shades discovered at Locusteni had been used in the kitchens. These vessels, generally made of semi-rough paste, were probably kitchen items, along with the rough Roman pottery that was present both in the settlement and cemetery of Locusteni.

IV.1.5.4. The Decoration

Relief decoration

Relief decoration (as opposed to incised) is predominant. The most frequent motifs are the cordon (simple, with alveoli, notched), alveolar segments, caesurae, and various shapes of buttons.

1.1. The relief cordon

1.1.1. The simple relief cordon is rare (7, 35, 45, 49, 52). It was present throughout the classic Dacian period from the Late Iron Age (Ursachi 1995, 161, pl. 63:1).

1.1.2. The alveolar cordon is the most frequent motif found within the native hand-made pottery of the Dacia province. It is always present on tall vessels (1, 4-6, 10-13, 16, 28, 39-40, 42-44, 46, 53-58, 61, 65-66, 70, 74-78, 80, 82, 88) but it is rare on Dacian cups (132, 138). The motif was typical of the classic Dacian Late Iron Age period (Crişan 1969, 208; Preda 1986, 52; Ursachi 1995, 167).

1.1.3. The relief notched cordon is less frequent than the alveolar one (47, 94). This kind of decoration was also used in the Dacian Late Iron Age (Crişan 1969, 209).

1.2. Relief segments

Relief segments are less frequent compared with the classic Dacian Late Iron Age period.

1.2.1. The oblique alveolar segment was first found on a vessel discovered at Slimnic (71). The motif was also used during

the classic Dacian Late Iron Age period (Ursachi 1995, 161, pl. 64:13).

1.2.2. The alveolar hook-like segment is present on vessels discovered at Râşnov (1), and in the Locusteni cemetery (66). Such motifs are present on Dacian pottery dating from the Late Iron Age (Crişan 1969, 209, pl. 106:8; Ursachi 1995, 161, pl. 61:3).

1.2.3. The "W"-shaped alveolar segment was found on a large cylindrical jar discovered in the Locusteni cemetery (97).

1.3. Caesurae were observed on several jars (15, 22, 48, 84-85).

1.4. Button decoration

Buttons decorated several jars. Of the relief motifs, buttons come second to cordons in terms of frequency of application. By their shape, and by their association with one or more alveoli (or incised lines), several types and versions can be classified.

1.4.1. Flat, round buttons

1.4.1.1. Small, simple, round buttons (24, 42, 69). Buttons of this shape were also used for vessel decoration during the classic Dacian Late Iron Age period (Crişan 1969, 208, pl. 105:16; Ursachi 1995, 167, pl. 61:3, 5).

1.4.1.2. Round buttons decorated with alveoli. According to their dimensions, they can be: a) small (38); b) or medium (11-12, 59, 71). The buttons with alveoli were also used throughout the Dacian pre-Roman period (Crişan 1969, 208, pl. 105:1,3; Ursachi 1995, 167, pl. 64:11-13).

1.4.1.3. Large, round buttons, decorated with four alveoli (37). Such buttons were used to decorate vessels from the classic Dacian Late Iron Age period (Crişan 1969, 208, pl. 106:1).

1.4.2. Half-moon buttons. These are medium-sized (44).

1.4.3. Rectangular, medium-sized buttons (12). Rectangular buttons were also used in vessel decoration at all the classic Dacian sites from the Late Iron Age (Crişan 1969, 208, pl. 105:13).

2. Decorative incised motifs

Incised motifs are less frequent than relief ones. They have the closest parallels in the classic Dacian Late Iron Age period.

2.1. Incised lines

2.1.1. A single incised horizontal line (67)

2.1.2. Two or three incised horizontal lines (27, 64, 66). This motif was also found on Dacian vessels from the Late Iron Age (Crişan 1969, 210, pl. 109:3; Preda 1986, pl. 9:3).

2.1.3. A strip of horizontal incised lines (42, 72). Strips of horizontal incised lines were also found during the classic Dacian Late Iron Age period (Crişan 1969, 210, pl. 109:4-5).

2.2. Waved lines

2.2.1. A single waved incised line (34, 61). The motif is also present on classic Dacian vessels (Crişan 1969, 210, pl. 110:1).

2.2.2. Two or three waved incised lines (27, 41). Some Dacian vessels dating from the classic Late Iron Age period (Crişan 1969, 210, pl. 110:2) were decorated with this motif.

2.2.3. A strip of waved incised lines (11, 13, 57, 72). The motif appeared during the Dacian pre-Roman period (Crişan 1969, 210, pl. 110:11; Berciu 1981, 34, pl. 11:1, 5, 8).

2.3. The fir tree branch motif (131, 150).

This is a frequently used motif throughout the classic Dacian Late Iron Age period (Crişan 1969, 210, pl. 97:3, 5, 7; Berciu 1981, pls. 11:2; 19:5-6).

2.4. Oblique notches (131, 150)

3. Motifs made by carving

3.1. Alveoli

3.1.1. Alveoli disposed in a horizontal row (47, 50). The motif was also used during the classic Dacian Late Iron Age period (Berciu 1981, 171, pl. 73:1).

3.1.2. Alveoli disposed in a double wave (60)

3.1.3. Alveoli disposed in vertical rows (47, 50). Vertical rows of alveoli were also found on vessels from the classic Dacian Late Iron Age period (Crişan 1969, 210, pl. 107:13; Berciu 1981, 171, pl. 73:1).

Of the decorative motifs, relief, applied are more frequent than incised ones. The alveolar cordon, applied on the shoulder or at the maximum diameter, is also present, and sometimes appears on Dacian cups as well.

The most frequently used incised motifs are horizontal, or waved, stripes of lines. Some of the vessels were decorated with irregularly incised lines, and others with alveoli.

The decoration was made on the upper part of the vessels. The alveolar cordon was set on the maximum diameter area or slightly above it, more rarely on the rim, and only in two cases of Dacian cups was it applied on the base.

Sometimes relief decorative elements were combined with incised ones. I should also mention that, while most of the vessels were decorated, in the case of Dacian cups most had no decoration.

The decorative elements used are identical to those used throughout the classic Dacian Late Iron Age period (Crişan 1969, 207-210, pls. 105-111; Ursachi 1995, 167-168).

IV.1.5.5. Dimensions

The overwhelming majority of the vessels are medium-sized (200-350 mm); small vessels (100-200 mm) are also present. Large vessels (over 400 mm) are very rare.

IV.1.5.6. Usage

The uses for hand-made pottery were varied. It is certain that some of the vessels had a well-defined use, but one cannot exclude two or more functions for the same shape of vessels.

Some vessels were used in food preparation (kitchen ware). Such were the vessels and lids made of rough paste, which, because of their porosity, were fire resistant (Opaiţ 1995, 19).

Vessels were covered with special lids (98-109), or with improvised lids - that is by using conical-shaped vessels with flaring upper parts (167, 175). This is one of the reasons why special lids are rarely observed - except for the discoveries at Gilău, Tibiscum and Timişoara-Freidorf - compared to the classic Dacian sites of the Late Iron Age. Another reason for their rarity would, of course, be the presence of Roman pottery lids.

Food was probably preserved in large or medium-sized provision vessels (1-4), according to contents and the duration of the storage period (Crişan 1969, 162; Bichir 1973, 68).

The use of the miniature vessels is not known exactly (53-54). I believe they were also items of kitchen ware, being used for food that was consumed in smaller quantities.

Most specialists consider that Dacian cups were also used as lamps (Crişan 1969, 156; Bichir 1984, 31). I believe that very large numbers of Dacian cups so far discovered (and dating from the classic Dacian Late Iron Age period and from the 2nd-4th centuries AD) suggest the multiple use of this category of vessels.

At Sprâncenata, almost 40 Dacian cups (whole or fragmentary) were discovered in just four dwellings (Preda 1986, 55), and this leads me to believe that they would have been used for other purposes than lamps. 1480 Dacian cup fragments (whole or identifiable) were also discovered in the Brad-Zargidava and open settlement (Ursachi 1995, 163).

Silviu Sanie further differentiated between these vessels. He observed the fact that "conical-shaped vessels, the lamp-cups, were first of all used as censers, or as cult vessels". His ideas were based on priority, not exclusive, usage (Sanie 1995, 106).

Effective function is a distinct matter compared to the destination of the vessels found. In most cases, while the function is suggested by shape, in several instances within the Locusteni cemetery, the vessels appeared to have different functions than usual. One cannot exclude the possibility that these "secondary" functions were also practiced in everyday life. Thus, in the above-mentioned cemetery, the Dacian cups were also used as lids (Popilian 1980, 82). Silviu Sanie suggests that, in some cases, the Dacian cups could have had a ritual function (Sanie 1995, 105-106).

Conical-shaped, hand-made vessels, similar in form to those from Roman Dacia, were found in Pannonia Inferior. They were considered as lids (Sirmium: Brukner 1981, 186, pl. 3:10-11; Gomolava: Brukner 1990, 34, pl. 20:143; Pannonia: Bónis 1942, 36, pls. 1:8; 2:3-4; 3:11). This could also suggest a common origin of this type of vessel. On the other hand, according to Silviu Sanie, some of the conical-shaped vessels might have had a ritual function (Sanie 1995, 105-106).

IV.1.6. The origins of the categories of hand-made pottery

Some Dacian traditional hand-made vessels seem to have had their origin during the Bronze Age. Among such vessels I list some of the bell-shaped jars (26) and the cylindrical vessel with a wide body and narrow base (97).

Certainly, however, most of the discovered categories and shapes had their origin in the Early Iron Age. Among our vessels, the following can be said to have originated in this period: biconical-shaped jars (5-16), convex-bodied pots of type 2 (41-42), some ovoid jars (68-70), cylindrical jars with wide body type 1 (86-96), and some cylindrical jars with tall bodies (79-84).

Some vessel shapes did not appear until the Late Iron Age. These include the pear-shaped jars (35-37), most of the pots with curved bodies (39-65), the ovoid jars (72-74), some tall cylindrical jars (76-77), the Dacian cups (111-150), the conical-shaped vessels with flaring or inward turning rims (161-163), the hemispherical lids (102-104), and the conical-shaped vessels with curved walls (106).

IV.1.7. Chronology

The native hand-made pottery discovered in Roman Dacia covers the whole period between the first and final decades of Roman rule in Dacia.

Thus, the native hand-made pottery from the Buza rural settlement (Bădău-Wittenberger 1994, 369), the Cătunele (Petolescu 1986, 162), Bologa (Gudea, Uzum 1988, 234), Buciumi Roman fortifications (Gudea, Uzum 1988, 234), and in the civilian settlement of the Tibiscum Roman camp (Benea 1981, 311), appears during the first decades of the 2nd century AD. Numerous fragments of hand-made Dacian vessels discovered in the Roman City of Napoca (Cociş, Voişian, Paki, Rotea 1996, 635-636) were dated from the Traian-Hadrian period. A series of vessels discovered in the Locusteni (Popilian 1980, 80-81) and Soporu de Câmpie cemeteries (Protase 1976, 81-82) date from the 2nd century AD.

Dacian pottery was also discovered in Moesia Inferior, in the Roman fortifications of Rucăr (Bogdan-Cătăniciu 1985-1986,

201) and Drajna de Sus (Ştefan 1945-1947, 132-134), and was also dated from the beginning of the 2nd century AD.

The Scorniceşti (No. 1) and Coloneşti-Gueşti settlements were dated from the middle of the 2nd century AD to the first half of the 3rd century AD (Bichir 1984, 105).

Most of the settlements where the discoveries were made (including the Soporu de Câmpie cemetery, the rural settlement of Slimnic, the villa rustica of Aiud, the Roman camps of Buciumi, Bologa, Breţcu, Râşnov, and others) were dated from the 2nd-3rd centuries AD (see the repertory of native pottery).

A suggestive fact, and one worth remembering, is that, in the Stolniceni-Buridava Roman camp, the Dacian pottery fragments discovered cover all of the six habitation levels, from the 2nd century AD to the 3rd century AD (Bichir 1983, 12). Also, the Soporu de Câmpie cemetery functioned from the 2nd century AD to the end of the 3rd century AD (Protase 1976, 81-82). At the same time, I should mention that, in the Bologa and Buciumi Roman camps, the hand-made pottery was used from the first decades of the Roman conquest to, at least, the middle of the 3rd century AD (Gudea, Moţu 1988, 234).

In this context, I recall the presence of the Dacian pottery within some indigenous rural settlements that continued the classic Dacian Late Iron Age period at Cernatu, Ocna Sibiului, Rosia Sibiului, and Slimnic (Protase 1980, 261).

The discoveries of the Scorniceşti (No. 2), and Colonesti-Maruntei settlements, and those of the Chilia cemetery, were dated after the end of the Roman rule (Morintz 1961, 441-447; Morintz 1963, 513-518; Bichir 1984, 92; Bichir 1986, 126). Continuity in the tradition of the indigenous pottery during the 4th century AD can also be observed in the Locusteni-La Gropan settlement (Popilian, Nica 1980, 254-260).

The conical-shaped vessels (decorated with alveoli at the base and similar to the Dacian cups discovered in the intra-Carpathian Roman Dacia, and in the extra-Carpathian area at Colonesti-Maruntei and Matasaru) were dated by Coriolan Opreanu to within the post-Roman Period (Opreanu 1993).

One biconical-shaped jar (6) was dated from the first half of the 2nd century AD, the same as the bell-shaped jar (20), and conical-shaped vessel (152).

Two biconical-shaped jars (6-7), three pots (45, 59, 65), and one cylindrical jar (83) were dated from the 2nd century AD.

One biconical jar (14), a bell-shaped jar (17), 17 pots with curved bodies (28, 33-36, 39, 42, 44, 46, 48, 51, 54-57, 61, 64), 4 ovoid jars (4, 66, 70, 74), 4 sack-jars (89-90, 93, 97), 2 cylindrical jars (76, 80) and 7 Dacian cups (113, 119, 127, 130, 132, 147, 149) were dated from the 2nd century AD to the first half of the 3rd century AD.

One lid found at Dedrad (107) was dated from the 2nd century AD to the middle of the 3rd century AD.

One provision jar (2) and one Dacian cup (133) were dated from the end of the 2nd century AD to the beginning of the 3rd century AD.

One pot (52), 2 tall cylindrical jars (82, 87), 5 Dacian cups (114, 135, 138, 141, 144) and the small conical-shaped jars (158) were dated from the second half of the 2nd century AD to the first half of the 3rd century AD.

One globular jar (38) was dated from the middle of the 2nd century AD to the end of the 3rd century AD.

The following were dated to the beginning of the 3rd century AD: one biconical jar (10), one pot (62), one ovoid jar (73), one tall cylindrical jar (86) and one Dacian cup (148).

Other vessels, such as 2 pear-shaped jars (67, 69), a Dacian cup (142), 8 conical-shaped vessels (154, 156, 162-163, 168, 170, 174-175) and 2 lids (108-109) were dated to the 3rd century AD.

The remaining vessels were widely dated to the 2nd-3rd centuries AD.

IV.1.8. Considerations concerning the local traditional pottery in Roman Dacia and in the classic Dacian Late Iron Age period

The indigenous pottery in Roman Dacia represents a natural continuation of that of the pre-Roman period in this region. The fundamental change that had taken place when a part of Dacia had become a Roman province must have had a strong impact upon the local population – from a political, military, economic, and cultural point of view. This impact was not necessarily reflected by the Late Iron Age traditional pottery of this local population, especially within rural indigenous areas situated far from the Roman cities or Roman camps. Therefore, if taken out of the context it was discovered in, a vessel dating from before the Roman conquest (1st century BC – 1st century AD) is hard to distinguish from one dating from the period of Roman rule (Popilian 1980, 78).

Sometimes it was observed that in the Roman Period the native hand-made pottery became more slender than it had been before the Roman conquest (Crişan 1969, 162-163; Bichir 1973, 68; Bichir 1984, 33). The latest research from the Dacian archaeological sites of the Late Iron Age shows that this change had already started before the Roman conquest. (Crişan 1969, 162-163, figs. 74, 76).

During both the classic Dacian Late Iron Age and Roman periods, the overwhelming majority of Dacian cups were hand-made, wheel-made examples being extremely rare. The double-handled items – rare throughout the Late Iron Age – became even lesser frequent during the Roman period. So far Dacian cups with two handles have only been discovered in the Obreja settlement and in the Locusteni and Soporu de Câmpie cemeteries (vessels nos. 146-149). A unique Dacian cup with three handles was discovered in the Obreja settlement.

A special case is represented by the Dacian cup discovered in the settlement no. 1, at Scornicești – a cup with a button at the base, instead of a handle (vessel no. 144). The discovery of an identical cup in the Dacian fortified settlement ("dava") of Sprâncenata is a significant piece of evidence concerning ethnic and cultural continuity in Western Wallachia during the 1st-3rd centuries AD (Preda 1986, pl. 19:8; Negru 1997a, 98).

Regarding the vessel's profile, no evident changes can be noticed compared to the classic Dacian Late Iron Age period. Instead, one notices a general (exceptions are few) simplification of decoration and an increase in the number of non-decorated vessels. Only three of the complete vessels, and two of the other restored ones, had alveoli on the rim; a single example had a fir tree branch as a decorative motif and notches on the base and rim.

The first Dacian cups appeared during the 2nd century BC, as proved by the discoveries at Schela Cladovei (Boroneanţ, Davidescu 1968, 225) and Zimnicea (Alexandrescu 1980, 47). They were produced throughout the classic Dacian sites from the Late Iron Age (Crişan 1969, 156-160).

The lack, or rarity, of some vessel shapes during the Roman Period, the apparition of some versions with no identical analogies during the classic Dacian Late Iron Age period, give rise to problems that cannot be solved at present. They can only be resolved by future discoveries.

One can only formulate conclusions after the intensive research of several Roman period settlements superposed over pre-Roman ones, as was the case with the Slimnic site (Glodariu 1981).

The paste, of which the classic Dacian Late Iron Age period pottery was made, had the same composition, generally, as that used for other vessels dating from the 2nd-3rd centuries AD.

The idea that the indigenous pottery persisted because it was more resistant (being used to preserve food) is invalidated by the fact that, in the Locusteni cemetery, hand-made vessels were generally so friable that some were actually reduced to a grainy-powder when discovered (Popilian 1980, 13-53).

During the Roman period it is usually considered that a simplification of hand-made vessel decoration was noticeable. The assertion is correct, but it should be mentioned that this phenomenon had began before the Roman conquest of Dacia. Thus, I observe the appearance, during the classic Dacian Late Iron Age period, of some pots that are only decorated with an alveolar cordon. Cordons of waved or horizontal incised strips were signaled during the classical Late Iron Age.

In the Ocniţa-Buridava (Berciu 1981, 26, pl. 7:3) and Sprâncenata (Preda 1986, pls. 9:3; 12:7; 13:5) "davae", vessels were found decorated with round buttons and incised horizontal lines identical to one of the vessels found at Locusteni (vessel no. 64).

I note that the use of alveoli was known in the classic Dacian Late Iron Age period (Crişan 1969, 209, pl. 106:7).

One may notice a considerable diminution of the complicated decoration that covered much of the body surface present in the Late Iron Age. This kind of decoration only persisted on a few vessels found at Scornicești (vessel no. 138), Locusteni (vessel no. 66), Slimnic (vessel no. 71) and Obreja (vessel no. 131). With these exceptions (to which one can add those from Drajna de Sus (Ștefan 1945-1947, 132-134, fig. 15:2) and from the free Dacian area (Bichir 1973, 67, fig. 11; pls. 42:1; 43:1)) during the Roman Period, the decoration was concentrated on the upper half of the vessels and up to the outer part of the rim inclusively (Bichir 1984, 32). During the classic Dacian Late Iron Age period, the decoration was also frequently placed on the upper part of the vessel (Crișan 1969, 208).

IV.1.9. Considerations on Celtic and Roman hand-made pottery discovered in Dacia

A hand-made identification was, until recently, a safe enough criterion to allow vessels to be assigned to the Late Iron Age local pottery tradition. It may now be theoretically possible to assign a few vessels to the Celtic colonists. Versions of some hand-made, Roman provincial vessels were neglected, being considered as unlikely from the outset.

Hand-made Celtic-type pottery is represented by some bell-shaped jars decorated with the "small broom". The jars found at Tibiscum (Benea 1981, fig. 16; Bona, Petrovszky, Petrovszky 1982, 410, pl. 2:2, 5; Rogozea 1988, 166, figs. 3:1; 12:1) have analogies within the Celtic pottery tradition (dating to the 2nd-3rd centuries AD) found in Pannonia (Bónis 1942, 36, pls. 2:3; 3:1). I should mention that the "small broom" decoration was only present in extremely few Dacian examples compared with the situation found in the Celtic settlements.

The conical-shaped vessels discovered in the Dacia province have numerous analogies within the traditional Late Iron Age pottery in Pannonia (Brukner 1987, pls. 33:2; 33:15-17). Unlike the pottery in the neighboring province, however, the Dacian vessels were not decorated with the well-known Celtic motif of irregular striations. To add to this, one should point out the closer analogies that exist with the classic Dacian Late Iron Age period pottery.

The dishes that were so numerous within the Roman camps in Dacia, and in their civilian settlements, undoubtedly imitated wheel-made Roman prototypes. For the time being, such vessels remain undiscovered at those sites that belong to the classic Dacian Late Iron Age period. Some of the vessels found on the upper course of the Tisa River (Kotigoroško 1996, pls. 115:8-11, 18-19; 116:46-47) have almost the same shape, but the link with these is not as strong as it is with samples from the Roman pottery discovered in the Dacia province.

The cylindrical examples discovered within the Buciumi (Gudea 1970, 304, fig. 4:12, 14) Roman camp are similar to an item of Roman provincial pottery found at the Râșnov camp (Gudea, Pop 1971, pl. 10:2). Other cylindrical dishes with flaring rims, discovered at the Buciumi and Bologa

Roman camps (Buciumi: Gudea 1970, 304, fig. 4:11; Bologa: Gudea 1977, 184, fig. 16:2), are similar to Roman wheel-made dishes discovered in the Roman camp of Porolissum (Gudea 1996, pl. 24:6, 7). The cylindrical dishes with curved walls, discovered in the Bologa and Buciumi Roman camps (Bologa: Gudea 1977, 184, pl. 16:5; Buciumi: Chirilă, Gudea, Lucăcel, Pop 1972, 54, figs. 47:3; 50:3), are similar to the Roman dishes found in the Râșnov and Buciumi Roman camps (Râșnov: Gudea, Pop 1971, figs. 10:6; 12:23; Buciumi: Chirilă, Gudea, Lucăcel, Pop 1972, pl. 19:2).

Conical-shaped vessels, with a flared rim continuing up from the walls, were discovered in the Buciumi and Gilău Roman camps (Buciumi: Gudea 1970, 305, figs. 6:4; 7:3; Gilău: Gudea, Moțu 1988, 233, fig. 11:1; Țentea, Marcu 1997, 245, pls. 10:5; 11:4).

Most of the hand-made dishes found in the Roman camps of the Dacia province have their rims, or upper sections, flaring (Bologa: Gudea 1973b, 52, fig. 23:20; Gilău: Rusu 1979, 160, pl. 2:14; Țentea, Marcu 1997, 245, pls. 10:6; 11:1-3, 5; Buciumi: Gudea 1970, 305, figs. 6:5; 7:4).

A series of hand-made lids discovered in Roman Dacian camps also imitated wheel-made Roman pottery shapes. Conical-shaped lids, with a button instead of a handle, were discovered at Tibiscum, Gilău, and Bologa (Gilău: Gudea, Moțu 1988, 233, fig. 13:1-2; Țentea, Marcu 1997, 245, pl. 10:2; Tibiscum: Rogozea 1988, 311, pls. 7:1-2, 4-5; 27:1; Benea 1985, 12-13, figs. 4:6; 27:2; Bologa: Gudea 1973, 52, fig. 23:22). These are similar, and sometimes identical, to certain vessels typical of the Roman pottery in Dacia and Pannonia (Sirmium: Brukner 1981, figs. 130:12-13; 131:25; Pannonia: Bónis 1942, 56, pl. 31:8; Slimnic: Glodariu 1981, 48-49, fig. 50:6-7; Oltenia: Popilian 1976, nos. 898, 916, 923, 931, 933, 935-936).

A pail discovered at Tibiscum also imitates a Roman shape (Rogozea 1988, 176, fig. 5). However, a plate found at Locusteni does not conform to the pre-Roman Dacian pottery repertory, nor does it have analogies during the Roman period (Popilian 1980, 26, pl. 14, M 92, 1).

Hand-made, conical-shaped tureens were found in the Roman camp of Ilișua and in the civilian settlement of the Tibiscum Roman camp (Ilișua: Protase, Gaiu, Marinescu 1997, 55, pl. 58:1; Tibiscum: Benea 1981, 311, fig. 27:4; Rogozea 1988, 166, fig. 2:3). Roughly similar vessels were found in several Dacian sites, where they were dated from the Dacian pre-Roman period (Răcătău: Căpitanu 1976, 57, fig. 8:2; Piscu Crăsani: Andrieșescu 1924, 51-52, figs. 116, 117; Brad-Zargidava Ursachi 1995, 158, pl. 60:2; Upper Tisa River area: Kotigoroško 1996, figs. 5:7, 9; 45:14). This type of vessel (exclusively wheel-made) was part of the pre-Roman Dacian pottery register of motifs (Gropșani: Popilian 1999, 88, pl. 58:6) and Celtic (Pișcolt: Nemeti 1992, fig. 2, M 13, 6; fig. 5, M 48, 4; M 49, 6; fig. 14, M 95, 5). Such vessels are rare, to date, within the 2nd-4th centuries AD (Nijnovo Strutinja: Smisko 1960, 122, pl. 10:6), but they can be found within the provincial Roman pottery in Dacia (Popilian 1976, nos. 789, 791) and Pannonia (Bónis 1942, 51, pl. 23:1, 3; Brukner 1981, 181, pl. 82:56). The fact that, in Dacia, they were found exclusively within a military milieu leads me to consider they were imitating a widely spread Roman shape from the middle and lower courses of the Danube.

At the present state of research, I consider it premature to give a verdict concerning the "Dacian manner" (Gudea, Moțu 1988, 231) in which pottery was made, as these vessels were worked using a paste similar to the one found with the Roman provincial pottery (Țentea, Marcu 1997, 240; Gudea, Moțu 1988, 231). In any event, these vessels cannot form part of this study, as they do not belong to the repertory of shapes of local tradition pottery found in the Roman Dacia.

IV.1.10. A comparative study of the hand-made pottery discovered within the Locusteni and Soporu de Câmpie cemeteries

Until now, the Locusteni and Soporu de Câmpie cemeteries are the only such sites of Roman Dacia that have been intensively investigated and published.

As no wheel-made local tradition vessels were discovered in the Soporu de Câmpie cemetery, I shall only analyze the hand-made pottery found within the two cemeteries.

The native hand-made pottery represents about 17% of the total pottery inventory of the Soporu de Câmpie cemetery, and 32.73% of that from Locusteni.

The main shapes of hand-made pottery discovered in the two cemeteries are the tall vessels and Dacian cups.

The paste can be analyzed from the point of view of its composition (degreasing substances) and consistency (resistance).

From the 62 vessels discovered at Locusteni, 95.16% contain sand as the degreasing agent. In the case of Soporu de Câmpie, I have collected information on the paste composition of some 14 vessels, of which 7 used sand as a degreasing agent.

A common attribute of the hand-made pottery discovered at Locusteni and Soporu de Câmpie is its friability. According to the information I hold, 65.62% of the Locusteni vessels, and 83.33% of those from Soporu de Câmpie, are friable.

Colour is another means of comparing the hand-made vessels discovered within the two mentioned cemeteries. An analysis of 77.47% of the Locusteni vessels shows that the brick-red colour is dominant with 95.34% of them. At Soporu de Câmpie, from a sample of 29 vessels (almost 37.18%), 41.37% are grey, and 24.13% are red, or brick-coloured. Thus, while the red-brick colour clearly prevails at Locusteni, at Soporu de Câmpie the majority belongs to grey vessels.

Decoration is present on 63.06% of the Locusteni vessels, and 61.53% of the Soporu de Câmpie finds.

Relief decorative elements prevail within the pottery of both cemeteries (80% of the decorated vessels at Locusteni, and 62.5% at the Soporu de Câmpie).

The most frequent motif is the alveolar cordon. At Locusteni, it is present on 62.85% of the total decorated vessels, and on 33.33% at Soporu de Câmpie. This difference could be due to the fact that the Soporu de Câmpie cemetery had ceased its evolution by the end of the 3rd century AD, when the relief decoration - the alveolar cordon inclusively - was used more seldom.

In both cemeteries, the next most popular relief decoration was the round, flat button, present on more than 14% of vessels.

Incised decoration is evident on 17.15% of Locusteni vessels and 36.94% of Soporu de Câmpie vessels. The most frequent motif is the strip of waved or horizontal incised lines. These are found together on 13% of the Locusteni decorated vessels, and on almost 20% of those found at Soporu de Câmpie.

Chronology is another criterion in the comparative analysis of the Dacian hand-made pottery found in the two cemeteries.

Both cemeteries started their existence in the 2nd century AD. At the Soporu de Câmpie cemetery, almost 13.15% of the hand-made vessels were dated to the 2nd century AD, and 73.67% were dated from the 2nd century AD to the end of the 3rd century AD. At Locusteni, 96.15% of the published vessels were dated to the 2nd and the first half of the 3rd centuries AD.

As for usage, the statistical situation is almost identical for both cemeteries. At Locusteni, almost 73% of the vessels were used as urns, 25% as lids, and 2% as ritual vessels. At Soporu de Câmpie, 78.43% of the vessels were used as urns, 17.64% as lids, and 3.92% as ritual vessels.

I insist on the fact that no "special" lid was found in either of the two cemeteries, and that Dacian cups, pots, or pot fragments were used as lids.

IV.2. Wheel-made pottery

IV.2.1. The typology of native wheel-made pottery

Research undertaken up until now shows an extremely small number of indigenous wheel-made ceramic vessels in Roman Dacia. The most plausible explanation of this situation might be the fact that it was replaced by Roman provincial pottery. The great pottery centres of Romula, Enoşeşti-Acidava, Apulum, Micăsasa, Micia, and others, were producing important amounts of cheaper and better quality pottery that were reaching even the rural indigenous communities. At a certain moment, this kind of pottery was also being produced within pottery centres of the native population. Ceramic workshops like these existed in the rural settlements of Slimnic and Locusteni, where Roman provincial pottery was made as well as the traditional ware.

The shapes of this kind of pottery that have been discovered so far include: the jar, the cup, the fruit bowl, the strainer, the pot, the lid, and the Dacian cup.

IV.2.2. Frequency

IV.2.3. The geography of the discoveries

Native wheel-made pottery is, according to the present state of research, a modest presence within the pottery of Roman Dacia. It was found in rural settlements at Slimnic, Săcelu, Scorniceşti, Ocna Sibiului, Blandiana, in the Locusteni and Daneţi cemeteries, and in the villa rustica of Aiud.

The extremely small number of complete vessels discovered, on each side of the Carpathians, does not permit me to make observations concerning regional features.

IV.2.4. Technical details

IV.2.4.1. Paste categories

The wheel-made vessels were worked by using a fine grey, or brick-coloured paste.

In spite of the small number of wheel-made vessels, I consider it necessary to present some observations concerning the vessels found in the Locusteni cemetery.

A. Fine paste

A.1. Fine paste containing sifted sand and mica

The firing is complete or incomplete (183, 187). It has a thin, light-grey film.

A.2. Rough, sandy paste

This contains much sifted sand and mica. The firing is complete (177-178). These vessels are brick-coloured. The paste is identical to that of the "A" category vessels found with the hand-made examples discovered in the same cemetery.

The presence of vessels made of such paste, within the Daco-Roman cemetery of Locusteni, might be the result of some influence coming from Roman-provincial, rough-style pottery.

IV.2.4.2. Decoration

A. Relief decoration

A.1. The relief notched cordon (176)

B. Incised decoration

B.1. Incised lines

B.1.1. Strip of incised lines (177-178)

B.1.2. Strip of waved incised lines (177-178)

The decoration motifs of the wheel-made Dacian traditional pottery can be found within classic Dacian Late Iron Age period (Crişan 1969, 210, pls. 109-111), as with the native hand-made pottery discovered at Locusteni, Breţcu, or Enoşeşti-Acidava (see vessels nos. 11, 57 and 72).

IV.2.4.3. Dimensions

Vessels found so far are of medium size, except for one provision vessel, which is large (176).

IV.2.4.4. Usage

As with the case of the hand-made pottery, the uses of wheel-made pottery can be deduced from their shapes. Food could have been preserved in jars for longer or shorter periods of the time. Pots, cups, and fruit bowls were used as table ware. Special wheel-made lids, of fine, grey paste, were used as coverings for the table ware.

Finally, I should mention scientist Silviu Sanie's opinion that "The fruit bowls … must have had a ritual destination", evidence being the use of similar vessels for libations in the Ancient Orient (Sanie 1995, 106, note 274).

IV.2.5. The origins of the native wheel-made pottery

Emil Moscalu considered that the pots with inward rim (189) are imitations of Greek forms. On the middle and low courses of the Danube River, they appeared during the 6th-5th centuries BC (Moscalu 1983, 115-117, type 10c).

Biconical-shaped fruit-bowls (186-188) were also taken by the Dacians from the Greek milieu (Moscalu 1983, 97-98, 132-136, 140-141).

The wheel-made, biconical-shaped jugs found at Scorniceşti and Daneţi, appeared at the Dacian sites from the Late Iron Age (181-185). As far as it seems, they, too, had a Greek prototype as origin (Crişan 1969, 118-119, 124, type 1).

Two of the jars found at Locusteni (177-178) imitate local shapes of the hand-made Dacian pottery (Popilian 1980, 83-84).

The wheel-made strainers and the conical-shaped cup (197) also originated during the Dacian Late Iron Age. It is certain that the strainers were, in their turn, taken from a Greek milieu (Moscalu 1983, 145).

From the above-mentioned features, one may observe that most of the wheel-made shapes from the Roman Dacia, identified so far, continued their existence from the classic Dacian Late Iron Age period, and that, in most cases, they originated from Greek pottery prototypes.

IV.2.6. Chronology

A curved-bodied jug (188) and a pot (193) were dated to the beginning of the 2nd century AD. A slightly curved jar (178) and a fruit bowl (186) were dated from the 2nd century AD.

An ovoid-shaped jar (177), two jugs (181, 184), a fruit-bowl (188), two lids (194-195) and a Dacian cup (197) were dated from the 2nd century AD and the first half of the 3rd century AD.

Two biconical shaped strainers (179-180), a biconical-shaped jug (182), and three pots (189-190, 192) were dated from the second half of the 2nd century AD to the first half of the 3rd century AD.

IV.2.7. Comparative analysis of the native wheel-made pottery in Roman Dacia and the classic Dacian Late Iron Age period

Compared to the classic Dacian Late Iron Age period, and according to present discoveries, the native wheel-made pottery did not evolve in a readily discernable way. The only observations concern their frequency in the 2nd-3rd centuries AD.

The fruit-bowls – a typical Dacian vessel - was discovered within the Locusteni cemetery, and within the settlements of Ocna Sibiului, Govora-Sat, Săcelu, Blandiana, at the villa rustica of Aiud, and in the Roman camps of Olteni and Sărăţeni. Throughout the 2nd-3rd centuries AD, it was an extremely rare shape in Roman Dacia, and it has not yet been found in the discoveries made in Wallachia (Bichir 1984, 36); it is present within the Carpian milieu (Bichir 1973, 76-78). The presence of this type of vessel in Roman Dacian territory does not necessarily provide proof of Carpian expansion, but it may be cited as evidence of local Dacian Late Iron Age survival (Popilian 1976, 138; Popilian 1980, 84-85).

It is worth remembering the discovery of some wheel-made Dacian cups at Locusteni (Popilian 1980, 36, pl. 23, M 155, 2) and Stolniceni-Buridava (Bichir 1983, 13). Wheel-made "Dacian" cups were an exceptional presence during the Dacian Late Iron Age (Crişan 1969, 307, pl. 47:4, 7), and also throughout the 3rd-4th centuries AD - at Hotnitza (Sultov 1980, 384, fig. 110), in Moesia Inferior.

The small number of indigenous, traditional wheel-made vessels discovered in Roman Dacia does not allow me to remark on changes in shape, as they are identical to some vessels coming from archaeological sites dating from the classic Dacian Late Iron Age period.

IV.3. Considerations concerning native pottery production in Roman Dacia

The native pottery production in the Dacia province formed part of the overall pottery production of the province and, in a wider context, contributed to its economy.

Professor Ioan Glodariu asserts that there was an "abrupt, simultaneous cessation of the activity of the pottery production centres that had been active before the Roman conquest. The survival of hand-made pottery was explained by the fact that it was home-made" (Glodariu 1981, 75).

The above-mentioned explanation seems tempting but it is hard to accept, as the possibility of producing hand-made pottery within the Dacian house-economy is not at all certain.

It is also the opinion of scientist Victor Baumann, who considered that the great amount of local tradition vessels found at Teliţa-Amza, for instance, could only have been fired in special furnaces. But, somehow contradicting the above, the same author showed that the pottery in question "was produced separately, and was only fired in special furnaces that belonged to the whole rural community" (Baumann 1995, 47).

The abrupt and simultaneous disappearance of native wheel-made pottery could have been possible only in conditions that gave brought about an abrupt disappearance of the respective population. I have no data at this time concerning some dictate of the new authorities that would have forbidden the local potters to produce these kinds of vessels. In any event, native hand-made pottery is present within the Roman camps at Cătunele, Drajna de Sus and Rucăr, in the civilian settlements of the Roman fortifications of Tibiscum, and also at Napoca, from the first decades of the Roman Period.

On the other hand, neither did the common use Roman provincial pottery abruptly disappear once the Roman army, administration, and most of the urban inhabitants - potters included - had left Dacia.

Ioan Glodariu's assertion can, at most, refer exclusively to luxury pottery (painted pottery included), and only partially to the usual wheel-made Dacian ware (for example fruit-bowls).

Within all the sites investigated, native pottery forms a minority compared to Roman ware. At the same time, I should stress that the presence of wheel-made Dacian tradition pottery is very infrequent, and that, up until now, it is completely absent from Roman camps and their civilian settlements.

The native hand-made pottery represents about 10% to 45% of the finds within rural settlements, and 17% to 32.27% within Daco-Roman cemeteries. Thus, at the Locusteni rural settlement, these vessels represent 10% of the total pottery inventory (Popilian 1980, 86), 10%-15% at Obreja (Protase 1980, 58), 40% at Scorniceşti settlement no. 1 (Bichir 1986, 118), and 45% at Noşlac (Macrea, Protase, Dănilă 1967, 116). In the Soporu de Câmpie cemetery, the native hand-made pottery represents about 17% of the total (Protase 1976, 47 and the table no. 2), while at the Locusteni cemetery the percentage is 32.73% (Popilian 1986, 86).

The situation is similar to that of other Dacian inhabited territories during the 2nd-3rd centuries AD. Thus, in the Sânicolaul Mare (Satu Mare county), native hand-made pottery represents about 39% (Dumitraşcu, Crişan 1988, 45), 25% in the Chilia cemetery (Morintz 1961, 397), and 45.9% in the Lipitza cemeteries (Bichir 1983a, 63).

In several complexes within the Locusteni settlement, the Dacian hand-made and wheel-made pottery represents 10%, while within its cemetery the percentage is 41% (Popilian 1980, 85). It was right to explain the difference by the idea that traditional pottery was preferred for funerary practices (Popilian 1980, 86).

The persistence of indigenous pottery within the Roman period was generally explained as a consequence of local conservatism, being considered as the survival of a tradition. Without ignoring this supposition, I consider the survival might also have economic and social explanations.

The hand-made pottery might have survived because of local demand. The reasons might include: a) lower prices compared to wheel-made pottery; b) the uses required of some kinds of vessels; c) the fact that the indigenous population was accustomed to such pottery.

Instead, Roman provincial ware replaced native wheel-made pottery. The key to this phenomenon is the quality/price relationship; in the case of wheel-made pottery, the balance inclined in favour of Roman pottery, but this relationship also allowed the continuity of production of the hand-made common Dacian ware, which was cheaper and more accessible to a rural population that was to some degree excluded from the monetary economy based on the urban areas.

My opinion does not exclude Ioan Glodariu's idea that, at Slimnic, the cause of the replacement of the fruit-bowls during the Roman period would have been: "Some change or transformation of the usual furniture of the inhabitants, as the later rarity of a shape that was always present in pre-Roman settings can hardly be explained by reasons other than those of functionality (Glodariu 1981, 55)". It is not easy to understand that one shape could have had a particular reason for disappearing, while different shapes had others.

The presence of Dacian pottery shows: a) the presence of a population that preferred Dacian traditional products (in most cases they were native people, though I do not exclude other ethnic groups); the presence of Dacian potters in the province; c) the functioning of a market economy and the relationship of supply and demand.

The presence of Dacian hand-made pottery within the Roman camps of Dacia suggests: a) its production in order to fulfil a lack (be it temporary) of some kinds of vessels within the Roman provincial pottery; b) the presence of some Dacian potters within the Roman army (not a very frequent occurence); c) a decrease in Roman production resulting from the general economic crisis in middle of the 3rd century AD.

The research and discoveries made up until the present, obliges me to consider that the local tradition pottery was generally produced in rural settings. Evidence for this is provided by the pottery kilns discovered in the rural settlement of Locusteni (Popilian 1980, 85), and the evidence of local native pottery production in the rural settlement at Slimnic (Glodariu 1981, 58).

The next sites for such production (and a ready market) would have been the military camps of the province. Dacian hand-made pottery was not only used in these camps (and their civilian settlements) but it was also produced there. Evidence for this lies in the remains of potters' furnaces found within the Roman camp of Orheiul Bistriţei (Protase, Dănilă 1964, 557-563), and those from the civilian settlements of the

Slăveni (Popilian 1971, 634), Enoşeşti-Acidava (Preda, Grosu 1996, 42), and Tibiscum (Benea 1981; Benea 1985) Roman camps. Within these camps and settlements, and in their close vicinity, vessels and fragments of native style pottery were found.

The presence of whole, or fragmentary, Dacian-tradition vessels in some Roman cities - such as Apulum or Napoca – must, for the time being at least, have rather an accidental explanation. It would have been natural, for the urban markets, to be dominated by the pottery made within the great urban pottery centres. So, the most probable hypothesis is that the hand-made vessels were brought, not made, there.

The local potters must have borrowed Roman pottery shapes and techniques when working in the rural, or civilian, settlements of the Roman camps. Professor Ioan Glodariu must have been right to assume that provincial Roman pottery was produced, at a certain moment, in local pottery centres somewhere near Slimnic (Glodariu 1981, 58). Victor Baumann, with regard to the Roman style of provincial pottery made at Teliţa-Amza, also supported this supposition for Moesia Inferior (Baumann 1995, 47).

The persistence of native pottery in Roman Dacia was not a singular phenomenon within the Roman Empire. I can refer to the continuation of indigenous pottery production in Moesia Inferior (Ohcearov 1965, 34-37; Scorpan 1968, 341-346; Scorpan 1970, 55-65; Babeş 1971, 19-45; Scorpan 1973, 137-151; Sultov 1980, 381-384; Opaiţ 1980, 328-360; Kabakcieva 1997, 33-40) and Pannonia (Bónis 1942, pls. 1-15; Brukner 1981, pls. 2-5; Brukner 1987, 40-41, pl. 12). These regions neighboured Dacia, with whom they formed a special cultural unit within the Empire. The continuation of local Late Iron Age traditions was, in fact, observed in several Roman Empire provinces, i.e. Noricum (Schindler-Kaudelka 1997, 116-125; Zabehlicky-Scheffenegger 1997, 127-132; Perko 1997, 165-172), Gallia Belgica (Deru, Grasset 1997, 151-156), and Britannia (Richmond 1966, 129-131; Salway 1981, 642-643; Jobey 1982, 9-10; Swan 1988, 7; Swan 1996, 81-85; Tyers 1996, 63-64).

Even though the situation in Dacia was not exactly similar to some regions in Britannia, where, due to the island's isolation, local pottery centres fulfilled 70%-80% of the civilian market's needs (Swan 1988, 8), the local Dacian potters continued producing hand-made pottery for the rural populations and for the army (and also wheel-made, Roman provincial pottery). The potters supplied rural buyers and the army as well, because, probably, the urban market must have been monopolized by the great urban pottery producing centres.

From this point of view the situation in Dacia could not have been unique within the Roman Empire. Paul Salway is not the only one to consider that there were two markets in Britannia: "one directly served the army needs, the other those of the civilian population. The army brought along a stock with it, or immediately afterwards. Subsequently a few potters arrived and soon local potters were also used" (Salway 1981, 641).

In turn, Vivien Swan observed that the great pottery industry concentrated on serving the needs of the army and that local producers supplied the civilian market. These local artisans made kitchen ware and were often influenced by Late Iron Age local traditions, "and many vessels were hand-made, or partly hand-made, throughout the whole of the Roman period" (Swan 1988, 8; Jobey 1982, 9-10, fig. 5).

Referring to the arrival of the army in Yorkshire, Vivien Swan showed that "the Roman army had little choice. They either had to import pottery from the Continent, or from south-eastern Britannia, or they had to open up their own figlinae, using soldiers or contractors, or else they had to encourage native locals to improve and enlarge their production. Of these options, only the latter ones could have brought long-term benefits. The fact that the Romans chose all three possibilities shows their pragmatism and adaptability" (Swan 1996, 81).

Although continuing a pre-Roman tradition, the production of native pottery could not avoid getting integrated within the general pottery production of Roman Dacia. No doubt future research will reveal new discoveries to help clarify the problems that remain in this area of economic life of the province.

Chapter V
THE REPERTORY OF WHOLLY NATIVE POTTERY FOUND IN ROMAN DACIA

Abbreviations:

H = High
RD = Rim diameter
MD = Maximum diameter
BD = Base diameter
M = Grave (an abreviation used in Romanian literature)

Storage ware

I. Storage jars

1. Jar. Almost complete. The paste contains sand and gravel. Incomplete firing. Brick colour. Little secondary burning inside and out (on the upper part). Dimensions: H=460 mm, RD=220 mm, MD=322 mm, BD=156 mm. Curved body. Bent outside rim. In the maximum area of diameter an applied alveolar cordon. Râşnov. Rural settlement. 2nd-3rd centuries AD. Muzeul de Istorie, Braşov (Alexandrescu 1974-1975, 11, fig. 5).

2. Jar. Almost complete. The paste contains sand and a very little gravel. Complete firing. Light-brick colour. Little secondary burning outside (all over body). Dimensions: H=360 mm, RD=254 mm, MD=267 mm, BD=135 mm. Tall, ovoid body. Everted rim. Narrow base. Stolniceni-Buridava. The civilian settlement of the Roman camp. Discovered in 1962. End of 2nd century AD to beginning of 3rd century AD. Muzeul Govora, inv. no. V.460 (Petre-Govora 1968, 147, fig. 2:1).

3. Jar. Almost complete. Paste contains sand. Brick colour. Dimensions: H=460 mm, RD=220 mm, MD=322 mm, BD=156 mm. Tall, ovoid body. Enlarged rim. Flat, narrow base. Locusteni. Cemetery, M 13. 2nd century AD. Muzeul Olteniei, Craiova, inv. no. 19.402 (Popilian 1976, 221, pl. 74, no. 950; Popilian 1976a, 285, fig. 3:14; Popilian 1980, 15, 103, pl. 3, M 13, 2).

4. Jar. Almost complete. Rough paste. Brick colour. Dimensions: H=380 mm, RD=222 mm, MD=270 mm,

BD=109 mm. Tall, ovoid body. Everted rim. Flat, narrow base. Over the maximum diameter area an applied alveolar cordon. Locusteni. Cemetery, M 15. 2nd century AD to first half of 3rd century AD. Muzeul Olteniei, Craiova (Popilian 1976, 221, pl. 74, no. 949; Popilian 1976a, 285, fig. 3:13; Popilian 1980, 15, 103, pl. 3, M 15, 1).

Storage and kitchen ware

II. Biconical jars

5. Jar. Almost complete. Brick colour. Dimensions: H=107 mm, RD=70 mm, MD=88 mm, BD=32 mm. Biconical body. Short, everted rim. Flat, narrow base. Decorated with an alveolar cordon on the rim and other on the shoulder. Locusteni. Cemetery, M 207. 2nd century AD. Muzeul Olteniei, Craiova (Popilian 1980, 44, pl. 29, M 207, 3).

6. Jar. Complete. The paste contains sand as a degreasing agent. Grey-blackish colour. Secondary burning. Dimensions: H=101 mm, RD=65 mm, MD=88 mm, BD=53 mm. Biconical body. The maximum diameter is at the middle of the vessel. The short rim is everted. The base is flat. Above the maximum diameter two alveolar cordons. Feldioara. Rural settlement. Beginning of 2nd century AD. Muzeul de Istorie, Braşov (Costea 1971, 30-31, fig. 4:1).

7. Jar. Almost complete. The rough paste contains sand. Grey colour. Dimensions: H=185 mm, MD=110 mm, BD=80 mm. Biconical body. Short, enlarged rim. Flat base. Above the maximum diameter an applied relief cordon. Daneţi. Cemetery, M 6. 2nd century AD. Muzeul Olteniei, Craiova (Popilian 1982, 50, fig. 2, M 6, 1).

8. Jar. Almost complete. The paste contains sand and gravel. Dark-reddish colour inside and brown outside. Dimensions: H=72 mm, RD=43 mm, MD=77 mm. Flat

base. Biconical body. Short, everted rim. 2nd-3rd centuries AD. Buciumi. Roman camp. Hut no. 5, 1943 (Chirilă, Gudea, Lucăcel, Pop 1972, 54, fig. 47:1, 48:2).

9. Jar. Almost complete. Biconical body. Rim diameter larger than that of base. Maximum diameter at lower part of vessel. The short rim is everted. The base is large and flat. Ilişua. Roman camp. 2nd-3rd centuries AD (Protase, Gaiu, Marinescu 1997, 55, pl. 61:2).

10. Jar. Almost complete. The paste contains much sand and mica. Complete firing. Grey colour. Little secondary burning outside (on the upper and middle parts) and inside (on the lower and middle parts). Dimensions: H=250 mm, DG 135 mm, MD=189 mm, BD=140 mm. Curved body. Almost vertical rim. On the shoulder an applied alveolar cordon. Stolniceni-Buridava. "La priză" (the civilian settlement of the Roman camp), Section S 4, Pit no. 4/1965. The beginning of 3rd century AD. Muzeul de Istorie, Râmnicu Vâlcea, inv. no. E.106 (Tudor 1967, 656, fig. 2:4).

11. Jar. Almost complete. Fine paste. Incomplete firing. Brick colour. Dimensions: H=140 mm, RD=115 mm, BD=75 mm. Everted rim. Flat base. On the maximum diameter area an applied alveolar cordon. On the shoulder cordon of waved lines and on neck four alveolar, rounded buttons. Breţcu. Roman camp. 2nd-3rd centuries AD. Muzeul Naţional de Istorie a Transilvaniei, Cluj-Napoca, inv. no. V.475 (Daicoviciu 1936-1942, 231, pl. 1:2).

12. Jar. Almost complete. The rough paste contains gravel. Curved body. Greatly everted rim. Flat base. On the maximum diameter area an applied alveolar cordon, and four alveolar rounded buttons (under rim). Breţcu. Roman camp. 2nd-3rd centuries AD. Muzeul Naţional de Istorie a Transilvaniei, Cluj-Napoca (Daicoviciu 1936-1940, 231, fig. 1:5; Protase 1966, 10, fig. 3:3).

13. Jar. Almost complete. The paste contains sand and gravel. Dark-reddish colour. Dimensions: H=165 mm, RD=125 mm, BD=80 mm. Curved body. Everted rim. Flat base. On shoulder an incised cordon of waved lines. On maximum diameter area an applied alveolar cordon. Breţcu. Roman camp. 2nd-3rd centuries AD. Muzeul Naţional de Istorie a Transilvaniei, Cluj-Napoca (Gudea 1980, 314, fig. 41:1).

14. Jar. Almost complete. Paste contains sand. Yellowish colour. Dimensions: H=292 mm, RD=212 mm, MD=228, BD=141 mm. Curved body. Everted rim. Flat base. Decorated with four asymmetric protuberances applied to the area of maximum diameter. Locusteni, Cemetery, M 47. 2nd century AD to first half of 3rd century AD. Muzeul Olteniei, Craiova, inv. no. I:2.137 (Popilian 1976, 221, pl. 74, no. 952; Popilian 1976a, 285, fig. 3:2; Popilian 1980, 20, pl. 8, M 47, 1).

15. Jar. Almost complete. Rough, friable paste. Blackish colour. Biconical body. Bent outside rim. Flat base, a little profilated. The maximum diameter was marked with

threshold. Soporu de Câmpie. Cemetery, M 77. 3rd century AD. Muzeul Naţional de Istorie a Transilvaniei, Cluj-Napoca (Protase 1976, 30-31, pl. 43:1).

16. Jar. Almost complete. Tall, biconical body. Maximum diameter located at centre of vessel. The rim diameter a little larger than that of base. Everted rim. Flat base. Obreja. Rural settlement. 2nd-3rd centuries AD. Muzeul Naţional de Istorie a Transilvaniei, Cluj-Napoca (Protase 1966, 43, fig. 17:4).

III. Bell-shaped jars

17. Jar. Almost complete. The paste contains sand and gravel. Incomplete firing. Brick colour. Little secondary burning outside and in. Dimensions: H=322 mm, RD=252 mm, MD=280 mm, BD=132 mm. Bell-shaped body. External rim enlarged. Flat, narrow base. Locusteni. Cemetery, M 38. 2nd century AD to first half of 3rd century AD. Muzeul Olteniei, Craiova, inv. no. 19766 (Popilian 1980, 19, 103, pl. 7, M 38, 1).

18. Jar. Almost complete. Bell-shaped body. Maximum diameter a little larger than that of base. Rim diameter greater than that of base. Enlarged rim. Flat base. Ilişua. Roman camp. 2nd-3rd centuries AD (Protase, Gaiu, Marinescu 1997, 55, pl. 59:4).

19. Jar. Almost complete. Bell-shaped body. Maximum diameter at upper half of vessel. Enlarged rim. Flat base. Filiaşi. Muzeul Ţării Secuilor, Sf. Gheorghe. Rural settlement. 2nd-3rd centuries AD (Székely 1980a, 360, fig. 2).

20. Jar. Almost complete. Rough paste. Bell-shaped body. Maximum diameter at upper half of vessel. Enlarged rim. Flat base. Buza. Rural settlement. First decades of 2nd century AD. Muzeul Naţional de Istorie a Transilvaniei, Cluj-Napoca (Bădău-Wittenberger 1994, 369, pl. 5:1).

21. Jar. Almost complete. Bell-shaped body. Everted rim. Bologa. Roman camp. S 18 c 26,50 - 0,70 m. 2nd-3rd centuries AD (Gudea 1973, 53, fig. 24:29).

22. Jar. Almost complete. Dark-blackish colour. Dimensions: H=205 mm, RD=160 mm, MD=175 mm, BD=110 mm. Bell-shaped body. Everted rim. Small, concave base. On maximum diameter a relief cordon. Soporu de Câmpie. Cemetery, M 95. 2nd-3rd centuries AD. Muzeul Naţional de Istorie a Transilvaniei, Cluj-Napoca (Protase 1976, 33, pls. 19:1 and 42:6).

IV. Pear-shaped jars

23. Jar. Almost complete. The paste contains sand. Dimensions: H=360 mm, RD=220, MD=280, BD=150mm. Pear-shaped body. Everted rim. Flat base. On maximum diameter area an applied alveolar cordon. Buciumi. Roman camp. 2nd-3rd centuries AD (Gudea

1970, 305, fig. 1:2; 5:6; Chirilă, Gudea, Lucăcel, Pop 1972, 54, figs. 47:4 and 48:5).

24. Jar. Almost complete. The paste contains sand and gravel. Brick colour. Dimensions: H=300 mm, RD=210 mm, MD=215 mm, BD=120 mm. Tall, pear-shaped body. Everted rim. Flat, narrow base. On shoulder three small, applied, rounded buttons. Soporu de Câmpie. Cemetery, M 116. 2nd-3rd centuries AD. Muzeul Național de Istorie a Transilvaniei, Cluj-Napoca, inv. no. 24073 (Protase 1976, 35, pls. 20:8 and 43:2).

25. Jar. Almost complete. Friable paste containing sand and gravel. Incomplete fiiring. Blackish colour. Dimensions: H=290 mm, MD=210 mm, BD=130 mm. Pear-shaped body. Short, everted rim. Flat base. Decorated with irregular incised lines. Soporu de Câmpie. Cemetery, M 89. 2nd-3rd centuries AD. Muzeul Național de Istorie a Transilvaniei, Cluj-Napoca, inv. no. 23224 (Protase 1976, 32, pls. 19:6 and 43:3).

26. Jar. Almost complete. Pear-shaped body. Maximum diameter at upper part of vessel. Everted rim. Mouth wider than base. Flat base, rather profilated. Ilişua. Roman camp. Middle of 3rd century AD (Protase, Marinescu, Gaiu 1981, 290-291, fig. 4; Protase, Gaiu, Marinescu 1997, 55, pl. 60:4).

27. Jar. Almost complete. Rough paste. Light-brick colour. Dimensions: H=240 mm, RD=155 mm, BD=98 mm. Little secondary burning inside and out (on the upper part). Pear-shaped body. Enlarged rim. Flat base. On shoulder a band of waved incised lines and two other bands of horizontal, incised lines. Olteni. Roman camp. Middle of the 3rd century AD. Muzeul Țării Secuilor, Sf. Gheorghe, inv. no. R9/1988 (Székely 1990-1994, 19, pl. 1:2).

28. Jar. Almost complete. The paste contains much sand. Brick colour. Dimensions: H=280 mm, RD=184 mm, MD=232 mm, BD=128 mm. Pear-shaped body. Short, everted rim. Flat base. On maximum diameter area an applied alveolar cordon. Locusteni. Cemetery, M 256. 2nd century AD to first half of 3rd century AD. Muzeul Olteniei, Craiova (Popilian 1980, 50, 103, pl. 35, M 256, 2).

29. Pear-shaped jar. Almost complete. Pear-shaped body. Maximum diameter at middle of vessel. Rim diameter greater than that of base. Short, everted rim. Flat base. Ilişua. Roman camp. 2nd-3rd centuries AD (Protase, Gaiu, Marinescu 1997, 55, pl. 59:3).

30. Jar. Almost complete. Rough paste. Dimensions: H=215 mm, RD=170 mm, MD=180 mm, BD=100 mm. Pear-shaped body. Everted rim. Flat, profilated base. Soporu de Câmpie. Cemetery, M 117. 2nd-3rd centuries AD. Muzeul Național de Istorie a Transilvaniei, Cluj-Napoca (Protase 1976, 35 pls. 21:2 and 41:2).

31. Jar. Almost complete. Small size. The paste contains sand and gravel. Dark-reddish colour. Dimensions: H=84 mm, RD=170 mm, BD=45 mm. Pear-shaped body. Bent outside rim. Flat base. Buciumi. Roman camp. Hut no. 5, - 0,40 m. 2nd-3rd centuries AD (Chirilă, Gudea, Lucăcel, Pop 1972, 54, figs. 47:2 and 48:1).

32. Jar. Almost complete. Pear-shaped body. Maximum diameter at upper part. Rim diameter greater than that of base. Everted rim. Flat, slightly profilated base. Ilişua. Roman camp. 2nd-3rd centuries AD (Protase, Gaiu, Marinescu 1997, 55, pl. 60:3).

33. Jar. Identifiable. Very friable paste. Brick colour. Dimensions: H=340 mm, RD=245 mm, BD=150 mm. Pear-shaped body. Everted rim. Base missing. Locusteni. Cemetery, M 76. 2nd century AD to first half of 3rd century AD. Muzeul Olteniei, Craiova (Popilian 1980, 23, pl. 11, M 76, 6).

34. Jar. Almost complete. The paste contains sand. Light-brick colour. Little secondary burning outside and in. Dimensions: H=344 mm, RD=238 mm, MD=236 mm, BD=84 mm. Pear-shaped body. Bent outside rim. Flat, narrow base. On the shoulder was an incised waved line. Locusteni. Cemetery, M 110. 2nd century AD to first half of 3rd century AD. Muzeul Olteniei, Craiova (Popilian 1976, 221, pl. 74, no. 951; Popilian 1976a, 285, fig. 3:1; Popilian 1980, 29, 103, pl. 17, M 110, 1).

35. Jar. Almost complete. The paste contains much sand. Brick colour. Dimensions: H=300 mm, RD=180 mm, MD=204 mm, BD=105 mm. Pear-shaped body. Bent outside rim. Flat, narrow base. On the shoulder was an applied relief cordon. Locusteni. Cemetery, M 195. 2nd century AD to first half of 3rd century AD. Muzeul Olteniei, Craiova (Popilian 1980, pl. 42, M 195, 1).

36. Jar. Almost complete. The paste contains sand and gravel. Incomplete firing. Brick colour. Dimensions: H=312 mm, RD=204 mm, MD=212 mm, BD=108 mm. Pear-shaped body. Bent outside rim. Flat, narrow base. Locusteni. Cemetery, M 54. On the maximum diameter were two applied buttons. 2nd century AD to first half of 3rd century AD. Muzeul Olteniei, Craiova, inv. no. I:2.092 (Popilian 1976, 221, pl. 74, no. 953; Popilian 1976a, 285, fig. 3:3; Popilian 1980, 21, 103, pl. 9, M 54, 1).

37. Jar. Almost complete. Pear-shaped body. Enlarged rim. Flat base. On the shoulder were four applied, flat, rounded buttons decorated with four alveoli each. Aiud. Villa rustica. 2nd-3rd centuries AD (Winkler, Vasiliev, Chitu, Bordea 1968, 72, fig. 7:1).

V. Globular jars

38. Jar. Identifiable. The friable paste contains sand and gravel. Incomplete firing. Brick colour. Little secondary burning outside (on the upper part) and inside (on the entire body). Dimensions: MD=282 mm, BD=134 mm. Globular body. Maximum diameter at the upper part. Flat base. On the shoulder were two bands of horizontal incised lines, one zigzag, and two flat, rounded buttons. Obreja.

Cemetery, M10. Middle of 2nd century AD to end of 3rd century AD. Muzeul Naţional de Istorie a Transilvaniei, Cluj-Napoca (Protase 1971, 151, fig. 13:1).

VI. Pots

39. Pot. Complete. The paste contains sand. Brick colour. Dimensions: H=280 mm, RD=170 mm, MD=185 mm, BD=113 mm. Curved body. Enlarged rim. Flat base. On shoulder an applied alveolar cordon. Locusteni. Cemetery, M 111. 2nd century AD to first half of the 3rd century AD. Muzeul Olteniei, Craiova (Popilian 1980, 29-30, 103, pl. 17, M 111, 1).

40. Pot. Complete. Dimensions: H=225 mm, RD=140 mm, MD=160 mm, BD=140 mm. Curved body. Bent outside rim. Flat base. In the maximum diameter area an applied alveolar cordon. Soporu de Câmpie. Cemetery, M 187. 2nd-3rd centuries AD. Muzeul Naţional de Istorie a Transilvaniei, Cluj-Napoca (Protase 1976, 36, pls. 21:6 and 42:2).

41. Pot. Almost complete. Rough paste. Blackish colour interior and dark-brick colour outside. Dimensions: H=270 mm, RD=160 mm, MD=180 mm, BD=120 mm. Slight curved body. Bent outside rim. Flat base. On the shoulder two waved incised lines. Soporu de Câmpie. Cemetery, M 187. 2nd-3rd centuries AD. Muzeul Naţional de Istorie a Transilvaniei, Cluj-Napoca (Protase 1976, 42, pls. 34:4 and 41:1).

42. Pot. Almost complete. The paste contains much sand. Brick colour. Dimensions: H=348 mm, RD=184 mm, MD=240 mm, BD=120 mm. Tall, curved body. Bent outside rim. Small, concave base. At base of neck a band of horizontal incised lines. At the maximum diameter area an applied alveolar cordon, and on it were four, applied, rounded and flat buttons. Locusteni. Cemetery, M 189. 2nd century AD to first half of 3rd century AD. Muzeul Olteniei, Craiova (Popilian 1980, 40, 103, pl. 27, M 189, 1).

43. Pot. Almost complete. The paste contains sand and gravel. Brick-light colour. Dimensions: H=318 mm, RD=187 mm, BD=132 mm. Curved body. The maximum diameter at the middle of vessel. Enlarged rim decorated with alveoli on the vertical edge. The base is flat. Over the maximum diameter area an applied alveolar cordon. Secondary burning. Enoşeşti-Acidava. The civilian settlement of the Roman camp. 2nd-3rd centuries AD. The school of Piatra Sat (Negru, Ciucă 1997, 23, pl. 1:1).

44. Pot. Almost complete. Rough paste. Brick colour. Dimensions: H=236 mm, RD=160 mm, MD=175 mm, BD=105 mm. Curved body. Everted rim. Flat base. Over maximum diameter area an applied alveolar cordon. Locusteni. Cemetery. 2nd century AD to first half of 3rd century AD. Muzeul Olteniei, Craiova, inv. no. I:2.134 (Popilian 1976, 220, pl. 74, no. 944; Popilian 1976a, 285, fig. 3:7; Popilian 1980, pl. 43:5).

45. Pot. Almost complete. Fine paste. Red colour. Dimensions: H=155 mm, RD=120/140 mm, BD=80 mm. Curved body. Enlarged rim. Flat base. On the middle section a relief cordon. Râşnov. Roman camp. 2nd century AD. Muzeul de Istorie, Braşov (Gudea 1973c, 28, fig. 2).

46. Pot. Almost complete. The paste contains sand. Brick colour. Dimensions: H=234 mm, RD=196 mm, BD=140 mm. Curved body. Enlarged rim. Flat base. On the shoulder an applied alveolar cordon. Locusteni. Cemetery, M 39. 2nd century AD to first half of 3rd century AD. Muzeul Olteniei, Craiova (Popilian 1980, 19, pl. 7, M 39, 1).

47. Pot. Almost complete. The fine paste contains sand, mica and little gravel. Brick colour. Outside secondary burning. Dimensions: H=250 mm, RD=180 mm, BD=138 mm. Curved body. Enlarged rim. Edge of rim decorated with notch. Impressions on the shoulder, under which is a notched cordon. Olteni. Roman camp. Middle of 3rd century AD. Muzeul Ţării Secuilor, Sf. Gheorghe, inv. no. R8/1988 (Székely 1990-1994, 19, pl. 1:3).

48. Pot. Almost complete. The paste contains much sand and little gravel. Dark-brick colour. Dimensions: H=236 mm, RD=160 mm, MD=184 mm, BD=83 mm. Curved body. Enlarged rim. Flat base. Maximum diameter area has a threshold mark. Locusteni. Cemetery, M 84. 2nd century AD to first half of 3rd century AD. Muzeul Olteniei, Craiova, inv. no. I:2133 (Popilian 1976, 220, pl. 74 no. 943; Popilian 1980, 25, pls. 13, M 84, 1 and 43:7).

49. Pot. Almost complete. The paste contains much sand. Brick colour. Dimensions: I=159 mm, RD=116 mm, MD=122 mm, BD=82 mm. Curved body. Enlarged rim. Flat, slightly profilated base. On the shoulder a relief cordon. Râşnov. Roman camp. 2nd-3rd centuries AD (Gudea, Pop 1971, 15, fig. 8).

50. Pot. Almost complete. Curved body. The maximum diameter is a little displaced in the lower half. Rim diameter greater than that of base. Shoulder decorated with a horizontal cordon of alveoli, and with vertical cordons of alveoli from rim to shoulder. Ilişua. Roman camp. 2nd-3rd centuries AD (Protase, Marinescu, Gaiu 1981, 290-291, fig. 4; Protase, Gaiu, Marinescu 1997, 55, pl. 59:10).

51. Pot. Almost complete. Paste contains sand and gravel. Brick colour. Dimensions: H=282 mm, MD=200 mm, BD=130 mm. Curved body. Small, enlarged rim. Flat base. On the maximum diameter area four small, applied, rounded buttons. Locusteni. Cemetery, M 91. 2nd century AD to first half of 3rd century AD. Muzeul Olteniei, Craiova (Popilian 1980, 26, pl. 13, M 91, 1).

52. Pot. Almost complete. Curved body. Flat base. On maximum diameter area an applied alveolar cordon. Scorniceşti. The rural settlement no. 1. Second half of 2nd century AD to first half of 3rd century AD (Bichir 1986, 118, pl. 4:1).

53. Pot. Small size. Complete. The paste contains chaff and gravel. Incomplete firing. Brick colour. Dimensions: H=75 mm, RD=60 mm, BD=40 mm. Curved body. Enlarged rim. Flat base. Decorated with an alveolar cordon applied above the maximum diameter. Enoşeşti-Acidava. The civilian settlement of the Roman camp. 2nd-3rd centuries AD. The school of Piatra Sat (Negru, Ciucă 1997, 25, pl. 2:10).

54. Pot. Almost complete. Small size. The paste contains much sand. Brick colour. Dimensions: H=94 mm, RD=64 mm, MD=74 mm, BD=42 mm. Curved body. Enlarged rim. Flat base. On maximum diameter area an applied alveolar cordon. Locusteni. Cemetery, M 257. 2nd century AD to first half of 3rd century AD. Muzeul Olteniei, Craiova (Popilian 1980, 50, pl. 35, M 257, 1).

55. Pot. Almost complete. The paste contains much sand and is very friable. Brick colour. Dimensions: H=324 mm, RD=228 mm, BD=160 mm. Curved body. Everted rim. The base is large and concave. On the shoulder an applied alveolar cordon. Locusteni. Cemetery, M 122. 2nd century AD to first half of 3rd century AD. Muzeul Olteniei, Craiova (Popilian 1980, 31, pl. 18, M 122, 2).

56. Pot. Almost complete. The paste contains much sand. Brick colour. Dimensions: H=250 mm, RD=165 mm, MD=185 mm, BD=115 mm. Curved body. Enlarged rim. Flat, slightly profilated base. On shoulder an applied alveolar cordon. Locusteni. Cemetery, M 196. 2nd century AD to first half of 3rd century AD. Muzeul Olteniei, Craiova (Popilian 1980, 42, pl. 28, M 196, 1).

57. Pot. Almost complete. The paste contains gravel. Brick colour. Dimensions: H=318 mm, RD=204 mm, MD=220 mm, BD=106 mm. Slight curved body. Slightly enlarged rim. Long neck. Slightly concave base. On shoulder an applied alveolar cordon, and above a band of waved incised lines. Locusteni. Cemetery, M 79. 2nd century AD to first half of 3rd century AD. Muzeul Olteniei, Craiova (Popilian 1980, 24, pl. 12, M 79, 1).

58. Pot. Almost complete. Slightly curved body. Enlarged rim. Slightly concave base. On shoulder an applied alveolar cordon. Enoşeşti-Acidava. The civilian settlement of the Roman camp. 2nd-3rd centuries AD (Preda, Grosu 1993, 50, pl. 8:2).

59. Pot. Almost complete. The paste contains much sand and little gravel. Brick colour. Dimensions: H=230 mm, RD=155 mm, MD=180 mm, BD=121 mm. Slightly curved body. Everted rim. Flat base. Above maximum diameter area an incised horizontal line and three small, flat, rounded buttons. Locusteni. Cemetery, M 197. 2nd century AD. Muzeul Olteniei, Craiova (Popilian 1980, 42, pl. 28, M197, 1).

60. Pot. Almost complete. Paste contains sand and mica. Incomplete firing. Grey-blackish colour. Secondary burning outside (entire body) and in (rim). Dimensions: H=170 mm, RD=116 mm, MD=120 mm, BD=66 mm.

Curved body. Bent outside rim. Short neck. Flat base. Decorated with two cordons of alveoli at maximum diameter area. Enoşeşti-Acidava. The civilian settlement of the Roman camp. 2nd-3rd centuries AD. Muzeul de Istorie, Slatina, inv. no. 8008 (Preda, Grosu 1993, 50, pl. 8:1).

61. Pot. Complete. The paste contains much sand. Brick colour. Dimensions: H=320 mm, RD=204 mm, MD=224 mm, BD=128 mm. Curved body. Enlarged rim. Short neck. Flat base. Decorated with alveoli on rim. Under rim a waved line, on shoulder an alveolar cordon and above four small, flat, rounded buttons. Locusteni. Cemetery, M 155. 2nd century AD to first half of 3rd century AD. Muzeul Olteniei, Craiova (Popilian 1976, 220, pl. 74, no. 944; Popilian 1976a, 285, pl. 2:8; Popilian 1980, 36, pls. 23, M 155, 1 and 43:6).

62. Pot. Almost complete. Smock colour. Curved body. Stolniceni-Buridava. The civilian settlement of the Roman camp ("La priză"). Beginning of 3rd century AD (Tudor 1967, 656, fig 2:3).

63. Pot. Identifiable. The fine paste contains a small quantity of sand and mica. Grey-dark colour. Dimensions: H=165 mm, RD=116 mm, MD=137 mm, BD=95 mm. Everted rim. Large, flat base. Olteni. Roman camp, S 8, - 0,40 m. Middle of 3rd century AD. Muzeul Ţării Secuilor, Sf. Gheorghe, inv. no. 1969 (Székely 1970, 53, fig. 1:1; Székely 1980, 62, fig. 6:6).

64. Pot. Almost complete. The paste contains much sand. Brick colour. Dimensions: H=207 mm, RD=172 mm, MD=220 mm, BD=124 mm. Curved body. Enlarged rim. Flat, slightly profilated base. On the maximum diameter area some incised horizontal lines and three small, flat, rounded buttons. On neck three incised irregular lines. Locusteni. Cemetery, M 239. 2nd century AD to first half of 3rd century AD. Muzeul Olteniei, Craiova (Popilian 1980, 48, pl. 34, M 239, 1).

65. Pot. Almost complete. The paste contains sand. Brick colour. Dimensions: H=266 mm, RD=146 mm, MD=184 mm, BD=112 mm. Curved body. Enlarged rim. Flat base. On shoulder an applied alveolar cordon. Locusteni. Cemetery, M 26. 2nd century AD. Muzeul Olteniei, Craiova (Popilian 1980, 17, pl. 5, M 26, 1).

VII. Ovoid jars

66. Jar. Identifiable. Rough paste. Brick colour. Dimensions: H=485 mm, RD=260 mm, MD=348 mm, BD=140 mm. Tall, ovoid body. Rim missing. Flat, narrow base. On shoulder an applied alveolar cordon, below which is a relief alveolar segment. On neck two incised waved lines. Locusteni. Cemetery. 2nd century AD to first half of 3rd century AD. Muzeul Olteniei, Craiova, inv. no. 19.558 (Popilian 1976, 221, pl. 74, no. 948; Popilian 1976a, 285, fig. 2:11).

67. Jar. Almost complete. Rough paste. Grey-blackish colour. Tall, ovoid body. Bent outside rim. Flat, narrow base. On shoulder an incised horizontal line. Soporu de Câmpie. Cemetery, M 46. 3rd century AD. Muzeul Naţional de Istorie a Transilvaniei, Cluj-Napoca (Protase 1976, 26, 81, pl. 43:6).

68. Jar. Almost complete. Rough paste. Dark-reddish colour. Polished outside. Dimensions: H=310 mm, RD=190 mm, MD=160 mm. Ovoid body. Short everted rim. Flat base. Tibiscum ("Pod Nord"), S 1 c 36/37, -1,70/1,85 m. 2nd-3rd centuries AD. Muzeul Caransebeş, inv. no. 9.614 (Bona, Petrovszky, Petrovszky 1982, 410, pl. 2:6).

69. Jar. Almost complete. Rough paste. Grey-blackish colour. Curved body. Bent outside rim. Flat base. On shoulder four applied, small rounded buttons. Soporu de Câmpie. Cemetery, M 46. 3rd century AD. Muzeul Naţional de Istorie a Transilvaniei, Cluj-Napoca (Protase 1976, 26, pl. 41:3).

70. Jar. Almost complete. The paste contains sand. Brick colour. Dimensions: H=320 mm, RD=204 mm, MD=224 mm, BD=132 mm. Tall, ovoid body. Vertical rim. Flat, narrow base. On shoulder an applied alveolar cordon. Locusteni. Cemetery. 2nd century AD to first half of 3rd century AD. Muzeul Olteniei, Craiova, (Popilian 1976, 221, pl. 74, no. 946; Popilian 1976a, 285, fig. 2:9).

71. Jar. Almost complete. Dark-yellowish colour. Tall, slightly curved body. Vertical rim. Slightly concave base. On shoulder four applied alveolar buttons. From every button an oblique alveolar segment. Slimnic. Rural settlement. Pit no. 18. 2nd-3rd centuries AD (Glodariu 1981, fig. 54:16).

72. Jar. Almost complete. The paste contains sand. Incomplete firing. Brick colour. Dimensions: H=292 mm, RD=170 mm, BD=125 mm. Ovoid body. Maximum diameter at middle of vessel. Flat base. On shoulder two bands of horizontal incised lines and another two of waved lines. Secondary burning on the outside upper part. Enoşeşti-Acidava. The civilian settlement of the Roman camp. 2nd-3rd centuries AD. The school of Piatra Sat (Negru, Ciucã 1997, 24, pl. 1:3).

73. Pot. Almost complete. The paste contains much sand and mica. Complete firing. Grey colour. Little secondary burning outside (on upper and middle parts) and inside (on lower and middle parts). Dimensions: H=251 mm, RD=142 mm, MD=160 mm, BD=107 mm. Ovoid body. Short, slightly enlarged rim. Flat base. On shoulder three applied oblique relief segments. Stolniceni-Buridava ("La prizã"). The civilian settlement of the Roman camp. Section S 4 Pit no. 4/1965. Beginning of 3rd century AD. Muzeul de Istorie, Râmnicu Vâlcea, inv. no. E.112 (Tudor 1967, 656, fig. 2:1).

74. Pot. Identifiable. Friable paste. Brick colour. Dimensions: H=(280) mm, MD=172 mm, BD=112 mm. Tall, ovoid body. Rim missing. Flat, profilated base. Over maximum

diameter area an applied alveolar cordon. Locusteni. Cemetery, M 149. 2nd century AD to first half of 3rd century AD. Muzeul Olteniei, Craiova (Popilian 1980, 35, 103, pl. 22 M 149, 1).

VIII. Tall cylindrical jars

75. Jar. Almost complete. Fine, very friable paste. Brick colour. Little secondary burning outside (on upper part) and in. Dimensions: H=275 mm, RD=170 mm, MD=200 mm, BD=130 mm. Curved middle body. At maximum diameter area an applied alveolar cordon, and on neck an incised waved line. Soporu de Câmpie. Cemetery, M 84. 2nd century AD to end of 3rd century AD. Muzeul Naţional de Istorie a Transilvaniei, Cluj-Napoca, inv. no. 24067 (Protase 1976, 32, pls. 19:8 and 43:5).

76. Jar. Almost complete. The paste contains much sand. Brick colour. Dimensions: H=238 mm, RD=160 mm, MD=175 mm, BD=135 mm. Cylindrical body. Enlarged rim. Flat base. Decorated with two alveolar cordons on neck. Locusteni. Cemetery, M 229. 2nd century AD to first half of 3rd century AD. Muzeul Olteniei, Craiova (Popilian 1980, 46/47, pl. 32, M 229, 1).

77. Jar. Almost complete. Rough friable paste. Brown-darkish colour. Dimensions: H=255 mm, RD=160, BD=100 mm. Curved body. Enlarged rim. Flat base. Decorated with an applied alveolar cordon at maximum diameter area. Soporu de Câmpie. Cemetery, M 16. 2nd century AD to end of 3rd century AD. Muzeul Naţional de Istorie a Transilvaniei, Cluj-Napoca (Protase 1976, 21, pls. 11:2 and 41:4).

78. Jar. Almost complete. The fine paste contains sand and mica. Complete firing. Brick colour. Little secondary burning outside. Dimensions: H=215 mm, RD=142 mm, MD=142 mm, BD=101 mm. Cylindrical body. Maximum diameter at middle of vessel. Everted rim. Flat base. Above maximum diameter an applied alveolar cordon. Boroşneul Mare. Roman camp. 2nd-3rd centuries AD. Muzeul Ţãrii Secuilor, Sf. Gheorghe, inv. no. 16685 (Székely 1980a, 360, fig. 1).

79. Jar. Almost complete. Rough paste. Blackish colour. Dimensions: H=154 mm, RD=98 mm, MD=113 mm, BD=75 mm. Cylindrical, slightly curved body. Enlarged rim. Flat base. Sãcelu. Rural settlement, hut L 1. 2nd-3rd centuries AD (Gherghe 1985, 52, fig. 3:2).

80. Jar. Almost complete. The paste contains much sand. Brick colour. Dimensions: H=263 mm, RD=180 mm, MD=174 mm, BD=110 mm. Cylindrical body. Everted rim. Slighty concave base. Over maximum diameter an applied alveolar cordon. Locusteni. Cemetery, M 225. 2nd century AD to first half of 3rd century AD. Muzeul Olteniei, Craiova (Popilian 1980, 46, pl. 31, M 225, 1).

81. Jar. Almost complete. Cylindrical body. Rim diameter larger than that of base. Everted rim. Flat, profilated base.

Ilişua. Roman camp. 2nd-3rd centuries AD (Protase, Gaiu, Marinescu 1997, 55, pl. 58:9).

82. Jar. Almost complete. Cylindrical body. Flat base. On shoulder an applied alveolar cordon. Scorniceşti. The rural settlement no. 1. Second half of 2nd century AD to first half of 3rd century AD (Bichir 1986, 118, pl. 4:6).

83. Jar. Almost complete. The paste contains sand and very little gravel. Light-brick colour. Little secondary burning outside and in (upper part). Dimensions: H=290 mm, RD=200 mm, MD=200 mm, BD=120 mm. Cylindrical body. Everted rim. Flat base. Rim decorated with alveoli, and at maximum diameter area an applied alveolar cordon. Soporu de Câmpie. Cemetery, M 169. Second half of 2nd century AD. Muzeul Naţional de Istorie a Transilvaniei, Cluj-Napoca, inv. no. 24066 (Protase 1976, 40, pls. 23:2 and 41:5).

84. Jar. Identifiable. Dark-yellowish colour. Cylindrical body. Everted rim. On maximum diameter area an applied alveolar cordon. Soporu de Câmpie. Cemetery, M 86. 2nd century AD to end of 3rd century AD. Muzeul Naţional de Istorie a Transilvaniei, Cluj-Napoca (Protase 1976, 32, pl. 42:3).

85. Jar. Complete. Paste contains sand, mica and gravel. Light-brick colour. Little secondary burning outside and in (upper part). Dimensions: H=250 mm, RD=154 mm, BD=120 mm. Cylindrical body. Enlarged rim, upper part with threshold. Olteni. Roman camp. The middle of the 3rd century AD. Muzeul Ţării Secuilor, Sf. Gheorghe, inv. no. 18348 (Székely 1990-1994, 19, pl. 1:1).

86. Jar. Identifiable. Paste contains sand and mica. Complete burning. Grey colour. Secondary burning outside (upper part). Dimensions: RD=175 mm, MD=190 mm. Cylindrical body with curved walls. Stolniceni-Buridava ("La priză"). The civilian settlement of the Roman camp. Discovered in the section S 4, Pit no. 4/1965. Beginning of 3rd century AD. Muzeul de Istorie, Râmnicu Vâlcea, inv. no. E.260 (Tudor 1967, 656, fig. 2:2).

87. Jar. Almost complete. Cylindrical body. Everted rim. Large, flat base. Scorniceşti. The rural settlement no. 1. Second half of 2nd century AD to first half of 3rd century AD (Bichir 1984, 32, pl. 17:10; Bichir 1986, 118, pls. 4:2 and 14:1).

88. Jar. Almost complete. Cylindrical body. Enlarged rim. Large, flat base. On middle an applied alveolar cordon. Enoşeşti-Acidava. The civilian settlement of the Roman camp. 2nd-3rd centuries AD (Preda, Grosu 1993, 50, pl. 8:3).

IX. Cylindrical large jars ("sack"-type)

89. Jar. Almost complete. The paste contains sand. Grey colour. Cylindrical body. Enlarged rim. Large, flat base.

Leu. Cemetery. 2nd century AD to first half of 3rd century AD (Popilian, Niţă 1982, 92, fig. 2:4).

90. Jar. Almost complete. Rough paste. Brick colour. Dimensions: H=254 mm, RD=192 mm, BD=120 mm. Cylindrical body. Everted rim. Flat base. Locusteni. Cemetery. 2nd century AD to first half of 3rd century AD. Muzeul Olteniei, Craiova, inv. no. I:2.140 (Popilian 1976, 221, pl. 74, no. 955; Popilian 1976a, 285, pl. 3:5).

91. Jar. Almost complete. The paste contains much sand. Complete firing. Little secondary burning outside and in. Blackish colour. Dimensions: MD= 86 mm, BD=62 mm. Cylindrical body. Maximum diameter at middle of vessel. Rim diameter almost equal to that of base. Slightly everted rim. Flat base. Obreja. Rural settlement. 2nd-3rd centuries AD. Muzeul Naţional de Istorie a Transilvaniei, Cluj-Napoca, inv. no. V.507 (Protase 1971, 137, fig. 5:1).

92. Jar. Almost complete. Cylindrical body. Maximum diameter a little displaced around lower part. Everted rim. Flat base. Gilãu. Roman camp. 2nd-3rd centuries AD (Isac 1997, 56; Ţentea, Marcu 1997, 243, pl. 1:2).

93. Jar. Almost complete. The paste contains sand and gravel. Brick colour. Dimensions: H=244 mm, RD=220 mm, MD=212 mm, BD=120 mm. Cylindrical body. Enlarged rim. Flat base. Locusteni. Cemetery, M 102. 2nd century AD to first half of 3rd century AD. Muzeul Olteniei, Craiova (Popilian 1976, 221, pl. 74, no. 954; Popilian 1976a, 285, fig. 3:4; Popilian 1980, 28, pls. 16, M 102, 1 and 45:2).

94. Jar. Almost complete. Cylindrical body. Maximum diameter at middle part. Mouth diameter equal to that of base. Enlarged rim. Flat base. On maximum diameter area an applied notched cordon. Ilişua. Roman camp. 2nd-3rd centuries AD (Protase, Gaiu, Marinescu 1997, 55, pl. 58:3).

95. Jar. Almost complete. The paste contains sand. Secondary burning. Dimensions: H=120 mm, RD=152 mm, BD=128 mm. Large cylindrical body. Enlarged rim. Flat base. Buciumi. Roman camp. 2nd-3rd centuries AD (Gudea 1970, 299, figs. 1: 1 and 5:2).

96. Jar. Almost complete. The paste contains much sand and gravel. Dark-reddish colour. Dimensions: H=180 mm, RD=108 mm, MD=150 mm. Cylindrical body. Everted rim. Flat base. Buciumi. Roman camp. Hut no. 5, - 0,60 m. 2nd-3rd centuries AD. Inv. no. 339/1969 (Chirilă, Gudea, Lucăcel, Pop 1972, 54, pls. 47:5 and 48:3).

97. Jar. Almost complete. The paste contains gravel. Brick colour. Dimensions: H=300 mm, RD=270 mm, MD=250 mm, BD=110 mm. Cylindrical body. Enlarged rim. Flat, narrow base. On shoulder four applied waved alveolar segments. Locusteni. Cemetery, M 286. 2nd century AD to first half of 3rd century AD. Muzeul Olteniei, Craiova (Popilian 1980, 53, pl. 38, M 286, 1).

Kitchen ware

X. Lids

98. Lid. Identifiable. Hemispherical-shaped body. Timişoara-Freidorf. Rural settlement. 2nd-3rd centuries AD (Benea 1997, 72, fig. 7:3).

99. Lid. Identifiable. Hemispherical-shaped body. Timişoara-Freidorf. Rural settlement. 2nd-3rd centuries AD (Benea 1997, 72, fig. 7:2).

100. Lid. Identifiable. Hemispherical-shaped body. Timişoara-Freidorf. Rural settlement. 2nd-3rd centuries AD (Benea 1997, 72, fig. 7:4).

101. Lid. Almost complete. The paste contains gravel. Dark-reddish colour. Dimensions: H=50 mm, RD=150 mm, BD=50 mm. Hemispherical-shaped body. Tibiscum. Roman camp, passim. 2nd-3rd centuries AD (Rogozea 1988, 177, fig. 7:3).

102. Lid. Almost complete. The paste contains gravel. Brick colour. Dimensions: H=63 mm, RD=200 mm, BD=65 mm. Hemispherical-shaped body. Tibiscum ("Pod Nord"), Building X (A). Hall D - 1,30/1,40 m. 2nd-3rd centuries AD (Rogozea 1988, 178, fig. 7:3).

103. Lid. Almost complete. Hemispherical-shaped body. Cylindrical button. Scorniceşti. The rural settlement no. 1. Second half of 2nd century AD to first half of 3rd century AD (Bichir 1984, pl. 17:1; Bichir 1986, 118, pl. 11:3).

104. Lid. Identifiable. Conical body. Timişoara-Freidorf. Rural settlement. 2nd-3rd centuries AD (Benea 1997, 72, fig. 7:5).

105. Lid. Complete Brick colour. Dimensions: H=85 mm, RD=185 m. Short, conical body. Tibiscum. Roman camp ("Pod Nord"), S 1 c 3. 2nd-3rd centuries AD (Bona, Petrovszky, Petrovszky 1982, 410, pl. 3:7).

106. Lid. Almost complete. Conical body. Ilişua. Roman camp. Middle of 3rd century AD (Protase, Marinescu, Gaiu 1981, 291-292, fig. 4).

107. Lid. Complete Paste with gravel. Dark-blackish colour. Enlarged, conical body. Dedrad. Rural settlement, S A. 2nd century AD to middle of 3rd century AD (Glodariu 1975, 229, fig. 13:1).

108. Lid. Almost complete. Dimensions: RD=132 mm, BD=43 mm, H=64 mm. Tall, conical body. Alveolar button. Gilău. Roman camp. Retendura dextra, sector A, m 6/7, -0,60 m (1984). Gilău III phase. 3rd century AD. Inv. no. 227 (Ţentea, Marcu 1997, 245, pl. 10:4).

109. Lid. Almost complete. Dimensions: RD=150 mm, BD=41 mm, H=82 mm. Conical body. Alveolar button. Gilău. Roman camp. Praetendura dextra, sector A, m 6/7, -0,60 m (1984). Gilău III phase. 3rd century AD. Inv. no. 332 (Ţentea, Marcu 1997, 245, pl. 10:3).

Table vessels

XI. Dish

110. Dish. Almost complete. Dimensions: H=33 mm, RD=58 mm, BD=27 mm. Tronconical body. Rim with rounded edge. Flat base. Scorniceşti. The rural settlement no. 1. Second half of 2nd century AD to first half of 3rd century AD (Bichir 1984, pl. 17:2).

Vessels of illumination

XII. Dacian cups

111. Dacian cup. Complete. The paste contains sand and gravel. Blackish colour. Dimensions: H=45 mm, RD=110 mm, BD=50 mm. Short, conical body. Flat base. The handle is attached by rim and line of base. Enoşeşti-Acidava. The civilian settlement of the Roman camp. 2nd-3rd centuries AD. The school of Piatra Sat (Negru, Ciucă 1997, 26, pl. 2:11).

112. Dacian cup. Almost complete. Dimensions: H=50 mm, RD=111 mm, BD=50 mm. Conical body. Flat base. The handle is attached under the rim and above the line of base. Olteni. Roman camp. Middle of 3rd century AD. Muzeul Ţării Secuilor, Sf. Gheorghe (Székely 1990-1994, 19, fig. 1:4).

113. Dacian cup. Rough paste. Brick-light colour. Dimensions: H=82 mm, RD=150 mm, BD=74 mm. Conical body. The handle is attached under rim and above line of base. Locusteni. Cemetery, M 15. 2nd century AD to first half of 3rd century AD. Muzeul Olteniei, Craiova (Popilian 1976, 220, pl. 74, no. 939; Popilian 1976a, 285, fig. 2:3; Popilian 1980, 15, pl. 3, M 15, 2).

114. Dacian cup. Almost complete. Conical body. Slight rim. Flat base. The handle is attached under rim and above line of base. Scorniceşti. The rural settlement no. 1. Second half of 2nd century to first half of 3rd century AD (Bichir 1986, 120, pl. 3:3).

115. Dacian cup. Almost complete. Paste with sand and gravel. Dark-reddish colour. Dimensions: H=65 mm, RD=135 mm, BD=65 mm. Conical body. The handle is attached by rim and line of base. Porolissum. Roman camp, principia, 1943. 2nd-3rd centuries AD (Gudea 1989, 501, fig. 94:5).

116. Dacian cup. Almost complete. Conical body. The handle is attached under rim and line of base. Obreja. Rural settlement. 2nd-3rd centuries AD. Muzeul Naţional de

Istorie a Transilvaniei, Cluj-Napoca (Protase 1966, 43, fig. 17:3).

117. Dacian cup. Almost complete. Conical body. The handle is attached under rim and line of base. Obreja. Rural settlement. 2nd-3rd centuries AD. Muzeul Naţional de Istorie a Transilvaniei, Cluj-Napoca (Protase 1966, 43, fig. 17:6).

118. Dacian cup. Complete. Conical body. The handle is attached under rim and above line of base. Obreja. Rural settlement. 2nd-3rd centuries AD. Muzeul Naţional de Istorie a Transilvaniei, Cluj-Napoca (Protase 1971, 137, fig. 6:7).

119. Dacian cup. Almost complete. Brick colour. Dimensions: H=66 mm, RD=141 mm, BD=65 mm. Conical body. Curved rim. Flat base. The handle is attached under rim and above line of base. Locusteni. Cemetery, M 283. 2nd century AD to first half of 3rd century AD. Muzeul Olteniei, Craiova (Popilian 1980, 52, pl. 37, M 283, 1).

120. Dacian cup. Almost complete. Conical body. Enlarged rim. The handle is attached under rim and above line of base. Orheiul Bistriţei. Roman camp, defensive fossa (south-eastern part). 2nd-3rd centuries AD (Macrea, Protase, Dănilă 1967, 116, fig. 6:4).

121. Dacian cup. Almost complete. Rough paste. Light-brick colour. Dimensions: H=63 mm, RD=132 mm, BD=72 mm. Conical body. Flat base. The handle is attached under rim and line of base. Drobeta. Roman camp. 2nd-3rd centuries AD (Popilian 1976, 220, pl. 74, no. 940).

122. Dacian cup. Almost complete. Rough paste. Grey colour. Dimensions: H=100 mm, RD=171 mm, BD=88 mm. Conical body. Flat, profilated base. The handle is attached under rim and above line of base. Leu-Albota. Rural settlement. 2nd-3rd centuries AD (Popilian 1976, 220, pl. 74, no. 938; Popilian 1976a, 285, fig. 2:2).

123. Dacian cup. Almost complete. The paste contains sand and gravel. Dark-reddish colour. Dimensions: H=80 mm, RD=142 mm, BD=65 mm. Conical body. Flat, profilated base. The handle is attached under rim and above line of base. Breţcu. Roman camp, S F, 1950. 2nd-3rd centuries AD. Muzeul Naţional de Istorie a Transilvaniei, Cluj-Napoca, inv. no. 6.694 (Gudea 1980, 314, fig. 41:4).

124. Dacian cup. Almost complete. Conical body. Slightly curved rim. Flat, profilated base. The handle is attached under rim and above line of base. Gilău. Roman camp. C I, 1956. 2nd-3rd centuries AD (Macrea, Rusu, Winkler 1959, 453, fig. 1:11).

125. Dacian cup. Conical body. The handle is attached under rim and above line of base. Obreja. Rural settlement. 2nd-3rd centuries AD. Muzeul Naţional de Istorie a Transilvaniei, Cluj-Napoca (Protase 1971, 137, fig. 7:4).

126. Dacian cup. Almost complete. The paste contains sand. Dark-reddish colour. Dimensions: H=45 mm, RD=65 mm, BD=20 mm. Conical body. The handle broken from ancient period. Porolissum. Roman camp, principia 1943. 2nd-3rd centuries AD (Gudea 1989, 501, pl. 94:3).

127. Dacian cup. Almost complete. Dimensions: H=88 mm, RD=139 mm, BD=49 mm. Tall conical body. Slightly curved rim. Flat, narrow base. The handle attached by middle part of body. Locusteni. Cemetery. 2nd century AD to first half of 3rd century AD. Muzeul Olteniei, Craiova (Popilian 1980, 82-83, M, pl. 45:8).

128. Dacian cup. Almost complete. Dimensions: H=78 mm, RD=138 mm, BD=61 mm. Tall conical body. Enlarged rim. Very short, flat base. The handle attached under rim and above line of base. Obreja. Rural settlement. 2nd-3rd centuries AD. Muzeul Naţional de Istorie a Transilvaniei, Cluj-Napoca (Protase 1971, 137, fig. 6:4).

129. Dacian cup. Almost complete. The paste contains much sand. Brick colour. Dimensions: H=70 mm, RD=145 mm, BD=60 mm. Conical body with enlarged upper part. Flat base. The handle is attached under rim and above line of base. Locusteni. Cemetery, M 196. 2nd century AD to first half of 3rd century AD. Muzeul Olteniei, Craiova (Popilian 1980, 42, pl. 28, M 196, 2).

130. Dacian cup. Almost complete. Rough paste. Brick colour. Dimensions: H=80 mm, RD=182 mm, BD=80 mm. Conical body with enlarged upper part. Flat base. The handle is attached under rim and above line of base. Locusteni. Cemetery, M 17. 2nd century AD to first half of 3rd century AD. Muzeul Olteniei, Craiova (Popilian 1976, 220, pl. 74, no. 937; Popilian 1976a, 285, fig. 2:1; Popilian 1980, 15-16, pl. 4, M 17, 2).

131. Dacian cup. Complete. The paste contains sand and gravel. Complete firing. Light-brick colour. Little secondary burning inside and out (rim). Dimensions: H=42 mm, RD=87 mm, BD=40 mm. Enlarged upper section. The handle is attached under rim and line of base. Decorated with incised motifs. Obreja. Rural settlement. 2nd-3rd centuries AD. Muzeul Naţional de Istorie a Transilvaniei, Cluj-Napoca, inv. no. V.503 (Protase 1971, 137, fig. 6:5).

132. Dacian cup. Almost complete. Rough paste. Brick colour. Dimensions: H=96 mm, RD=170 mm, BD=86 mm. Conical body with enlarged upper part. Flat base. The handle is attached under rim and above line of base. The base was decorated with an alveolar cordon. Locusteni. Cemetery, M 108. 2nd century AD to the first half of 3rd century AD. Muzeul Olteniei, Craiova (Popilian 1980, 29, pl. 16, M 108, 2).

133. Dacian cup. Almost complete. The paste contains sand. Incomplete firing. Grey coloured. Exterior secondary burning (lower and middle parts). Dimensions: H=75 mm, RD=145 mm, BD=72 mm. Conical body with enlarged upper part. Flat base. Stolniceni-Buridava. The civilian settlement of the Roman camp. Discovered in 1962. End of 2nd century AD to beginning of 3rd century AD. Muzeul Govora, inv. no. 415 (Petre 1968, 147, fig. 2:4).

134. Dacian cup. Almost complete. Conical body with enlarged upper part. The handle is attached under rim and above line of base. Micia. Roman camp. 2nd-3rd centuries AD (Floca 1968, 52-53, fig 1).

135. Dacian cup. Almost complete. Conical body with enlarged upper part. Flat base. The handle is attached by rim and above line of the base. Scorniceşti. Cemetery, M 5. Second half of 2nd century AD to first half of 3rd century AD (Bichir 1986, 117, pl. 3:2, 4).

136. Dacian cup. Almost complete. The rough paste contains sand, mica and gravel. Incomplete firing. Yellowish-brick colour. Conical body with enlarged upper part. The handle is attached under rim and line of base. Olteni. Roman camp. 2nd-3rd centuries AD. Muzeul Ţării Secuilor, Sf. Gheorghe, inv. no. 6910 (Székely 1970, 53 fig. 1:3).

137. Dacian cup. Almost complete. The rough paste contains sand and gravel. Dark-reddish colour. Dimensions: H=65 mm, RD=125 mm, BD=55 mm. Conical body with enlarged upper part. The handle is attached under rim and line of base. Breţcu. Roman camp, S F, 1950. 2nd-3rd centuries AD. Muzeul Naţional de Istorie a Transilvaniei, Cluj-Napoca, inv. no. 6.704 (Gudea 1980, 314, fig. 41:3).

138. Dacian cup. Almost complete. Paste contains sand, mica and a very little gravel. Complete firing. Brick colour. Secondary burning outside (except the rim) and in (at base). Dimensions: H=104 mm, RD=186 mm, BD=86 mm. Conical body with enlarged upper part. Flat base. An alveolar cordon was applied on rim and another at the base of the vessel. Scorniceşti. The rural settlement no. 1. Discovered in 1967. Second half of 2nd century AD to first half of 3rd century AD. Muzeul de Istorie, Slatina, inv. no. 8688 (Bichir 1984, 31, pl. 17:8; Bichir 1986, 117, pls. 3:1 and 12:5).

139. Dacian cup. Almost complete. Conical body with enlarged upper part. The handle is attached under rim and line of the base. Orheiul Bistriţei. Roman camp, in the foundation of the praetorium. 2nd-3rd centuries AD (Protase 1960, 190, fig. 1:2; Macrea, Protase, Dănilă 1967, 116, fig. 6:5).

140. Dacian cup. Almost complete. Conical body. Flat base. The handle is attached under rim and above line of base. Decorated with an incised motif. Ilişua. Roman camp. 2nd-3rd centuries AD (Protase, Gaiu, Marinescu 1997, 55, pl. 60:7).

141. Dacian cup. Almost complete. Tall conical body with enlarged upper part. Flat, narrow base. The handle is attached under rim and above line of base. Scorniceşti. The rural settlement no. 1. Second half of 2nd century AD to first half of 3rd century AD (Bichir 1984, 31-32, pl. 17:7; Bichir 1986, 117, pls. 3:8 and 11:6).

142. Dacian cup. Almost complete. The paste contains sand and gravel. Dark-reddish colour. Dimensions: H=60 mm, RD=100 mm, BD=45 mm. Conical body with enlarged upper part. The handle is attached by rim and above line

of base. Porolissum. Roman camp, S A 1943. 3rd century AD. Muzeul Naţional de Istorie a Transilvaniei, Cluj-Napoca (Gudea 1989, 501, pl. 94:4).

143. Dacian cup. Almost complete. Fine paste contains sand and mica. Complete firing. Brick colour. Little secondary burning outside and in. Dimensions: H= 90 mm, RD=112 mm, BD=40/54 mm. Conical body with enlarged upper part. Olteni. Roman camp. 2nd-3rd centuries AD. Muzeul Ţării Secuilor, Sf. Gheorghe, inv. no. 11978 (Székely 1970, 53, fig. 1:2; Székely 1980, 60, fig. 6:2).

144. Dacian cup. Almost complete. Tall conical body with enlarged upper part. Flat, narrow base. Base has button instead of handle. Scorniceşti. The rural settlement no. 1. Second half of 2nd century AD to first half of 3rd century AD (Bichir 1984, 31, pl. 17:4; Bichir 1986, 117, pls. 3:6 and 11:5).

145. Dacian cup. Almost complete. Conical body. Two handles are attached by rim and line of the base. Obreja. Rural settlement. 2nd-3rd centuries AD. Muzeul Naţional de Istorie a Transilvaniei, Cluj-Napoca (Protase 1971, 137, fig. 6:6).

146. Dacian cup. Almost complete. The paste contains sand and gravel. Complete firing. Brick colour. Secondary burning outside. Dimensions: H=90 mm, RD=210 mm, RD=85 mm. Slightly curved rim. Flat base. Two handles are attached by rim and above line of base. Soporu de Câmpie. Cemetery, M 6. 2nd century AD to end of 3rd century AD. Muzeul Naţional de Istorie a Transilvaniei, Cluj-Napoca, inv. no. 9700 (Protase 1976, 19, fig. 6:2).

147. Dacian cup. Almost complete. The paste contains sand. Brick colour. Dimensions: H=111 mm, RD=210 mm, BD=96 mm. Flat base. Two handles attached by middle part of body. Decorated with alveoli on rim. Locusteni. Cemetery, M 162. 2nd century AD to first half of 3rd century AD. Muzeul Olteniei, Craiova (Popilian 1980, 36-37, pl. 23, M162, 2).

148. Dacian cup. Complete. Rough paste. Brick colour. Dimensions: H=96 mm, RD=216 mm, BD=94 mm. Conical body with enlarged upper part. Flat base. Two handles are attached by rim and above line of base. Locusteni. Cemetery, M 110. First decades of 3rd century AD. Muzeul Olteniei, Craiova, inv. no. 30.018 (Popilian 1976, 220, pl. 74, no. 942; Popilian 1980, 29, pl. 17, M 110, 2).

149. Dacian cup. Almost complete. The paste contains sand. Brick colour. Dimensions: H=110 mm, RD=220 mm, BD=67 mm. Tall, conical body with very curved upper part. Two handles attached under rim and above line of base. Decorated with alveoli on rim. Locusteni. Cemetery. 2nd century AD to first half of 3rd century AD. Muzeul Olteniei, Craiova (Popilian 1976, 220, pl. 74, no. 941; Popilian 1976a, 285, fig. 2:4; Popilian 1980, 68, pl. 45:6).

150. Dacian cup. Small size. Almost complete. Rough paste with sand. Brick colour. Little secondary burning outside

and in. Tall conical body with enlarged upper part. Two handles attached under rim and on line of base. Decorated with incised motifs. Obreja. Rural settlement. 2nd-3rd centuries AD. Muzeul Naţional de Istorie a Transilvaniei, Cluj-Napoca, inv. no. A4/5 (Protase 1966, 43, fig. 17:5; Protase 1971, 137, fig. 6:3).

XIII. Conical vessel

151. Conical vessel. Almost complete. Conical body. Rim exterior enlarged. Base flat, profilated. Ilişua. Roman camp. 2nd-3rd centuries AD (Protase, Gaiu, Marinescu 1997, 55, pl. 60:6).

152. Conical vessel. Complete. Grey-blackish colour. Tibiscum. Civilian settlement, near kiln mouth. First half of 2nd century AD (Benea 1981, 311, fig. 27:3).

153. Conical vessel. Almost complete. Conical body. Base flat, slightly profilated. Ilişua. Roman camp. 2nd-3rd centuries AD (Protase, Gaiu, Marinescu 1997, 55, pl. 58:8).

154. Conical vessel. Almost complete. Dimensions: H=73 mm, RD=152 mm, BD=73 mm. Tall, conical body. Base flat, slightly profilated. Gilău. Roman camp. Praetendura sinistra, Building A, surface I, -1,30/1,40 m (1979). Gilău III. 3rd century AD. Inv. no. 34 (Ţentea, Marcu 1997, 245, pl. 12:3).

155. Conical vessel. The paste contains sand and gravel. Dimensions: H= 56 mm, RD=130 mm, BD=64 mm. Conical body. Flat, profilated base. Enoşeşti-Acidava. The civilian settlement of the Roman camp. 2nd-3rd centuries AD. School of Piatra Sat (Negru, Ciucă 1997, 26, pl. 2:13).

156. Conical vessel. Almost complete. Dimensions: H=26 mm, RD=55 mm, BD=26 mm. Conical body. Flat, profilated base. Gilău. Roman camp. North-western tour, B room, -1,80/2,00 m. Gilău III phase. 3rd century AD. Inv. no. 311 (Ţentea, Marcu 1997, 245, pl. 12:6).

157. Conical vessel. The paste contains sand and gravel. Brown colour. Dimensions: H=55 mm, RD=132 mm, BD=47 mm. Conical body with enlarged upper part. Enoşeşti-Acidava. The civilian settlement of the Roman camp. 2nd-3rd centuries AD. The school of Piatra Sat (Negru, Ciucă 1997, 26, pl. 2:14).

158. Conical vessel. Small size. Complete. Dimensions: H=35 mm, RD=58 mm, BD=27 mm. Conical body. Scorniceşti. The rural settlement no. 1. Second half of 2nd century AD to first half of 3rd century AD (Bichir 1984, pl. 17:3).

159. Conical vessel. Almost complete. Paste with gravel. Slimnic. Rural settlement. 2nd-3rd centuries AD (Glodariu 1981, fig. 29:7).

160. Conical vessel. Complete. Paste with gravel. Slimnic. Rural settlement. 2nd-3rd centuries AD (Glodariu 1981, fig. 29:9).

161. Conical vessel. Almost complete. Rough paste. Incomplete firing. Brick colour. Dimensions: H=65 mm, RD=116 mm, BD=47 mm. Conical body. Enlarged rim. Flat base. Enoşeşti-Acidava. The civilian settlement of the Roman camp. 2nd-3rd centuries AD. School of Piatra Sat (Negru, Ciucă 1997, 27, pl. 2:15).

162. Conical vessel. Almost complete. Dimensions: H=66 mm, RD=125 mm, BD=60 mm. Tall, conical body. Base flat, slightly profilated. Gilău. Roman camp. Retendura dextra, sector B, m 4/5, -0,35 m (1984). Gilău phase III. 3rd century AD. Inv. no. 354 (Ţentea, Marcu 1997, 245, pl. 12:7).

163. Conical vessel. Slightly conical body. Enlarged rim. Flat base. Gilău. Roman camp. 3rd century AD (Macrea, Rusu, Winkler 1959, 453, fig. 1:15).

164. Conical vessel. Almost complete. The paste contains sand and gravel. Blackish colour. Dimensions: H=65 mm, RD=108 mm, BD=47 mm. Slightly conical body. Flat base. Enoşeşti-Acidava. The civilian settlement of the Roman camp. 2nd-3rd centuries AD. School of Piatra Sat (Negru, Ciucă 1997, 28, pl. 2:16).

165. Conical vessel. Almost complete. Conical body. Flat base. Ilişua. Roman camp. 2nd-3rd centuries AD (Protase, Gaiu, Marinescu 1997, 55, pl. 58:7).

166. Conical vessel. Almost complete. Conical body. Exterior rim enlarged. Flat base. Ilişua. Roman camp. 2nd-3rd centuries AD (Protase, Gaiu, Marinescu 1997, 55, pl. 60:5).

167. Conical vessel. Almost complete. Dimensions: H=63 mm, RD=150 mm, BD=75 mm. Conical body with enlarged upper part. Flat base. Buciumi. Roman camp. 2nd-3rd centuries AD (Chirilă, Gudea, Lucăcel, Pop 1972, 54, fig. 50:1).

168. Conical vessel. Almost complete. Dimensions: H=82 mm, RD=186 mm, BD=93 mm. Tall, conical body with enlarged upper part. Flat base. Gilău. Roman camp. Retendura sinistra, sector A, -0,40/0,50 m (1984). Gilău phase III. 3rd century AD. Inv. no. 199 (Ţentea, Marcu 1997, 246, pl. 13:2).

169. Conical vessel. Conical body with enlarged upper part. Flat, profilated base. Gilău. Roman camp. 2nd-3rd centuries AD (Isac 1997, 56; Ţentea, Marcu 1997, 245, pl. 12:5).

170. Conical vessel. Almost complete. Dimensions: H=64 mm, RD=134 mm, BD=50 mm. Tall, conical body with enlarged upper part. Flat base. Gilău. Roman camp. Praetendura sinistra, Building A, sector II, -0,75 m (1979). Gilău phase III. 3rd century AD. Inv. no. 19 (Ţentea, Marcu 1997, 245, pl. 12:2).

171. Conical vessel. Almost complete. Flat base. Obreja. Rural settlement. 2nd-3rd centuries AD. Muzeul Naţional

de Istorie a Transilvaniei, Cluj-Napoca (Protase 1971, 137, fig. 6:2).

172. Conical vessel. Almost complete. Paste contains sand. Dark-reddish colour. Dimensions: H= 75 mm, RD=135 mm. Pojejena. Roman camp. Section 2. 2nd-3rd centuries AD (Gudea 1973, 89, fig. 6:7).

173. Conical vessel. Almost complete. Fine paste contains sand and mica. Complete firing. Brick colour. Dimensions: H=32 mm, RD=59 mm, BD=24 mm. Everted upper half. Tall body. Flat, profilated base. Obreja. Rural settlement. 2nd-3rd centuries AD. Muzeul Național de Istorie a Transilvaniei, Cluj-Napoca (Protase 1966, 43, fig. 17:2; Protase 1971, 137, fig. 6:1).

174. Conical vessel. Almost complete. Conical body. Enlarged upper part. Flat, profilated base. Gilău. Roman camp. 3rd century AD (Rusu 1979, 160-161, pl. 3:20).

175. Conical vessel. Almost complete. Dimensions: H=68 mm, RD=150 mm, BD=50 mm. Tall, conical body with enlarged upper part. Flat base. Gilău. Roman camp. Principia, section S 29, m 2/3, -0,20/0,30 m (1980). Gilău phase III. 3rd century AD. Inv. no. 271 (Țentea, Marcu 1997, 246, pl. 13:3).

Wheel-made pottery

Storage jars

A. Ovoid Jars

176. Jar. Ovoid body. Maximum diameter at middle part. Diameter of mouth is greater than that of base. Everted rim. Above maximum diameter area a notched cordon. Obreja. Cemetery. M 2. Middle of 2nd century AD to end of 3rd century AD. Muzeul Național de Istorie a Transilvaniei, Cluj-Napoca (Protase 1971, 151, fig. 13:2).

177. Jar. Identifiable. Paste contains sand. Brick colour. Ovoid body. Everted rim. On shoulder a band of horizontal incised lines and other of waved lines. Locusteni. Cemetery, M 12. 2nd century AD to first half of 3rd century AD. Muzeul Olteniei, Craiova, inv. no. I:2.136 (Popilian 1976, 220, pl. 74, no. 947; Popilian 1976a, 285, fig. 2:12; Popilian 1980, 15, pl. 3, M 12, 1).

Kitchen ware

B. Pots

178. Pot. Almost complete. The paste contains sand. Grey colour. Dimensions: H=210 mm, RD=157 mm, MD=172 mm, BD=99 mm. Curved body. Enlarged rim. Flat base. On shoulder a band of horizontal incised lines and other of waved lines. Locusteni. Cemetery, M 11. 2nd century

AD. Muzeul Olteniei, Craiova, inv. no. I:2.141 (Popilian 1976, 220, pl. 74, no. 956; Popilian 1976a, 285, fig. 2:10; Popilian 1980, 14, pl. 2 M, 11, 1).

C. Strainers

179. Strainer. Almost complete. Biconical body. Short, cylindrical neck. Flat base. Scornicești. The rural settlement no. 1. Second half of 2nd century AD to first half of 3rd century AD (Bichir 1984, 36, pl. 17:11; Bichir 1986, 119, pls. 4:1 and 12:6).

180. Strainers. Almost complete. Biconical body. Short, cylindrical neck. The handle attached by shoulder and rim. Scornicești. The rural settlement no. 1. Second half of 2nd century AD to first half of 3rd century AD (Bichir 1984, 36, pl. 18:10; Bichir 1986, 119, pl. 13:10).

Table ware

D. Jugs

181. Jug. Small size. Almost complete. Fine paste. Grey-light colour. Short, biconical body. Everted rim. The handle attached by rim and shoulder. Danéti. Cemetery, M 2. 2nd century AD to first half of 3rd century AD (Popilian 1982, 48, fig. 1 M 2, 2).

182. Jug. Identifiable. Fine paste. Biconical body. Everted rim. The handle attached by rim and shoulder. Scornicești. The rural settlement no. 1. Second half of 2nd century AD to first half of 3rd century AD (Bichir 1984, 35, pl. 17:14; Bichir 1986, 119, pl. 14:11).

183. Jug. Biconical body. Everted rim. The base has a ring. Obreja. Rural settlement. 2nd-3rd centuries AD. Muzeul Național de Istorie a Transilvaniei, Cluj-Napoca (Protase 1966, 43, fig. 17:7).

184. Jug. Small size. Almost complete. Fine paste. Grey colour. Dimensions: H=84 mm, RD=55 mm, BD=80 mm. Biconical body. Everted rim. Base broken. The broken handle is attached by rim and shoulder. Locusteni. Cemetery, M 182. 2nd century AD to first half of 3rd century AD. Muzeul Olteniei, Craiova (Popilian 1980a, 40 pl. 26, M 182, 3).

185. Jug. Almost complete. Curved body. Base has a ring. The handle attached by rim and shoulder. Tibiscum. Civilian settlement, near to the pottery kiln next to Building no. 2. Beginning of 2nd century AD (Benea 1981, 311, fig. 20:1).

E. Fruit-bowls

186. Fruit-bowl. Identifiable. Fine paste. Grey colour. Dimensions: H=180 mm, RD=180 mm. Biconical, shallow

cup. Horizontal, everted rim. Locusteni. Cemetery, M 24. 2nd century AD. Muzeul Olteniei, Craiova (Popilian 1980, 16, pl. 4, M 24, 2).

187. Fruit-bowl. Almost complete. The fine paste contains sand and mica. Light-grey colour. Dimensions: H=170 mm, RD=260 mm. Globular deep cup. Short stem with ring at base. Horizontal rim. Obreja. Rural settlement, S5, 1962. 2nd-3rd centuries AD. Muzeul Naţional de Istorie a Transilvaniei, Cluj-Napoca (Protase 1966, 43, fig. 17:9; Protase 1971, 137, fig. 5:3).

188. Fruit-bowl. Identifiable. Fine paste. Grey colour. Dimensions: H=(120) mm, RD=308 mm. Hemispherical deep cup. Horizontal rim. Locusteni. Cemetery, M 204. 2nd century AD to first half of 3rd century AD. Muzeul Olteniei, Craiova (Popilian 1980, 43, pl. 28, M 204, 2).

F. Dishes

189. Dish. Almost complete. Tronconical curved body. Rounded rim. Scorniceşti. The rural settlement no. 1. Second half of 2nd century AD to first half of 3rd century AD (Bichir 1984, 36, pl. 18:1; Bichir 1986, 119, pls. 4:2 and 13:1).

190. Dish. Identifiable. Tronconical body. Everted oblique rim. Scorniceşti. The rural settlement no. 1. Second half of 2nd century AD to first half of 3rd century AD (Bichir 1984, 36, pl. 18:3; Bichir 1986, 119, pl. 12:1 and 13: 3).

191. Dish. Identifiable. Tronconical body. Everted, oblique rim. Timişoara-Freidorf. Rural settlement. 2nd-3rd centuries AD (Benea 1997, 75, fig. 10:3).

192. Dish. Identifiable. Curved body. Short, everted rim. Scorniceşti. The rural settlement no. 1. Second half of

2nd century AD to first half of 3rd century AD (Bichir 1984, pl. 18:5; Bichir 1986, 119, pl. 13:5).

193. Dish. Almost complete. Tall, conical body. Vertical rim with rounded edge. Buza. Rural settlement. The first decades of 2nd century AD. Muzeul Naţional de Istorie a Transilvaniei, Cluj-Napoca (Bădău-Wittenberger 1994, 369, pl. 5:2).

G. Lids

194. Lid. Almost complete. Dimensions: I=62 mm, RD=192 mm, BD=39 mm. Hemispherical body. Short button. Locusteni. Cemetery, M 74. 2nd century to first half of 3rd century AD (Popilian 1980, 23, pl. 11, M 74, 2).

195. Lid. Conical body. Short button. Daneţi. Cemetery. 2nd century AD to first half of 3rd century AD (Popilian 1982, 51, fig. 2, M8, 2).

196. Lid. Almost complete. Dimensions: I=44 mm, RD=124 mm, MD=165 mm, BD=50 mm. Conical body. Short button. Locusteni. Cemetery, M 130. 2nd century to first half of 3rd century AD (Popilian 1980, 33, pl. 20, M 130, 2).

Illumination vessel

H. Dacian cup

197. Dacian cup. Almost complete. The paste contains much sand. Yellowish-brick colour. Dimensions: H=146 mm, RD=295 mm, BD=100 mm. Turned inside rim. The handle is attached by middle part. Locusteni. Cemetery, M 155. 2nd century AD to first half of 3rd century AD. Muzeul Olteniei, Craiova (Popilian 1980, 36, pl. 23, M 155, 2).

Abbreviations

ACMIT - Anuarul Comisiunii Monumentelor Istorice. Secția pentru Transilvania, Cluj, 1-4, 1926-1938.

ActaMN - Acta Musei Napocensis, Cluj-Napoca.

ActaMP - Acta Musei Porolissensis, Zalău.

Aluta - Aluta. Muzeul de Istorie Sf. Gheorghe.

AISC - Anuarul Institutului de Studii Clasice, Cluj, 1-5, 1928-1949

AnBan - Analele Banatului, Timişoara.

AO (SN) - Arhivele Olteniei, Craiova, 1-19, 1920-1939; New Series, 1, 1981and follows.

AÖG - Archiv für Künde österreichhischer Geschichtquellen, Wien.

Apulum - Apulum. Buletinul Muzeului regional Alba Iulia.

Arheologija - Arheologija. Organ na Arheologikeskaia Institut i Muzei pri Bălgerskata Akademia na Naukita, Sofia.

ArchAeliana - Archaeologia Aeliana, Newcastle.

ArchKozl - Archeologiai Kozlemenyek, Budapest, 1-22, 1859-1899.

AVSL - Archiv des Vereins für Siebenbürgische Landeskunde, Sibiu, 1843-1915.

Banatica - Banatica. Muzeul judeţean de Istorie Reşita.

Buridava - Buridava. Muzeul de Istorie Râmnicul Vâlcea.

Crisia - Crisia. Buletinul Muzeului "Ţării Crişurilor", Oradea.

Carpica - Carpica. Muzeul judeţean Bacău.

CA - Cercetări arheologice. Muzeul Naţional de Istorie a României, Bucureşti.

CAB - Cercetări arheologice în Bucureşti. Muzeul de Istorie (şi Artă) al Oraşului Bucureşti.

Cronica - Cronica cercetărilor arheologice, Bucuresti.

Cumidava - Cumidava. Buletinul Muzeului de Istorie Braşov.

Dacia - Dacia. Recherches et découvertes archéologiques en Roumanie, Bucureşti, 1-12, 1924-1948.

Dacia, NS - Dacia. Revue d'archéologie et histoire ancienne, Nouvelle série, Bucureşti, 1, 1957 and follows.

DissPann - Dissertationes Pannonicae, Budapest.

DolgozatokCluj - Dolgozatok - Travaux de la section numismatique et archeologique du Musee national de Transylvanie, Koloszvar (Cluj), 1-10, 1910-1919.

Drobeta - Drobeta. Muzeul Regiunii Porţile de Fier, Turnu Severin.

Ephemeris Napocensis - Ephemeris Napocensis, Cluj-Napoca.

FI - File de istorie. Muzeul judeţean de Istorie Bistriţa-Năsăud.

IDR - Inscripţiile Daciei romane, Bucureşti, I, 1975.

Izvestia - Izvestia na Arheologiceskija Institut, Sofia.

JCC - Jahrbuch der Kaiserl. Königl. Central-Commision zur Erforschung und Erhaltung der Badenkmale, Wien.

Litua - Litua. Muzeul judeţean de Istorie Gorj.

Marisia - Marisia. Muzeul judeţean de Istorie Mureş.

Materiale - Materiale şi cercetări arheologice, Bucureşti.

MemAnt - Memoria Antiquitatis. Muzeul judeţean de Istorie Piatra Neamţ.

MCC - Mitellungen der. K.K. Central-Commision zur Erforschung und Erhaltung der Baudenkmale, Wien.

OlteniaStCom - Oltenia. Studii şi comunicări, Craiova.

Peuce - Peuce. Studii şi comunicări. Muzeul judeţean (Institutul de Studii Eco-Muzeale) Tulcea.

Pontice (a) - Pontice (a). Muzeul de Istorie şi Arheologie Constanţa.

Potaissa - Potaissa. Studii şi comunicări, Turda.

RadVojv - Rad Vojvodine Muzei, Beograd.

RCRFActa - Rei Cretariae Romanae Fautores Acta, Abingdon.

RESEE – Revue de l'Etudes Sud-Est Europene, Bucureşti.

RI – Revista istorică, Bucureşti.

RevMuz - Revista muzeelor, Bucureşti.

RRH - Revue romaine d'histoire, Bucureşti.

RevŞtiinţifică - Revista Ştiinţifică, Bucureşti.

Sargetia - Sargetia. Buletinul Muzeului judeţean Hunedoara.

SlovArch - Slovenska Archeologia, Bratislava.

SCIV (A) - Studii şi cercetări de istorie veche (şi arheologie), Bucureşti.

StComCaransebeş - Studii şi comunicări de istorie, Caransebeş.

SIB - Studii de Istorie a Banatului, Timişoara.

SMMIM - Studii şi materiale de muzeografie şi Istorie militară, Bucureşti.

SV - Studii vâlcene. Muzeul judeţean Vâlcea, Râmnicu Vâlcea.

Thraco-Dacica - Thraco-Dacica. Institutul Român de Tracologie, Bucureşti.

Tibiscum - Tibiscum. Revista Muzeului judeţean de Istorie Timiş, Timişoara.

Literature

Ackner 1857 - M. J. Ackner, *Die Colonien und militärischen Standlager der Römer in Siebenbürgen*, JCC, II, 1857, 95.

Ackner 1858 - M. J. Ackner, *Correspondenz*, MCC, III, 3, 1858, 82-83.

Alexandrescu 1974-1975 - A. Alexandrescu, *Aşezarea dacică de la Hărman*, Cumidava, 8, 1974-1975, 9-21.

Alexandrescu 1980 - A. Alexandrescu, *La nécropole gète de Zimnicea*, Dacia, NS, 24, 1980, 19-126.

Alicu, Bota, Voişian 1997 - D. Alicu, E. Bota, V. Voişian, Cronica, 1997, 14.

Andrieşescu 1924 - I. Andrieşescu, *Piscul Crăsani*, Bucureşti, 1924.

Angelov 1952 - N. Angelov, *Novootkratia seliţa po brega na Dunava mejdu Ruse i Tutrakan*, Izvestia, XVIII, 1952, 370-378.

Ardeţ, Ardeţ 1997 - A. Ardeţ, L. C. Ardeţ, Cronica, 1997, 67-68.

Aschbach 1858 - J. Aschbach, *Über Trajan's steinerne Donaubrücke*, MCC, III, 10, 1858, 257-262.

Babeş 1971 - M. Babeş, *Necropola daco-romană de la Enisala*, SCIVA, 22, 1971, 1, 19-45.

Baumann 1995 - V. Baumann, *Aşezări rurale antice în zona gurilor Dunării. Contribuţii arheologice la cunoaşterea habitatului rural (sec. I-IV p. Chr.)*, Tulcea, 1995.

Bădău-Wittenberger 1994 - M. Bădău-Wittenberger, *Şantierul arheologic Buza (jud. Cluj)*, ActaMN, 31, 1, 1994, 367-377.

Benea 1981 - D. Benea, *Cercetări arheologice de la Tibiscum*, Materiale, 15, 1981, 306-323.

Benea 1982 - D. Benea, *Atelierele ceramice de la Tibiscum (Contribuţii la istoria atelierelor ceramice din sud-vestul Daciei)*, Potaissa, 3, 1982, 22-39.

Benea 1985 - D. Benea, *Römische Töpferwörksteten im Tibiscum*, SIB, 11, 1985, 11-21.

Benea 1996 - D. Benea, *Dacia sud-vestică în secolele III-IV*, Timişoara, 1996.

Benea 1997 - D. Benea, *Quelques observations sur la cèramique de l'aglomeration daco-romaine de Freidorf-Timişoara*, in *Études sur la ceramique romaine et daco-romaine de la Dacie et Mésie Inférieure,* Timişoara, 1997, 55-76.

Bejan, Benea 1981 - A. Bejan, D. Benea, *Şantierul arheologic Hodoni-Pustă*, Materiale, 15, 1981, 388-394.

Bejan, Benea 1981a - A. Bejan, D. Benea, *Aşezarea din secolele III-IV e.n. de la Timişoara-Cioreni*, Materiale, 15, 1981, 381-383.

Berciu 1981 - D. Berciu, *Buridava dacică*, Bucureşti, 1981.

Berciu 1989 - D. Berciu, *Descoperiri şi însemnări de la Buridava dacică*, VII, Thraco-Dacica, X, 1989, 205-214.

Berciu, Iosifaru, Diaconescu 1992 - D. Berciu, M. Iosifaru, M. Diaconescu, *Descoperiri şi însemnări de la Buridava dacică*, Thraco-Dacica, XIII, 1-2, 1992, 113-120.

Berciu et al. 1952 - D. Berciu et al., *Şantierul Verbicioara*, SCIV, III, 1952, 141-190.

Berciu 1965 - I. Berciu, *Contribuţie la studiul chiupurilor de factură dacică din secolul IV e.n.*, Apulum, 5, 1965, 597-610.

Bichir 1973 - G. Bichir, *Cultura carpică*, Bucureşti, 1973.

Bichir 1983 - G. Bichir, *Continuitatea şi romanizarea populaţiei geto-dace în lumina cercetărilor de la Stolniceni-Rm.Vîlcea*, Studii vîlcene, 6, 1983, 9-13.

Bichir 1983a - G. Bichir, *Ramura nordică a dacilor - costobocii*, Thraco-Dacica, IV, 1983, 59-68.

Bichir 1984 - G. Bichir, *Geto-dacii din Muntenia în epoca romană*, Bucureşti, 1984.

Bichir 1986 - G. Bichir, *Cercetări arheologice la Scorniceşti*, Thraco-Dacica, VII, 1-2, 1986, 112-126.

Bichir, Bardaşu 1980 - G. Bichir, Bardaşu, *Şantierul arheologic Stolniceni-Buridava (judetul Vîlcea)*, Materiale, 14, 1980, 336-339.

Blăjan, Stoicovici, Georoceanu, Păcurariu 1978 - I. Blăjan, E. Stoicovici, Georoceanu, C. Păcurariu, *Descoperiri romane inedite în Transilvania*, Marisia, VIII, 1978, 57-74

Blăjan 1989 - M. Blăjan, *Contribuţii la repertoriul arheologic al aşezărilor rurale antice (secolele II-III e.n.) din Dacia romană*, Apulum, 26, 1989, 283-330.

Bogdan-Cătăniciu 1985-1986 - I. Bogdan-Cătăniciu, *Ceramica dacică din castellum de la Rucăr*, ActaMN, XXII-XXIII, 1985-1986, 201-209.

Bolliac 1869 - C. Bolliac, *Excursiune arheologică din anullu 1869*, Bucureşti, 1869.

Bolliac 1861 - C. Bolliac, *Călletorie arheologică în România*, Bucureşti, 1861.

Bona, Petrovszky, Petrovszky 1982 – P. Bona, R Petrovszky, M. Petrovszky, *Tibiscum, Cercetări arheologice (II)*, ActaMN, XX, 1982, 405-432.

Bónis 1942 - E. Bónis, *Die kaiserzeitliche Keramik von Pannonien*, Diss.Pann., Ser. II, 20, Budapest, 1942.

Boroneanţ, Davidescu 1968 - V. Boroneanţ, M. Davidescu, *Două bordeie dacice de la Schela Cladovei*, Apulum, VII-1, 1968, 253- 259.

Bozu 1990 - O. Bozu, *Aşezarea daco-romană de la Grădinari-"Sălişte"(judetul Caraş-Severin)*, Banatica, 10, 1990, 158-186.

Bozu 1999 - O. Bozu, Cronica, 127-128.

Bozu, Sousi 1987 - O. Bozu, G. El Sousi, *Aşezarea romană târzie de la Moldova Veche din punctul "Vinograda-Vlaskicrai" (judetul Caraş-Severin)*, Banatica, 9, 1987, 239-268.

Branga 1986 - N. Branga, *Italicii şi veteranii din Dacia*, Timişoara, 1986.

Brătianu 1988 - G. Brătianu, *O enigmă şi un miracol istoric: poporul român*, Bucureşti, 1988.

Brukner 1981 - O. Brukner, *Rimska keremika u Jugoslovenskom delu provincje Dolnje Pannonije*, Beograd, 1981.

Brukner 1987 - O. Brukner, in O. Brukner, V. Dautova-Rusevljan, P. Milosović, *Poceti romanizatie u Jugoistocinom delu provintije Pannonije*, Novi Sad, 1987, 25-44.

Brukner 1988 - O. Brukner, *Kontinuiteiu domorodacikiv naselja u dominatije rimske*, GradVoijv, XV, 1988, 95-102.

Brukner 1990 - O. Brukner, *Keramicka proisvodja*, in Dautova-Rusevljan, O. Brukner, *Gomolava. Rimski period*, Beograd, 1990, 11-59.

Buday 1913 - A. Buday, *Romai villak Erdelyben*, Dolgozatok, Cluj, 1, 1913, 109-165.

Budinsky-Krička 1960 - V. Budinsky-Krička, *Vinkum 1958 na Vrchu Bochegyh Strede nad Bodrogom*, Slov. Arch., VIII-1, 1960, 217-230.

Bujor 1970 - E. Bujor, *Aşezarea romană de la Bumbeşti-Jiu*, Materiale, 9, 1970, 107-115.

Buzilă 1970 - A. Buzilă, *Ceramica dacică din dava de la Bîtca Doamnei*, MemAnt, 2, 1970, 237-250.

Calotoiu 1982 - Gh. Calotoiu, *Repertoriul arheologic al judeţului Gorj*, Litua, I, 1982, 43-58.

Căpitanu 1976 - V. Căpitanu, *Aşezarea geto-dacă de la Răcătău*, Carpica, VIII, 1976, 49-121.

Chirilă, Gudea 1970 - E. Chirilă, N. Gudea, *Şantierul arheologic Bologa, judeţul Cluj (1967)*, Materiale, 9, 1970, 115-120.

Chirilă, Gudea, Lucăcel, Pop 1972 - E. Chirilă, N. Gudea, V. Lucăcel, C. Pop, *Das Römerlager von Buciumi*, Cluj, 1972.

Cichorius 1896-1900 - C. Cichorius, *Die Reliefs des Traianssaule*, Berlin, 1896-1900.

Cociş, Opreanu 1998 - S. Cociş, C. Opreanu, *Barbarische Fibeln aus dem römischen Dakien: ihre Historische Bedeütung*, ActaMN, 35, 1, 1998, 195-228.

Cociş, Voişian, Paki, Rotea 1996 - S. Cociş, V. Voişian, A. Paki, M. Rotea, *Raport preliminar privind cercetările arheologice din strada Victor Deleu în Cluj-Napoca, I, Campaniile 1992-1994*, ActaMN, 33, 1, 1996, 635-636.

Costea 1971 - F. Costea, *Sondajul arheologic de la Feldioara-Braşov (1970)*, Cumidava, 5, 1971, 25-44.

Costea 1974-1975 - F. Costea, *Persistenţa elementului autohton în sud-estul Transilvaniei în timpul stăpînirii romane*, Cumidava, 8, 1974-1975, 66-70.

Costea 1974-1975a - F. Costea, *Prezenţe romane în sud-estul Transilvaniei*, Sargetia, 11-12, 1974-1975, p.269-276.

Crişan 1955 - I. H. Crişan, *Ceaşca dacică. Contribuţie la cunoaşterea culturii materiale şi a istoriei dacilor*, Studii şi Cercetări ştiinţifice, Serie III, tom VI, nos. 3-4, 1955, 128-157.

Crişan 1969 - I. H. Crişan, *Ceramica daco-getică. Cu privire specială la Transilvania*, Bucureşti, 1969.

Crişan 1978 - I. H. Crişan, *Ziridava*, Arad, 1978.

Daicoviciu 1936-1940 - C. Daicoviciu, *Problema continuităţii în Dacia*, AISC, III, 1936-1940, 200-270.

Daicoviciu 1937-1940 - C. Daicoviciu, *Neue Mittelungen aus Dacien*, Dacia, VII-VIII, 1937-1940, 299-336.

Daicoviciu 1940 - C. Daicoviciu, *Problema continuităţii în Dacia romană*, Cluj, 1940.

Daicoviciu 1945 - C. Daicoviciu, *La Transylvanie dans l'antiquite*, Bucureşti, 1945.

Daicoviciu, Malasz 1930-1931 - C. Daicoviciu, I. Malasz, *Micia. I. Cercetări asupra castrului*, ACMIT, III, 1930-1931, 1-44.

Daicoviciu 1961 - C. Daicoviciu, *Dăinuirea populaţiei dacice*, in *Din istoria Transilvaniei*, Second edition, Bucureşti, 1961.

Daicoviciu, Miloia 1930 - C. Daicoviciu, I. Miloia, *Cercetări arheologice în Banatul de Sud*, AnBan, III, 4, 7, 1930, 10-25.

Deru, Grasset 1997 - X. Deru, L. Grasset, *The Roman pottery workshop in the Saint-Remi district (Reims, Marne). Preliminary report*, RCRFActa, 35, 1997, 151-156.

Dumitraşcu, Crişan 1988 - S. Dumitraşcu, I. H. Crişan, *Cuptoare de ars oale descoperite la Sînnicolau Român, judeţul Bihor*, Crisia, 18, 1988, 41-119.

Dumitraşcu, Bader 1967 - S. Dumitraşcu, T. Bader, *Aşezarea dacilor liberi de la Medieşu Aurit*, Satu Mare, 1967.

Fabritius 1862 - K. Fabritius, *Bericht über die Auffindung und öffnung eines Dakischen Grabes*, AVSL, 5, 3, 1862, 287-313.

Ferenczi, Ferenczi 1976 - G. Ferenczi, I. Ferenczi, *Săpături arheologice la Mugeni. Studiu preliminar*, ActaMN, 13, 1976, 239-256.

Ferenczi 1926-1928 - Al. Ferenczi, *Dare de seamă asupra săpăturilor arheologice de la Cristeşti*, ACMIT, II, 1926-1928, 216-217.

Floca 1938 - O. Floca, *Sisteme de înmormântare în Dacia Superioară romană*, Sargetia, II, 1938, 1-116.

Floca 1968 - O. Floca, *Pagus Miciensis*, Sargetia, 5, 1968, 49-58.

Floca, Mărghitan 1970 - O. Floca, L. Mărghitan, *Noi consideraţii privitoare la castrul roman de la Micia*, Sargetia, 7, 1970, 43-57.

Floca, Valea 1965 - O. Floca, M. Valea, *Villa rustica şi necropola daco-romană de la Cinciş*, ActaMN, II, 1965, 163-193.

Florescu 1931 - G. Florescu, Inst. Arh. Olteană, Memoriul I.

Florescu 1930 - G. Florescu, *Castrul roman de la Răcari*, AO, 1930, 373-395.

Florescu 1937 - Gr. Florescu, *La camp romain de Arcidava (Vărădia)*, Istros, I, 1, 1937, 60-72.

Gavela 1952 - B. Gavela, *Keltski oppidum Židovar*, Beograd, 1952.

Georgieva 1952 - S. Georgieva, *Razkopki na obekt "Gorno Gradişte" pri Kadikai*, Izvestia, XVIII, 1952, 259-284.

Gherghe 1983 – P. Gherghe, *Cercetări şi descoperiri cu privire la civilizaţia geto-dacică pe teritoriul judeţului Gorj*, AO, SN, 2, 1983, 49-73.

Gherghe 1985 – P. Gherghe, *Dovezi ale continuităţii dacice în aşezarea romană de la Săcelu (jud. Gorj)*, AO, SN, 4, 1985, 47-52.

Gherghe 1986 – P. Gherghe, *Descoperiri arheologice din epoca geto-dacică la Socu-Bărbăteşti (jud. Gorj)*, AO, SN, 5, 1986, 77-88.

Glodariu 1972 - I. Glodariu, *Aşezarea dacică şi daco-romană de la Slimnic*, ActaMN, 9, 1972, 119-140.

Glodariu 1975 - I. Glodariu, *Cercetări arheologice la Dedrad*, Apulum, 13, 1975, 227-243.

Glodariu 1981 - I. Glodariu, *Aşezări dacice şi daco-romane la Slimnic*, Bucureşti, 1981.

Glodariu, Moga 1989 - I. Glodariu, V. Moga, *Cetatea dacică de la Căpâlna*, Bucureşti, 1989.

Goos 1876 - C. Goos, *Chronik der archäologischen Funde Siebenbürgens*, Hermannstadt, 1876.

Gudea 1969 - N. Gudea, *Ceramica dacică din castrul roman de la Bologa*, ActaMN, VI, 1969, 503-508.

Gudea 1970 - N. Gudea, *Ceramica dacică din castrul roman de la Buciumi*, SCIVA, 21, 1970, 2, 299-311.

Gudea 1973a - N. Gudea, *Castrul roman de la Bologa*, Crisia, 1973, 109-138.

Gudea 1973b - N. Gudea, *Castrul roman de la Bologa*, SMMIM, 6, 1973, 27-56.

Gudea 1973c - N. Gudea, *Ceramica dacică din castrul roman de la Rîşnov*, Cumidava, VII, 1973, 23-30.

Gudea 1977 - N. Gudea, *Materiale arheologice din castrul roman de la Bologa*, Apulum, XV, 1977, 169-215.

Gudea 1977 - N. Gudea, *Gornea. Aşezarea din epoca romană şi romană tîrzie*, Reşiţa, 1977.

Gudea 1979 - N. Gudea, *Castrul roman de la Inlănceni. Încercare de monografie*, ActaMP, 3, 1979, 149-273.

Gudea 1980 - N. Gudea, *Castrul roman de la Breţcu*, ActaMP, IV, 1980, 255-332.

Gudea 1989 - N. Gudea, *Porolissum - Un complex arheologic daco-roman la marginea de nord a Imperiului Roman*, ActaMP, XIII, 1989.

Gudea 1996 - N. Gudea, *Porolissum. Vama romană*, Cluj-Napoca, 1996.

Gudea 1997a - N. Gudea, *Das Römergrenzenkastell von Bologa-Rescvlvm/Castrul roman de la Bologa-Rescvlvm*, Zalău, 1997.

Gudea 1997b - N. Gudea, *Castrul roman de la Buciumi/Das Römergrenzenkastell von Buciumi*, Zalău, 1997.

Gudea 1996 - N. Gudea, *Porolissum. Vama romană*, Cluj-Napoca, 1996.

Gudea, Pop 1971 - N. Gudea, I. Pop, *Castrul roman de la Rîşnov-Cumidava. Contribuţii la cercetarea limesului de sud-est al Daciei romane*, Braşov, 1971.

Gudea, Pop 1973 - N. Gudea, I. I. Pop, *Castrul roman de la Rîşnov. Săpăturile arheologice din anul 1971*, Cumidava, VII, 1973, 13-46.

Gudea, Pop 1974-1975 - N. Gudea, I. Pop, *Cercetări arheologice recente în castrul roman de la Rîşnov*, SMMIM, 7-8, 1974-1975, 55-78.

Gudea, Uzum 1973 - N. Gudea, I. Uzum, *Castrul roman de la Pojejena. Săpăturile arheologice din anul 1970*, Banatica, 2, 1973, 85-101.

Gudea, Moţu 1988 - N. Gudea, I. Moţu, *Despre ceramica provincială modelată cu mîna din castre. Observaţii arheologice cu specială privire la Dacia Porolissensis*, ActaMP, 12, 1988, 229-250.

Hunyady 1942 - I. Hunyady, *Die Kelten im Karpatenbecken*, DissPann, Ser. II, 18, 1942.

Isac 1980 - D. Isac, *Castrul roman de la Gilău*, Materiale, 14, 1980, 292-297.

Isac 1997 - D. Isac, *Castrele de cohortă şi ală de la Gilău/ Die Kohorten und Alenkastelle von Gilău*, Zalău, 1997.

Isac, Diaconescu, Opreanu 1980 - D. Isac, A. Diaconescu, C. Opreanu, *Săpături arheologice la Gilău*, Potaissa, 2, 1980, 29-54.

Isac, Diaconescu, Opreanu 1981 - D. Isac, A. Diaconescu, C. Opreanu, *Castrul roman de la Gilău*, Materiale, 15, 1981, 293-296.

Jobey 1982 - G. Jobey, *The settlement at Doubstead and Romano - British settlement on the coastal plain between Tyne and Forth*, ArchAeliana, Fifth series, 10, 1982, 1-23.

Jovanović 1971 - B. Jovanović, *Nasele Scordiska na Gomolavi*, RadVojv, 20, 1971, 123-145.

Jung 1894 - J. Jung, *Fasten der Provinz Dacien*, Innsbruck, 1894.

Kabakcieva 1997 - G. Kabakcieva, *Keramikversorgung in den Militärstützpunkten an der unteren Donau im 1 Jh n. Ch. und die Politik Roms*, RCRFActa, 35, 1997, 33-40.

Kenner 1860 - F. Kenner, *Beiträge zu einer Chronik der archäeologischen Funde in der österreichischer Monarchie (1856-1858)*, AOG, 1860, XXIV, 2, 225-424.

Kolnik 1972 - T. Kolnik, *Prehlad a stere badania o dobe rimski a Stahovani narodov*, SlovArch, XIX-2, 1972, 499-550.

Laurian 1846 - A. T. Laurian, *Istriana*, Magazin istoric pentru Dacia, 2, 1846, 73-119.

Lamiová-Schmiedlova 1969 - M. Lamiová-Schmiedlova, *Römerzeitliche Siedlung Keramik im der Südostslovakei*, SlovArch, XVII, 1969, 403-501.

Lazăr 1995 - V. Lazăr, *Repertoriul arheologic al Judeţului Mureş*, Târgu Mureş, 1995.

Leahu 1962 - V. Leahu, *Raport asupra cercetărilor arheologice efectuate în anul 1960 la Căţelu Nou*, CAB, I, 1962, 5-27.

Lupu 1968 - N. Lupu, *Aşezarea daco-romană de la Roşia (Sibiu Judeţul)*, ActaMN, 5, 1968, 445-450.

Lupu 1989 - N. Lupu, *Tilişca. Aşezările arheologice de pe Cătinaş*, Bucureşti, 1989.

Macrea 1941-1943 - M. Macrea, *Cumidava*, AISC, IV, 1941-1943, 234-253.

Macrea 1957 - M. Macrea, *Les Daces ŕ l''epoque romaine ŕ la lumière des recentes fouilles archèologiques*, Dacia, NS, 1, 1957, 205-220.

Macrea 1960 - M. Macrea, *Şantierul arheologic Caşolţ-Boiţa*, Materiale, VI, 1960, 407-419.

Macrea 1968 - M. Macrea, *Viaţa în Dacia romană*, Bucureşti, 1968.

Macrea, Buzdugan, Ferenczi, Horedt, Popescu, Russu 1951 - M. Macrea, L. Buzdugan, G. Ferenczi, K. Horedt, I. Popescu, I. I. Russu, *Despre rezultatele cercetărilor întreprinse pe şantierul arheologic de la Sf. Gheorghe-Breţcu*, SCIV, II, 1, 1951, 285-311.

Macrea, Rusu 1960 - M. Macrea, M. Rusu, *Der Dakische Friedhof von Porolissum und das Problem der dakischen Bestattungsbräuche in oder Spätlatenezeit*, Dacia, NS, 1960, 201-230.

Macrea, Rusu, Winkler 1959 - M. Macrea, M. Rusu, J. Winkler, *Şantierul arheologic Gilău*, Materiale, V, 1959, 453-460.

Macrea, Protase, Dănilă 1967 - M. Macrea, D. Protase, Ş. Dănilă, *Castrul roman de la Orheiul-Bistriţei*, SCIVA, 18, 1967, 1, 113-121.

Macrea, Gudea, Moţu 1993 - M. Macrea, N. Gudea, I. Moţu, *Castrul roman de la Mehadia*, Bucureşti, 1993.

Marcu 1968 - M. Marcu, *Săpături arheologice la Cristian-Braşov*, Cumidava, 2, 1968, 43-49.

Marcu 1973 - M. Marcu, *O nouă aşezare prefeudală la Hărman*, Cumidava, 6, 1973, 39-43.

Mare 1999 - M. Mare, Cronica, 1999, 122-123.

Marinescu 1989 - G. Marinescu, *Cercetări şi descoperiri arheologice de epocă romană în nord-vestul Transilvaniei*, FI, 6, 1989, 5-66.

Marinoiu 1992 - V. Marinoiu, *Cercetările arheologice de la Vîrtop Bumbeşti-Jiu. Campania 1991*, Litua, 4, 1992, 24-34.

Marinoiu, Camui 1986 - V. Marinoiu, I. Camui, *Castrul roman de la Bumbeşti-Jiu. probleme de conservare-restaurare*, Litua, 3, 1986, 138-158.

Marsigli 1726 - L. F. Marsigli, *Danubius Pannonico-Mysicus*, Haga, 1726

Marsigli 1740 - L. F. Marsigli, *Description du Danube*, Haga, 1740.

Matei 1974-1975 - A. Matei, *O aşezare rurală romană la Chinteni*, Sargetia, 11-12, 1974-1975, 299-302.

Matei, Bajusz - A. V. Matei, I. Bajusz, *Castrul roman de la Romiţa-Certiae/Das Römergrenzenkastell von Romita-Certiae*, Zalău, 1997.

Mănucu-Adameşteanu 1984 - M. Mănucu-Adameşteanu, *Necropola daco-romană de la Enisala, com. Sarichioi, jud. Tulcea*, Peuce, IX, 1984, 31-39.

Mărgărit-Tătulea 1984 - C. Mărgărit-Tătulea, *Cercetări arheologice la Bîzdîna*, Thraco-Dacica, V, 1-2, 1984, 92-110.

Mărghitan 1976 - L. Mărghitan, *Câteva consideraţii referitoare la ceramica din thermele de la Micia*, MN, 3, 1976, 133-142.

Mărghitan 1979 - L. Mărghitan, *O importantă contribuţie privitoare la problema continuităţii dacilor în provincia nord-dunăreană întemeiată de Traian*, Sargetia, 14, 1979, 133-136.

Mikov, Djambakov 1960 - V. Mikov, N. Djambazov, *Devetaşkata peşcera*, Sofia, 1960.

Mitrofan 1971 - I. Mitrofan, *Aşezarea daco-romana de la Noşlac (Aiud). Rezultatele săpăturilor din anii 1963-1964*, Sesiunea ştiinţifică a muzeelor de istorie, Bucureşti, 1, 440-453.

Mitrofan 1972 - I. Mitrofan, *Aşezări ale populaţiei autohtone în Dacia superioară*, ActaMN, 9, 1972, 141-162.

Mitrofan 1973 - I. Mitrofan, *Villae rusticae în Dacia Superioară*, ActaMN, 10, 1973, 127-150.

Mitrofan 1996 - I. Mitrofan, Cronica, 1996, 78, no. 90.

Moga 1976 - V. Moga, *Sondajul arheologic de la Blandiana*, Marisia, 6, 1976, 95-100.

Moga, Drîmboceanu 1996 - V. Moga, M. Drîmboceanu, Cronica, 1996, 3, no. 2.

Morintz 1961 - S. Morintz, *Săpăturile de la Chilia*, Materiale, 6, 1961, 443-447.

Morintz 1961a - S. Morintz, *Novîi oblik dakiiskoi culturî v rimskovo epohu (Otkrîtia v Killi, raion Vedea, obl. Piteşti)*, Dacia, NS, 5, 1961, 395-414.

Morintz 1963 - S. Morintz, *Săpăturile de la Chilia*, Materiale, 7, 1963, 513-518.

Moscalu 1968 - E. Moscalu, *Aşezarea dacică de la Cozia Veche*, SCIVA, 19, 1968, 4, 1968, 629-642.

Moscalu 1970 - E. Moscalu, *O aşezare dacică din secolul al III-lea e.n. la Govora*, SCIVA, 21, 1970, 4, 653-665.

Moscalu 1983 - E. Moscalu, *Ceramica traco-getică*, Bucureşti, 1983.

Müler 1857 - F. Müller, *Archäeologische Skizen aus Schäsburg*, MCC, II, 7, 1857, 194.

Müller 1858 - F. Müller, *Die Ruinen am Firtos im Siebenbürgen*, MCC, III, 10, 1858, 257-262.

Müler 1859 - F. Müler, *Römerspuren im Osten Sieberbürgens*, MCC, IV, 3, 1859, 69-73.

Negru 1994 - M. Negru, *Contribuţii la repertoriul arheologic al Judeţului Dolj. Cercetări arheologice de suprafaţă în bazinul inferior al Jiului*, AO, SN, 9, 1994, 61-80.

Negru 1996 - M. Negru, *Introduction in the study of provincial pottery of native tradition from South-Carpathian Roman Dacia*, in The Thracian World at the Crossroads of civilizations, Bucharest, 1996, 306-307.

Negru 1997 - M. Negru, *An introduction to the study of native hand-made pottery from Roman Dacia*, RCRF Acta, 35, Abingdon, 1997, 97-106.

Negru 1998 - M. Negru, *Consideraţii privind ceştile dacice modelate cu mâna descoperite în Dacia romană*, AO, SN, 13, 1998, 27-45.

Negru 1998a - M. Negru, *An introduction to the study of native pottery from South-Carpathian Roman Dacia*, The Thracian World at the crossroads of civilivilisations, II, Bucureşti, 1998, 630-643.

Negru 2000 - M. Negru, *Asezarea din secolul al III-lea p.Chr.*, in M. Negru, C. F. Schuster, D. Moise, *Militari-Câmpul Boja. Un sit arheologic pe teritoriul Bucurestilor*, Bucuresti, 2000, 57-152.

Negru 2000a - M. Negru, *Some considerations regarding the native wheel-made pottery from Roman Dacia*, RCRF Acta, 36, 2000, 235-240.

Negru, Ciucă 1997 - M. Negru, I. Ciucă, *Ceramica dacică lucrată cu mâna descoperită în aşezarea civilă a castrului roman de la Enoşeşti-Acidava*, AO, SN, 12, 1997, 23-29.

Neigebaur 1894 - J. F. Neigebaur, *Dacien*, Innsbruck, 1894.

Nica 1928 – C. Nica, *Monografia comunei Vărădia*, AnBan, I, 1928, 147-154.

Nica 1995 - M. Nica, Cronica, 1995, 31, no. 51.

Nica 1996 - M. Nica, Cronica, 1996, 30, no. 32.

Nikolov 1965 - B. Nikolov, *Trakiiski pametniti vîv vrasansko*, Izvestia, 28, 1965, 163-203.

Odobescu 1872 - A. Odobescu, *Arheologia preistorică: arme şi unelte de piatră şi de os din epocile preistorice aflate în România*, RevŞtiinţifică, Bucureşti, 1872, 143-144.

Odobescu 1872a - A. Odobescu, *Bibliografia Daciei*, Bucureşti, 1872.

Odobescu 1958 - A. Odobescu, *Opere*, 2, Bucureşti, 1958.

Ohcearov 1965 - D. Ohcearov, *Trako-rimski nekropol Tărgovişte*, Arheologia, 7, 1965, 1, 34-37.

Opaiţ 1980 - A. Opaiţ, *Consideraţii preliminare asupra ceramicii romane timpurii de la Troesmis*, Peuce, VIII, 1980, 328-366.

Opreanu 1993 - C. Opreanu, *Elemente ale culturii materiale dacice şi daco-romane târzii (sec. III-IV p. Chr.)*, Ephemeris Napocensis, III, 1993, 235-260.

Párducz 1956 - M. Párducz, *Dak leletek Jánosszaállásan*, A Móra Ferenc Múzeum Evkönue, Szeged, 1956, 15-31.

Paulovics 1944 - I. Paulovics, *Dacia keleti hotarvonala és az ugynevezeit "dak" ezüstikinesek érdése*, Cluj, 1944.

Pârvan 1926 - V. Pârvan, *Getica*, Bucureşti, 1926.

Pârvan 1928 - V. Pârvan, *Dacia*, Bucureşti, 1928.

Perko 1997 - V. V. Perko, *The Roman tiles factory at Vransko near Celeia (Noricum). Part two: Ceramic finds*, RCRFActa, 35, 1997, 165-172.

Petolescu 1971 - C. C. Petolescu, *Întinderea provinciei Dacia Inferior*, SCIV, 22, 3, 1971, 411-423.

Petolescu 1979 - C. C. Petolescu, *Contribuţii privind organizarea administrativă a Daciei romane*, RI, 32, 2, 1979, 359-376.

Petolescu 1982 - C. C. Petolescu, *Contribuţii la istoria Munteniei în secolul al II-lea e.n.*, RI, 35, 1, 1982, 65-77.

Petolescu 1983 - C. C. Petolescu, *Organisation de la province de Dacia Inférieure*, RESEE, 21, 3, 1983, 241-247.

Petolescu 1985 - *L'organisation de la Dacie sous Traian et Hadrien*, Dacia, NS, 29, 1-2, 1985, 45-55.

Petolescu 1986 - C. C. Petolescu, *Cercetări arheologice în castrul roman de la Cătunele*, Litua, 1986, 156-163.

Petolescu 1986a - C. C. Petolescu, *Procuratori ecveştri ai Daciei romane*, Dacia, NS, 30, 1-2, 1986, 159-165.

Petică 1979 - M. Petică, *Săpăturile arheologice de la Voivodeni (Mureş Judeţul)*, Marisia, 9, 1979, 126-133.

Petre-Govora 1966 - G. Petre-Govora, *Urme romane necunoscute la Govora-Sat*, SCIV, 17, 1, 1966, 171-173.

Petre 1968 - G. Petre-Govora, *Cuptor de ars vase la Stolniceni*, SCIVA, 19, 1968, 1, 147-158.

Petrescu, Rogozea 1990 - M. S. Petrescu, P. Rogozea, *Tibiscum - principia castrului roman*, Banatica, 10, 1990, 107-135.

Piso 1973 - I. Piso, *Certains aspects de l'organisation de la Dacie romaine*, RRH, 6, 1973, 999-1015.

Piso, Isac, Diaconescu, Opreanu 1981 - I. Piso, D. Isac, A. Diaconescu, C. Opreanu, *Castrul roman de la Căşei*, Materiale 15, 1981, 297-298.

Poenaru-Bordea, Vlădescu 1972 - G. Poenaru-Bordea, C. M. Vlădescu, *Primele săpături arheologice în fortificaţia romană de la Rădăcineşti*, SCIVA, 23, 3, 1972, 477-486.

Popescu 1925 - D. Popescu, *Fouilles de Lechinţa de Mureş*, Dacia, II, 1925, 304-344.

Popescu, Covaciu, Popescu, Puşcaş 1951 - D. Popescu, N. Covaciu, V. Popescu, I. Puşcaş, *Săpăturile de la Cristeşti*, SCIV, II, 1951, 279-285.

Popilian 1971 - G. Popilian, *Thermele de la Slăveni*, Apulum, 9, 1971, 627-640.

Popilian 1976 - G. Popilian, *Ceramica romană din Oltenia*, Craiova, 1976.

Popilian 1976a - G. Popilian, *Traditions autochtones dans la céramique provinciale romaine de la Dacie Méridionale*, Thraco-Dacica, I, 1976, 279-286.

Popilian 1980 - G. Popilian, *Necropola daco-romană de la Locusteni*, Craiova, 1980.

Popilian 1981 - G. Popilian, *L'atélier de céramique du camp romain de Slăveni*, OlteniaStCom, 3, 1981, 25-46.

Popilian 1982 - G. Popilian, *Necropola daco-romană de la Daneţi*, Thraco-Dacica, III, 1982, 42-67.

Popilian 1996 - G. Popilian, *Unitatea culturală din provinciile romane Dacia şi Moesia*, Drobeta, 7, 1996, 59-74.

Popilian 1997 - G. Popilian, *Les centres de production céramique d'Oltenie*, în *Ètudes sur la céramique romaine et daco-romaine de la Dacie et Mésie Inférieure*, Timişoara, 1997, 7-20.

Popilian 1998 - G. Popilian, in G. Popilian, M. Nica, *Gropşani - Monografie arheologică*, Bucureşti 1998, 43-95.

Popilian, Nica, Mărgărit-Tătulea 1980 - G. Popilian, M. Nica, C. Mărgărit-Tătulea, *Raport asupra cercetărilor arheologice de la Locusteni*, Materiale, 14, 1980, 254-260.

Popilian, Nica 1981 - G. Popilian, M. Nica, *Cercetările arheologice de la Locusteni-La Gropan*, Materiale, 1981, 395-397.

Popilian, Niță 1982 - G. Popilian, T. Niță, *Necropola daco-română de la Leu*, OlteniaStCom, 4, 1982, 87-92.

Preda 1986 - C. Preda, *Geto-dacii din bazinul Oltului inferior. Dava de la Sprîncenata*, București, 1986.

Preda, Grosu 1993 - C. Preda, A. Grosu, *Cercetările arheologice din așezarea civilă a castrului roman de la Enoșești-Acidava*, AO, SN, 8, 1993, 43-55.

Preda, Grosu 1996 - C. Preda, A. Grosu, Cronica, 1996, 41-42, no. 50.

Protase 1964 - D. Protase, *La permanence des Daces en Dacie romaine tell quelle resulte de l'archeologie*, RRH, 3, 2, 1964, 193-212.

Protase 1966 - D. Protase, *Problema continuității în Dacia în lumina arheologiei și numismaticii*, București, 1966.

Protase 1968 - D. Protase, *O așezare dacică din epoca romană la Ocna Sibiului*, Apulum, 7, 2, 1968, 229-239.

Protase 1968a - D. Protase, *Riturile funerare la daci și daco-romani*, București, 1968.

Protase 1969 - D. Protase, *Le cimetière de Soporu de Cîmpie*, Dacia, NS, 13, 1969, 291-317.

Protase 1971 - D. Protase, *Așezarea și cimitirul daco-roman de la Obreja (Transilvania)*, ActaMN, 8, 1971, 135-160.

Protase 1976 - D. Protase, *Soporu de Cîmpie. Un cimitir dacic din epoca romană*, București, 1976.

Protase 1980 - D. Protase, *Autohtonii în Dacia*, București, 1980.

Protase, Gaiu 1995 - D. Protase, C. Gaiu, Cronica, Cluj, 1995, 29.

Protase, Gaiu, Marinescu 1997 - D. Protase, C. Gaiu, G. Marinescu, *Castrul roman de la Ilișua*, Bistrița, 1997.

Protase, Marinescu, Gaiu 1981 - D. Protase, G. Marinescu, C. Gaiu, *Cercetările arheologice din castrul roman de la Ilișua (Județul Bistrița-Năsăud)*, Materiale 15, 1981, 289-291.

Protase, Țigăra 1959 - D. Protase, I. Țigăra, *Săpăturile arheologice de la Soporu de Cîmpie*, Materiale, 5, 1959, 425-434.

Protase, Țigăra 1960 - D. Protase, I. Țigăra, *Săpăturile arheologice de la Soporu de Cîmpie*, Materiale, 6, 1960, 383-395.

Protase, Zrinyi 1975 - D. Protase, A. Zrinyi, *Castrul roman de la Brîncovenești*, Marisia, 5, 1975, 57-69.

Protase, Zrinyi 1994 - D. Protase, A. Zrinyi, *Castrul roman și așezarea civilă de la Brâncovenești (jud. Mureș). Săpăturile din anii 1970-1987*, Târgu Mureș, 1994.

Richmond 1966 - I. A. Richmond, *Roman Britain*, London, 1966.

Rogozea 1988 - P. Rogozea, *Ceramica dacică din așezarea romană de la Tibiscum*, Tibiscum, 7, 1988, 165-176.

Roman, Dodd, Dogaru, Șimon 1992 - Roman, A. Dodd-Oprițescu, M. Dogaru, M. Șimon, *Descoperirile de la Ostrovul Corbului, județul Mehedinți*, Materiale, I, 1992, 101-108.

Rusu 1953 - M. Rusu, *Cercetări arheologice la Gilău*, Materiale, 2, 1953, 687-716.

Rusu 1979 - M. Rusu, *Castrul roman de la Gilău*, Stcom Caransebeș, 1979, 153-192.

Salway 1981 – P. Salway, *Roman Britain*, London, 1981.

Sanie, Dragomir 1980 - S. Sanie, I. T. Dragomir, *Aspects de la cohabitation des Daces et des Romains dans le Midi romain de la Moldaviae*, Actes du II-e International Congres de Thracologie, București, 1980, 2, 339-350.

Sanie 1995 - S. Sanie, *Din istoria culturii și religiei geto-dacice*, Iași, 1995.

Sandor 1960 - N. Sandor, *Za anticino iskopavanie na Gomolavi pod Vinkovta*, RadVojv, 9, 1960, 116-129.

Schindler-Kaudelka 1997 - E. Schindler-Kaudelka, *Tonnenförmige Kochtöpfe vom Magdalensberg*, RCRFActa, 35, 1997, 117-125.

Scorpan 1968 - C. Scorpan, *Contribuții arheologice la problemele etnice ale Dobrogei antice. Carpii în Scythia Minor*, Pontice, I, 1968, 341-364.

Scorpan 1970 - C. Scorpan, *Prezența și continuitatea getică în Tomis și Callatis*, SCIVA, 21, 1970, 1, 65-95.

Scorpan 1973 - C. Scorpan, *La continuité de la population et des traditions gètes les conditions de la romanization de la Scythie Minor*, Pontica, VI, 1973, 137-151.

Smisko 1960 - I. M. Smisko, *Karpatski kurgani. Pervoi polovini I tisiacelitija nasevoi eri*, Kiiv, 1960.

Soultov 1980 - B. Sultov, *Centres antiques de poteries en Mésie Inférieure*, Actes du II-e Congrès International de Thracologie, Bucurețti, 1980, 2, 379-388.

Stanciu 1995 - I. Stanciu, *Contribuții la cunoașterea epocii romane în bazinul mijlociu și inferior al râului Someș*, Ephemeris Napocensis, 5, 1995.

Stînga 1998 - I. Stînga, *Viața economică la Drobeta în secolele II-VI p. Ch.*, București, 1998.

Stînga 1999 - I. Stînga, Cronica, 1999, 43.

Stînga 1999a - I. Stînga, *Locuirea romană rurală de la Gârla Mare, jud. Mehedinți (sec. II-III e.n.)*, Drobeta, 8, 1999, 33-42.

Swan 1988 - V. Swan, *Pottery in Roman Britain*, Fourth edition, Aylesbury, 1988.

Swan 1996 - V. Swan, *The Roman pottery of Yorkshire and the North-East: A selective historical guide*, RCRF, XXth International Congress 1996, York and Newcastle, 1996, 81-93.

Székely 1962 - Z. Székely, *Sondaje executate de Muzeul regional din Sf. Gheorghe*, Materiale, VIII, 1962, 325-340.

Székely 1970 - Z. Székely, *Date referitoare la cucerirea sud-estului Transilvaniei de către romani și persistența elementului dacic*, Cumidava, IV, 1970, 49-55.

Székely 1980 - Z. Székely, *Castrul roman de la Olteni*, Aluta, X-XI, 1980, 55-76.

Székely 1980a - Z. Székely, *Les Daces et les Romains aux IIe-IVe siécles dans le Sud-Est de la Transylvanie*, Actes du II-e Congrès International de Thracologie, Bucurețti, 1980, 2, 359-361.

Székely 1990-1994 - Z. K. Székely, *Ceramica dacică din castrul roman de la Olteni*, Cumidava, 15-19, 1990-1994, 18-20.

Ştefan 1935-1936 - G. Ştefan, *Nouvelles dècouvertes dans le "castellum" romain de Barboşi*, Dacia, V-VI, 1935-1936, 341-349.

Ştefan 1945-1947 - G. Ştefan, *Le camp romain de Drajna de Sus*, Dacia, XI-XII, 1945-1947, 115-144.

Točik 1959 - A. Točik, *Ze soucesne probletiku evropsekeho praveku*, ArchRozhl, XI, 1959, 841-874.

Todorović 1962 - J. Todorović, *Jedan tip dacikik sobe*, RadVojv, 11, 1962, 145-147.

Trohani 1976 - G. Trohani, *Săpăturile arheologice în aşezarea geto-dacică de la Vlădiceasca*, CA, 2, 1976, 87-103.

Tudor 1961 - D. Tudor, in *Prefaţă* to *Al. Odobescu, Istoria archeologiei*, Bucureşti, 1961.

Tudor 1967 - D. Tudor, *Depozitul de vase dacice şi romane de la Stolniceni*, SCIVA, 18, 1967, 4, 655-656.

Tudor 1968 - D. Tudor, *Centrul militar roman de la Buridava*, SMMIM, 1, 1968, 17-29.

Tudor 1970 - D. Tudor, *Săpăturile arheologice de la Castra Traiana*, Materiale, 9, 1970, 245-251.

Tudor, Davidescu 1978 - D. Tudor, M. Davidescu, *Săpăturile arheologice din castrul roman de la Cătunele*, Drobeta, 1978, 62-79.

Tudor, Poenaru, Vlădescu 1969, 1970 - D. Tudor, G. Poenaru-Bordea, C. Vlădescu, *Rezultatele primelor două campanii de săpături arheologice în castrul de la Bivolari-Arutela*, SMMIM, 2-3, 1969, 1970, 8-46.

Tudor, Purcărescu 1976 - D. Tudor, D. Purcărescu, *Prima campanie de săpături arheologice la Buridava romană*, Buridava, 2, 1976, 41-44.

Turcu 1979 - M. Turcu, *Geto-dacii din Cîmpia Munteniei*, Bucureşti, 1979.

Tyers 1996 - P. Tyers, *Roman pottery in Britain,* First edition, London, 1996.

Tzony 1980 - M. Tzony, *Les établissements du type Militari (IIe-IIIe s.d.n.è) sur le teritoire de Bucarest*, Actes du II-e Congrès International de Thracologie, Bucureţti, 1980, 2, 308-312.

Ţentea, Marcu - O. Ţentea, F. Marcu, *Ceramica lucrată cu mâna din castru roman de la Gilău*, ActaMP, 21, 1997, 281-289.

Ursachi 1968 - V. Ursachi, *Cercetări arheologice efectuate de Muzeul din Roman*, Carpica, I, 1968, 111-189.

Visy 1970 - Z. Visy, *Die Daker am Gebiet von Ungarn*, A Móra Ferenc Müzeum Évkönyve, Szeged, 1970, 5-31.

Vlassa, Rusu, Protase, Horedt 1966 - N. Vlassa, M. Rusu, D. Protase, K. Horedt, *Săpăturile arheologice de la Iernut*, ActaMN, 3, 1966, 399-410.

Vlădescu 1986 - C. M. Vlădescu, *Complexul de fortificaţii de la Bumbeşti şi rolul lor în răspîndirea romanităţii*, Litua, 3, 1986, 132-137.

Vlădescu, Poenaru 1983 - C. Vlădescu, G. Poenaru Bordea, *Castra Traiana (Sîmbotin)*, Materiale, 1983, 223-231.

Voivozeanu, Voivozeanu 1970 - Z. Voivozeanu, P. Voivozeanu, *Patella cu inscriptia latină de la Socetu*, RevMuz, 1970, 6, 530.

Vulpe, Vulpe 1924 - R. Vulpe, E. Vulpe, *Les fouilles de Tinosu*, Dacia, I, 1924, 166-223.

Vulpe, Vulpe 1933 - R. Vulpe, E. Vulpe, *Les fouilles de Poiana*, Dacia, 3-4, 1933, 253-251.

Winkler, Takacs, Păiuş 1979 - J. Winkler, M. Takacs, G. Păiuş, *Aşezarea dacică şi daco-romană de la Cicău*, Apulum, 17, 1979, 145-148.

Winkler, Blăjan 1979 - J. Winkler, M. Blăjan, *Aşezarea dacică, daco-romană şi prefeudală de la Copşa Mică*, ActaMN, 16, 1979, 460-462.

Winkler, Vasiliev, Chiţu, Borda 1968 - J. Winkler, V. Vasiliev, L. Chiţu, A. Borda, *Villa rustica de la Aiud. Câteva observatii privind villae-le rusticae din Dacia Superior*, Sargetia, V, 1968, 59-86.

Zabehlicky-Scheffenegger 1997 - S. Zabehlicky-Scheffenegger, *Dreifußschusseln mit Töpfermarken vom Magdalensberg*, RCRFActa, 1997, 127-132.

List of figures and plates

Figures:

1. Roman Dacia. Archaeological sites with completely native pottery.

2. Hand-made storage jars. 1. Locusteni; 2. Stolniceni-*Buridava*; 3. Râşnov.

3. Hand-made biconical and bell-shaped jars: 1. Daneţi; 2. Locusteni; 3. Stolniceni-*Buridava*; 4. Feldioara; 5. Breţcu; 6. Filiaşi; 7. Obreja; 8. Soporu de Câmpie; 9. Ilişua; 10. Buza; 11. Bologa; 12. Buciumi.

4. Hand-made pear-shaped and globular jars: 1. Locusteni; 2. Olteni; 3. Obreja; 4. Aiud; 5. Soporu de Câmpie; 6. Ilişua; 7. Buciumi.

5. Hand-made pots: 1. Locusteni; 2. Leu; 3. Enoşeşti-*Acidava*; 4. Scorniceşti; 5. Stolniceni-*Buridava*; 6. Râşnov; 7. Olteni; 8. Boroşneul Mare; 9. Filiaşi; 10. Soporu de Câmpie; 11. Ilişua.

6. Hand-made ovoid jars: 1. Locusteni; 2. Enoşeşti-*Acidava*; 3. Soporu de Câmpie.

7. Hand-made cylindrical jars: 1. Locusteni; 2. Leu; 3. Enoşeşti-*Acidava*; 4. Scorniceşti; 5. Stolniceni-*Buridava*; 6. Olteni; 7. Breţcu; 8. *Drobeta*; 9. Buciumi; 10. Bologa.

8. Hand-made lids: 1. Scorniceşti; 2. *Tibiscum*; 3. Timişoara-Freidorf; 4. Gilău; 5. Dedrad.

9. Hand-made Dacian cups: 1. Locusteni; 2. Leu; 3. Enoşeşti-*Acidava*; 4. Scorniceşti; 5. Stolniceni-*Buridava*; 6. Olteni; 7. Breţcu; 8. *Drobeta*; 9. *Micia*; 10. Obreja; 11. Soporu de Câmpie; 12. Orheiul Bistriţei; 13. Ilişua; 14. *Porolissum*; 15. Gilău; 16. Bologa.

10. Hand-made conical vessels: 1. Enoşeşti-*Acidava*; 2. Scorniceşti; 3. Pojejena; 4. *Tibiscum*; 5. Slimnic; 6. Obreja; 7. Gilău; 8. Bologa; 9. Ilişua.

11. Wheel-made ovoid jars and pot: 1. Locusteni; 2. Obreja.

12. Wheel-made strainers and jugs: 1. Daneţi; 2. Locusteni; 3. Scorniceşti; 4. *Tibiscum*.

13. Wheel-made fruit-bowls and dishes: 1. Locusteni; 2. Scorniceşti; 3. Obreja; 4. Buza.

14. Wheel-made lids and Dacian cup: 1. Daneţi; 2. Locusteni.

15. Hand-made pottery. Vessel categories and types.

16. Hand-made pottery. Vessel categories and types.

17. Hand-made pottery. Vessel categories and types.

18. Hand-made pottery. Vessel categories and types.

19. Wheel-made pottery. Vessel categories and types.

20. Hand-made pottery. Decorative motifs.

21. Hand-made and wheel-made pottery. Decorative motifs.

22. Native hand-made and wheel-made pottery discovered in some rural settlements from Roman Dacia.

23. Native hand-made pottery discovered in the Locusteni and Soporu de Câmpie cemeteries.

24. Decoration on the native hand-made pottery discovered in the Locusteni and Soporu de Câmpie cemeteries.

25. Decorative techniques on the native hand-made pottery discovered in the Locusteni and Soporu de Câmpie cemeteries.

26. The functions of the native hand-made pottery discovered in the Locusteni and Soporu de Câmpie cemeteries.

Plates:

1. Ovoid jars: type 1 (1-4).

2. Ovoid jars: type 1 (5-10); type 2 (11-13).

3. Biconical jars: type 1 (14); type 2 (15, 16); bell-shaped jars: type 1 (17, 18, 20-22); pear-shaped jars: type 1 (23).

4. Pear-shaped jars: type 1 (24-32).

5. Pear-shaped jars: type 2 (33-36); globular jar (38); pots: type 1 (39, 40); type 2 (41, 42).

6. Pots: type 3 (43-51).

7. Pots: type 3 (52-61).

8. Pots: type 3 (63-65); ovoid jars: type 1 (66, 67); type 2 (68-70); type 3 (71).

9. Ovoid jars: type 3 (72-74); tall cylindrical jars: type 1 (75-78); type 2 (79-80).

10. Tall cylindrical jars: type 2 (81; 83-86); type 3 (87, 88); large cylindrical jars: type 1 (89, 90).

11. Large cylindrical jars: type 1 (91-96); type 2 (97).

12. Hemispherical lids: type 1 (98-100); type 2 (101-103).

13. Conical lids: type 1 (104-107); type 2 (108, 109); trays (110); Dacian cups with handle: type 1 (111, 112)

14. Dacian cups with handle: type 1 (113, 115-117, 119-122).

15. Dacian cups with handle: type 1 (123-128); type 2 (129, 130).

16. Dacian cups with handle: type 2 (131-133, 136-141).

17. Dacian cups with handle: type 2 (142-144); Dacian cups with two handles: type 1 (145-147); type 2 (148, 149); Dacian cup with three handles (150).

18. Conical vessels: type 1 (151, 153-159).

19. Conical vessels: type 2 (160-167).

20. Conical vessels: type 2 (168-175).

21. Wheel-made pottery. Ovoid vessels: type 1 (176); type 2 (177); pot: type 1 (179); strainers: type 1 (180); jugs: type 1 (181, 182).

22. Wheel-made pottery. Jugs: type 1 (183, 184); fruit-bowls: type 1 (186); type 2 (1887-188); dish: type 1 (189).

23. Wheel-made pottery. Dishes: type 1 (190-192); type 2 (193); lids: type 1 (194-195); type 2 (196); Dacian cup (197).

24. Hand-made pottery. Photographs (19, 37, 52, 62, 82, 106, 114, 118, 134).

25. Hand-made and wheel-made pottery. Photographs (135-136, 145, 152, 171, 185).

The bibliographical references and sources of illustrations

For technical reasons we have redesigned vessel profiles. We were unable to view certain vessels for drawing and photographs were used in these instances (nos. 19, 37, 52, 62, 82, 106, 114, 118, 134-136, 145, 152, 171, 185). I am grateful to Mrs. Cătălina Toma for her drawings (nos. 1, 2, 7, 10, 27, 38, 49, 57, 82, 85-87, 90, 127, 130, 142).

STORAGE WARE

I. Ovoid jars

1. Alexandrescu 1974-1975, 11, fig. 5.
2. Petre-Govora 1968, 147, fig. 2:1.
3. Popilian 1976, 221, pl. 74, no. 950; Popilian 1976a, 285, fig. 3:14. Popilian 1980, 15, 103, pl. 3, M 13, 2.
4. Popilian 1976, 221, pl. 74, no. 949; Popilian 1976a, 285, fig. 3:13. Popilian 1980, 15, 103, pl. 3, M 15, 1.

STORAGE AND KITCHEN WARE

II. Biconical jars

5. Popilian 1980, 44, pl. 29, M 207, 3.
6. Chirilă, Gudea, Lucăcel, Pop 1972, 54, figs. 47:1; 48:2.
7. Costea 1971, 30-31, fig. 4:1.
8. Popilian 1982, 50, fig. 2, M 6, 1.
9. Protase, Gaiu, Marinescu 1997, 55, pl. 61:2.
10. Tudor 1967, 656, fig. 2:4.
11. Daicoviciu 1936-1942, 231, pl. 1:2.
12. Daicoviciu 1936-1940, 231, fig. 1:5; Protase 1966, 10, fig. 3:3.
13. Gudea 1980, 314, fig. 41:1.
14. Popilian 1976, 221, pl. 74, no. 952; Popilian 1976a, 285, fig. 3:2; Popilian 1980, 20, pl. 8, M 47, 1.
15. Protase 1976, 30-31, pl. 43:1.
16. Protase 1966, 43, fig. 17:4.

III. Bell-shaped jars

17. Popilian 1980, 19, 103, pl. 7, M 38, 1.
18. Protase, Gaiu, Marinescu 1997, 55, pl. 59:4.
19. Székely 1980a, 360, fig. 2.
20. Bădău-Wittenberger 1994, 369, pl. 5:1.
21. Gudea 1973, 53, fig. 24:29.
22. Protase 1976, 33, pls. 19:1; 42:6.

IV. Pear-shaped jars

23. Gudea 1970, 305, figs. 1:2; 5:6; Chirilă, Gudea, Lucăcel, Pop 1972, 54, figs. 47:4; 48:5.
24. Protase 1976, 35, pls. 20:8; 43:2.
25. Protase 1976, 32, pls. 19:6; 43:3.
26. Protase, Gaiu, Marinescu 1997, 55, pl. 60:4; Protase, Marinescu, Gaiu 1981, 290-291, fig. 4.
27. Székely 1990-1994, 19, pl. 1:2.
28. Popilian 1980, 50, 103, pl. 35, M 256, 2.
29. Protase, Gaiu, Marinescu 1997, 55, pl. 59:3.
30. Protase 1976, 35 pls. 21:2; 41:2.
31. Chirilă, Gudea, Lucăcel, Pop 1972, 54, figs. 47:2; 48:1.
32. Protase, Gaiu, Marinescu 1997, 55, pl. 60:3.
33. Popilian 1980, 23, pl. 11, M 76, 6.
34. Popilian 1976, 221, pl. 74, no. 951; Popilian 1976a, 285, fig. 3:1; Popilian 1980, 29, 103, pl. 17, M 110, 1.
35. Popilian 1980, pl. 42, M 195, 1.
36. Popilian 1976, 221, pl. 74, no. 953; Popilian 1976a, 285, fig. 3:3; Popilian 1980, 21, 103, pl. 9, M 54, 1.
37. Winkler, Vasiliev, Chitu, Bordea 1968, 72, fig. 7:1.

V. Globular jar

38. Protase 1971, 151, fig. 13:1.

VI. Pots

39. Popilian 1980, 29-30, 103, pl. 17, M 111, 1.
40. Protase 1976, 36, pls. 21:6; 42:2.
41. Protase 1976, 42, pls. 34:4; 41:1.
42. Popilian 1980, 40, 103, pl. 27, M 189, 1.
43. Negru, Ciucă 1997, 23, pl. 1:1.
44. Popilian 1976, 220, pl. 74, no. 944; Popilian 1976a, 285, fig. 3:7; Popilian 1980, pl. 43, 5.
45. Gudea 1973c, 28, fig. 2.
46. Popilian 1980, 19, pl. 7, M 39, 1.
47. Székely 1990-1994, 19, pl. 1:3.
48. Popilian 1976, 220, pl. 74 no. 943; Popilian 1980, 25, pls. 13, M 84, 1; 43:7.
49. Gudea, Pop 1971, 15, fig. 8.
50. Protase, Gaiu, Marinescu 1997, 55, pl. 59:10; Protase, Marinescu, Gaiu 1981, 290-291, fig. 4.

51. Popilian 1980, 26, pl. 13, M 91, 1.

52. Bichir 1986, 118, pl. 4:1.

53. Negru, Ciucă 1997, 25, pl. 2:10.

54. Popilian 1980, 50, pl. 35, M 257, 1.

55. Popilian 1980, 31, pl. 18, M 122, 2.

56. Popilian 1980, 42, pl. 28, M 196, 1.

57. Popilian 1980, 24, pl. 12, M 79, 1.

58. Preda, Grosu 1993, 50, pl. 8:2.

59. Popilian 1980, 42, pl. 28, M 197, 1.

60. Preda, Grosu 1993, 50, pl. 8:1.

61. Popilian 1976, 220, pl. 74, no. 944; Popilian 1976a, 285, pl. 2:8; Popilian 1980, 36, pl. 23, M 155, 1; pl. 43:6.

62. Tudor 1967, 656, fig. 2:3.

63. Székely 1970, 53, fig. 1:1; Székely 1980, 62, fig. 6:6.

64. Popilian 1980, 48, pl. 34, M 239, 1.

65. Popilian 1980, 17, pl. 5, M 26, 1.

VII. Ovoid jars

66. Popilian 1976, 221, pl. 74, no. 948; Popilian 1976a, 285, fig. 2:11.

67. Protase 1976, 26, 81, pl. 43:6.

68. Bona, Petrovszky, Petrovszky 1982, 410, pl. 2:6.

69. Protase 1976, 26, pl. 41:3.

70. Popilian 1976, 221, pl. 74, no. 946; Popilian 1976a, 285, fig. 2:9.

71. Glodariu 1981, fig. 54:16.

72. Negru, Ciucă 1997, 24, pl. 1:3.

73. Tudor 1967, 656, fig. 2:1.

74. Popilian 1980, 35, 103, pl. 22, M 149, 1.

VIII. Tall cylindrical jars

75. Protase 1976, 32, pls. 19:8; 43:5.

76. Popilian 1980, 46-47, pl. 32, M 229, 1.

77. Protase 1976, 21, pls. 11:2; 41:4.

78. Gherghe 1985, 52, fig. 3:2.

79. Popilian 1980, 46, pl. 31, M 225, 1.

80. Protase, Gaiu, Marinescu 1997, 55, pl. 58:9.

81. Bichir 1986, 118, pl. 4:6.

82. Székely 1980a, 360, fig. 1.

83. Protase 1976, 40, pls. 23:2; 41:5.

84. Protase 1976, 32, pl. 42:3.

85. Székely 1990-1994, 19, pl. 1:1.

86. Tudor 1967, 656, fig. 2:2.

87. Bichir 1984, 32, pl. 17:10; Bichir 1986, 118, pls. 4:2; 14:1.

88. Preda, Grosu 1993, 50, pl. 8:3.

IX. Cylindrical jars

89. Popilian, Niţă 1982, 92, fig. 2:4.

90. Popilian 1976, 221, pl. 74, no. 955; Popilian 1976a, 285, pl. 3:5.

91. Protase 1971, 137, fig. 5:1.

92. Isac 1997, 56; Ţentea, Marcu 1997, 243, pl. 1:2.

93. Popilian 1976, 221, pl. 74, no. 954; Popilian 1976a, 285, fig. 3:4; Popilian 1980, 28, pls. 16, M 102, 1; 45:2.

94. Protase, Gaiu, Marinescu 1997, 55, pl. 58:3.

95. Gudea 1970, 299, figs. 1: 1; 5:2.

96. Chirilă, Gudea, Lucăcel, Pop 1972, 54, pls. 47:5; 48:3.

97. Popilian 1980, 53, pl. 38, M 286, 1.

KITCHEN WARE

X. Lids

98. Benea 1997, 72, fig. 7:3.

99. Benea 1997, 72, fig. 7:2.

100. Benea 1997, 72, fig. 7:4.

101. Rogozea 1988, 177, fig. 7:3.

102. Rogozea 1988, 178, fig. 7:2.

103. Bichir 1984, pl. 17:1; Bichir 1986, 118, pl. 11:3.

104. Benea 1997, 72, fig. 7:5.

105. Bona, Petrovszky, Petrovszky 1982, 410, pl. 3:7.

106. Protase, Marinescu, Gaiu 1981, 291-292, fig. 4.

107. Glodariu 1975, 229, fig. 13:1.

108. Ţentea, Marcu 1997, 245, pl. 10:4.

109. Ţentea, Marcu 1997, 245, pl. 10:3.

TABLE WARE

XI. Dish

110. Bichir 1984, pl. 17:2.

ILLUMINATION VESSELS

XII. Dacian cups

111. Negru, Ciucă 1997, 26, pl. 2:11.

112. Székely 1990-1994, 19, fig. 1:4.

113. Popilian 1976, 220, pl. 74, no. 939; Popilian 1976a, 285, fig. 2:3; Popilian 1980, 15, pl. 3, M 15, 2.

114. Bichir 1986, 120, pl. 3:3.

115. Gudea 1989, 501, fig. 94:5.

116. Protase 1966, 43, fig. 17:3.

117. Protase 1966, 43, fig. 17:6.

118. Protase 1971, 137, fig. 6:7.

119. Popilian 1980, 52, pl. 37, M 283, 1.

120. Macrea, Protase, Dănilă 1967, 116, fig. 6:4.

121. Popilian 1976, 220, pl. 74, no. 940.

122. Popilian 1976, 220, pl. 74, no. 938; Popilian 1976a, 285, fig. 2:2.

123. Gudea 1980, 314, fig. 41:4.

124. Macrea, Rusu, Winkler 1959, 453, fig. 1:11.

125. Protase 1971, 137, fig. 7:4.

126. Gudea 1989, 501, pl. 94:3.

127. Popilian 1980, 82-83, pl. 45:8.

128. Protase 1971, 137, fig. 6:4.

129. Popilian 1980, 42, pl. 28, M 196, 2.

130. Popilian 1976, 220, pl. 74, no. 937; Popilian 1976a, 285, fig. 2:1; Popilian 1980, 15-16, pl. 4, M 17, 2.
131. Protase 1971, 137, fig. 6:5.
132. Popilian 1980, 29, pl. 16, M 108, 2.
133. Petre 1968, 147, fig. 2:4.
134. Floca 1968, 52-53, fig 1.
135. Bichir 1986, 117, pl. 3:2, 4.
136. Székely 1970, 53 fig. 1:3.
137. Gudea 1980, 314, fig. 41:3.
138. Bichir 1984, 31, pl. 17:8; Bichir 1986, 117, pls. 3:1; 12:5.
139. Protase 1960, 190, fig. 1:2; Macrea, Protase, Dãnilã 1967, 116, fig. 6:5.
140. Protase, Gaiu, Marinescu 1997, 55, pl. 60:7.
141. Bichir 1984, 31-32, pl. 17:7; Bichir 1986, 117, pls. 3:8; 11:6.
142. Gudea 1989, 501, pl. 94:4.
143. Székely 1970, 53, fig. 1:2; Székely 1980, 60, fig. 6:2.
144. Bichir 1984, 31, pl. 17:4; Bichir 1986, 117, pls. 3:6; 11:5.
145. Protase 1971, 137, fig. 6:6.
146. Protase 1976, 19, fig. 6:2.
147. Popilian 1980, 36-37, pl. 23, M162, 2.
148. Popilian 1976, 220, pl. 74, no. 942; Popilian 1980, 29, pl. 17, M 110, 2.
149. Popilian 1976, 220, pl. 74, no. 941; Popilian 1976a, 285, fig. 2:4; Popilian 1980, 68, pl. 45:6.
150. Protase 1966, 43, fig. 17:5; Protase 1971, 137, fig. 6:3.

XIII. Conical vessels
151. Protase, Gaiu, Marinescu 1997, 55, pl. 60:6.
152. Benea 1981, 311, fig. 27:3.
153. Protase, Gaiu, Marinescu 1997, 55, pl. 58:8.
154. Țentea, Marcu 1997, 245, pl. 12:3.
155. Negru, Ciucã 1997, 26, pl. 2:13.
156. Țentea, Marcu 1997, 245, pl. 12:6.
157. Negru, Ciucã 1997, 26, pl. 2:14.
158. Bichir 1984, pl. 17:3.
159. Glodariu 1981, fig. 29:7.
160. Glodariu 1981, fig. 29:9.
161. Negru, Ciucã 1997, 27, pl. 2:15.
162. Țentea, Marcu 1997, 245, pl. 12:7.
163. Macrea, Rusu, Winkler 1959, 453, fig. 1:15.
164. Negru, Ciucã 1997, 28, pl. 2:16.
165. Protase, Gaiu, Marinescu 1997, 55, pl. 58:7.
166. Protase, Gaiu, Marinescu 1997, 55, pl. 60:5.
167. Chirilã, Gudea, Lucãcel, Pop 1972, 54, fig. 50:1.
168. Țentea, Marcu 1997, 246, pl. 13:2.
169. Isac 1997, 56; Țentea, Marcu 1997, 245, pl. 12:5.
170. Țentea, Marcu 1997, 245, pl. 12:2.
171. Protase 1971, 137, fig. 6:2.
172. Gudea 1973, 89, fig. 6:7.
173. Protase 1966, 43, fig. 17:2; Protase 1971, 137, fig. 6:1.
174. Rusu 1979, 160-161, pl. 3:20.
175. Țentea, Marcu 1997, 246, pl. 13:3.

WHEEL-MADE POTTERY

STORAGE WARE

A. Ovoid jars

176. Protase 1971, 151, fig. 13:2.
177. Popilian 1976, 220, pl. 74, no. 947; Popilian 1976a, 285, fig. 2:12; Popilian 1980, 15, pl. 3, M 12, 1.

KITCHEN WARE

B. Pots

178. Popilian 1976, 220, pl. 74, no. 956; Popilian 1976a, 285, fig. 2:10; Popilian 1980, 14, pl. 2 M, 11, 1.

C. Strainers

179. Bichir 1984, 36, pl. 17:11; Bichir 1986, 119, pls. 4:1; 12:6.
180. Bichir 1984, 36, pl. 18:10; Bichir 1986, 119, pl. 13:10.

TABLE WARE

D. Jugs

181. Popilian 1982, 48, fig. 1, M 2, 2.
182. Bichir 1984, 35, pl. 17:14; Bichir 1986, 119, pl. 14:11.
183. Protase 1966, 43, fig. 17:7.
184. Popilian 1980a, 40, pl. 26, M 182, 3.
185. Benea 1981, 311, fig. 20:1.

E. Fruit-bowls

186. Popilian 1980, 16, pl. 4, M 24, 2.
187. Protase 1966, 43, fig. 17:9; Protase 1971, 137, fig. 5:3.
188. Popilian 1980, 43, pl. 28, M 204, 2.

F. Dishes

189. Bichir 1984, 36, pl. 18:1; Bichir 1986, 119, pls. 4:2; 13:1.
190. Bichir 1984, 36, pl. 18:3; Bichir 1986, 119, pls. 12:1; 13:3.
191. Benea 1997, 75, fig. 10:3.
192. Bichir 1984, pl. 18:5; Bichir 1986, 119, pl. 13:5.
193. Bãdãu-Wittenberger 1994, 369, pl. 5:2.

G. Lids

194. Popilian 1980, 23, pl. 11, M 74, 2.
195. Popilian 1982, 51, fig. 2, M 8, 2.
196. Popilian 1980, 33, pl. 20, M 130, 2.

ILLUMINATION VESSELS

H. Dacian cups

197. Popilian 1980, 36, pl. 23, M 155, 2.

List of researched sites

Aiud - city, Cluj County

Alba Iulia-*Apulum* - city, Alba County

Amărăşti - village, Dolj County

Apele Vii - village, Dolj County

Băneasa - hamlet in Salcia village, Teleorman County

Bivolari - (ex-Poiana) hamlet in Păiuşa village, Vâlcea County

Blandiana - village, Alba County

Bologa - hamlet in Pieni village, Cluj County

Boroşneu Mare - village, Covasna County

Brâncoveneşti - village, Mureş County

Breţcu - village, Covasna County

Buciumi - village, Sălaj County

Bumbeşti - village, Gorj County

Buza - village, Cluj County

Cârcea - hamlet in Coşoveni village, Dolj County

Cătunele - village, Gorj County

Căşei - village, Cluj County

Castranova - village, Dolj County

Caşolţ - hamlet in Roşia village, Sibiu County

Celeiu - village in Corabia city, Olt County

Cenade - village, Alba County

Cernatu de Jos – hamlet in Vorţa village, Hunedoara County

Chilia - hamlet in Făgeţel village, Olt County

Chinteni - village, Cluj County

Cicău - hamlet in Mirăslău village, Alba County

Cinciş - hamlet in Teliucu Inferior village, Hunedoara city area, Hunedoara County

Ciunga - (ex-Vioara de Jos) village, Ocna Mureşului city area, Mureş County

Cluj-Napoca - city, Cluj County

Comalău - ex-hamlet in Reci village, Covasna County

Copşa Mică - city, Sibiu County

Cristeşti - hamlet in Mogoş village, Alba County

Daneţi - village, Dolj County

Dedrad - hamlet in Batoş village, Mureş County

Dobrun - hamlet in Osica de Jos village, Olt County

Drobeta-Turnu Severin - city, Mehedinţi County

Enoşeşti-*Acidava* - hamlet in Piata Olt village, Olt County

Feldioara - hamlet in Ucea village, Braşov County

Filiasi - village, in Cristuru Secuiesc city area, Harghita County

Gilău - village, Cluj County

Gligoreşti - hamlet in Vidra village, Alba County

Gornea - hamlet in Şicheviţa village, Caraş Severin County

Govora-Sat - hamlet in Mihăeşti village, Vâlcea County

Grădinari - village, Caraş Severin County

Gueşti - hamlet in Coloneşti village, Olt County

Guşteriţa - quarter of Sibiu city, Sibiu County

Hodoni - hamlet in Satchinez village, Timiş County

Ilişua - hamlet in Uriu village, Mureş County

Jupa-*Tibiscum* - village in Caransebeş city area, Caraş Severin County

Laslea - village, Sibiu County

Lechinţa de Mureş - hamlet in Iernut village, Mureş County

Leu - village, Dolj County

Locusteni - hamlet in Daneţi village, Dolj County

Mănerău - hamlet in Peştişu Mic village, Hunedoara County

Matei - village, Bistriţa Năsăud County

Medieşorul Mare - hamlet in Simoneşti village, Harghita County

Mehadia - village, Caraş Severin County

Micăsasa - village, Sibiu County

Moigrad-*Porolissum* - hamlet in Mirşid village, Sălaj County

Moldova Veche - village in Moldova Nouă city area, Caraş Severin County

Noşlac - village, Alba County

Obreja - hamlet in Mihalţ village, Alba County

Ocna Sibiului - city, Sibiu County

Ocnele Mari - city, Vâlcea County

Olteni - hamlet in Bodoc village, Covasna County

Orheiul Bistriţei - hamlet in Cetate village, Bistriţa Năsăud County

Ostrovul Corbului - hamlet in Hinova village, Mehedinţi County

Pojejena - village, Caraş Severin County

Râsnov - city, Braşov County

Răcari - hamlet in Brădeşti village, Dolj County

Rădăcineşti - hamlet in Berislăveşti village, Vâlcea County

Rădeşti - village, Alba County

Reşca - *Romula* - hamlet in Dobrosloveni village, Olt County

Românaşi - village, Sălaj County

Romiţa - hamlet in Românaşi village, Sălaj County

Roşia - village, Sibiu County

Rucăr - village, Argeş County

Sânbotin - *Castra Traiana* - hamlet in Dăeşti village, Vâlcea County

Sângeorgiu de Mureş - village in Târgu Mureş city area, Mureş County

Săcelu - village, Gorj County

Sărăţeni - village in Sovata city, Mureş County

Sava - hamlet in Palatca village, Cluj County

Scorniceşti - village, Olt County

Sf. Gheorghe - Iernut - hamlet in Iernut village, Mureş County

Sic - village, Cluj County

Sighişoara - city, Mureş County

Slăveni - hamlet in Stoeneşti village, Olt County

Slimnic - village, Sibiu County

Socetu - hamlet in Stejaru village, Teleorman County

Soporu de Câmpie - hamlet in Frata village, Cluj County

Stolniceni-*Buridava* - village in Râmnicu Vâlcea city area, Vâlcea County

Şeica Mică - village, Sibiu County

Şura Mică - village, Sibiu County

Târnava Mare - village in Mediaş city area, Mureş County

Timişoara-Cioreni - quarter of Timişoara city, Timiş County

Timişoara-Freidorf - quarter of Timişoara city, Timiş County

Turdaş - village, Alba County

Vărădia - village, Caraş Severin County

Verbicioara - hamlet in Verbiţa village, Dolj County

Veţel-*Micia* - village in Deva city area, Hunedoara County

Voivodeni - village, Mureş County

Vulcan - village, Braşov County

Vultureşti - village, Olt County

List of sites with native pottery

1. Daneţi
2. Locusteni
3. Leu
4. Scorniceşti
5. Enoşeşti-*Acidava*
6. Stolniceni-*Buridava*
7. Săcelu
8. *Drobeta*
9. Pojejena
10. *Tibiscum*
11. Timişoara-Freidorf
12. *Micia*
13. Aiud
14. Slimnic
15. Obreja
16. Râşnov
17. Feldioara
18. Boroşneu Mare
19. Breţcu
20. Filiaşi
21. Olteni
22. Dedrad
23. Orheiul Bistriţei
24. Soporu de Câmpie
25. Gilău
26. Buza
27. Ilişua
28. *Porolissum*
29. Buciumi
30. Bologa

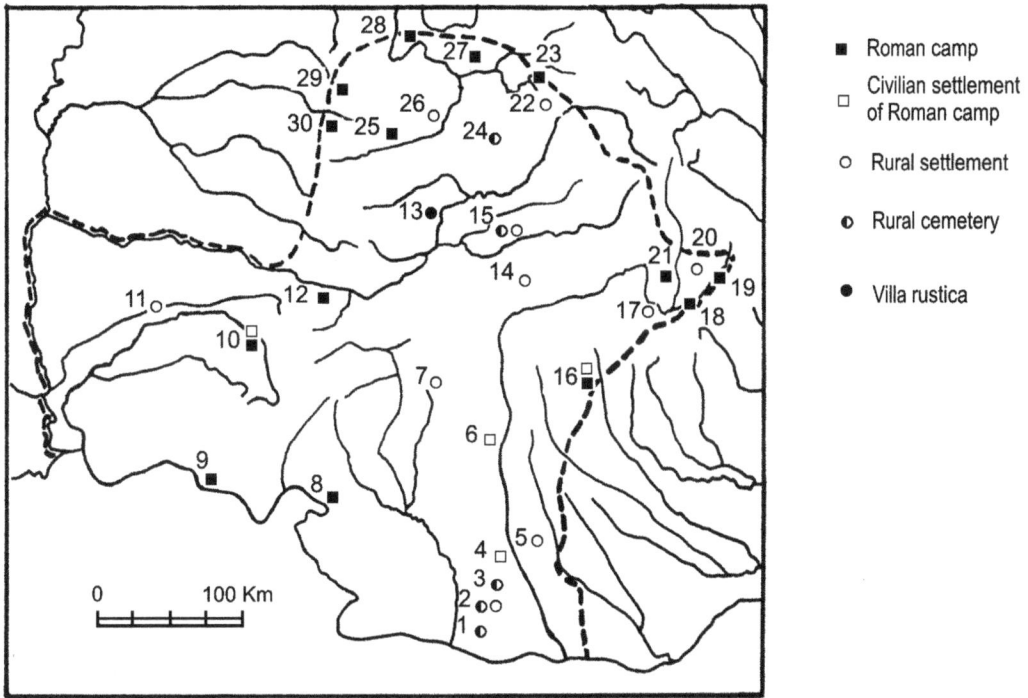

Figure 1. Roman Dacia. Archaeological sites with completely native pottery.

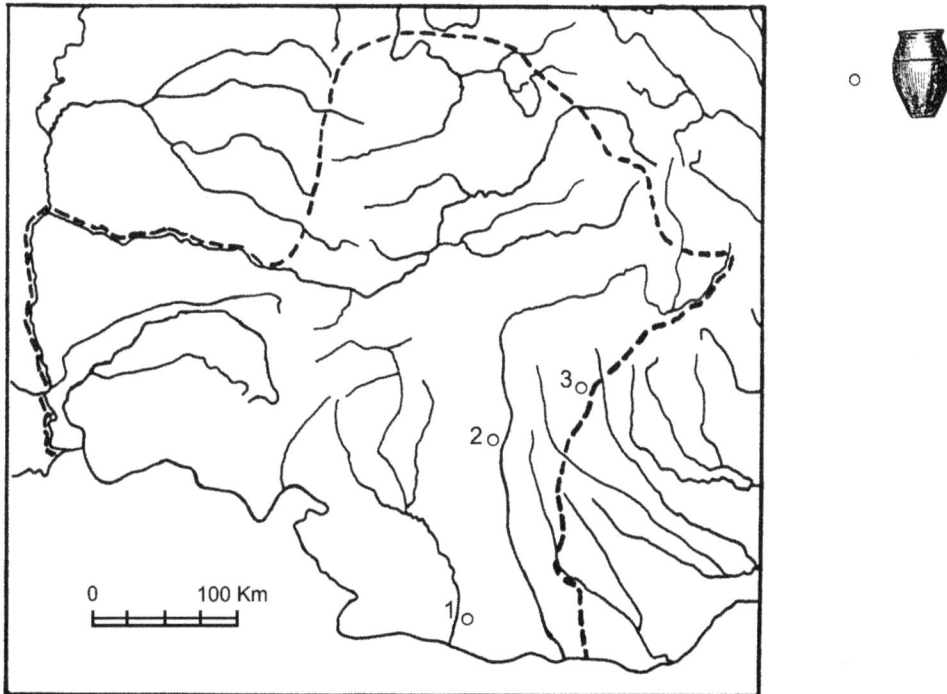

Figure 2. Hand-made storage jars. 1. Locusteni; 2. Stolniceni-*Buridava*; 3. Râşnov.

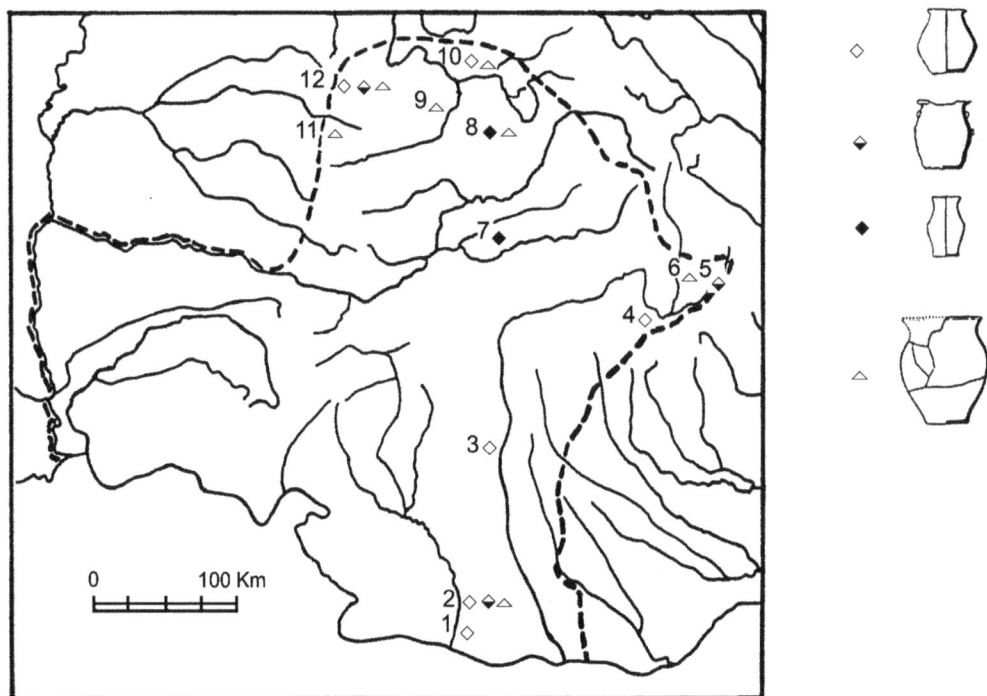

Figure 3. Hand-made biconical and bell-shaped jars: 1. Daneţi; 2. Locusteni; 3. Stolniceni-*Buridava*; 4. Feldioara; 5. Breţcu; 6. Filiaşi; 7. Obreja; 8. Soporu de Câmpie; 9. Ilişua; 10. Buza; 11. Bologa; 12. Buciumi.

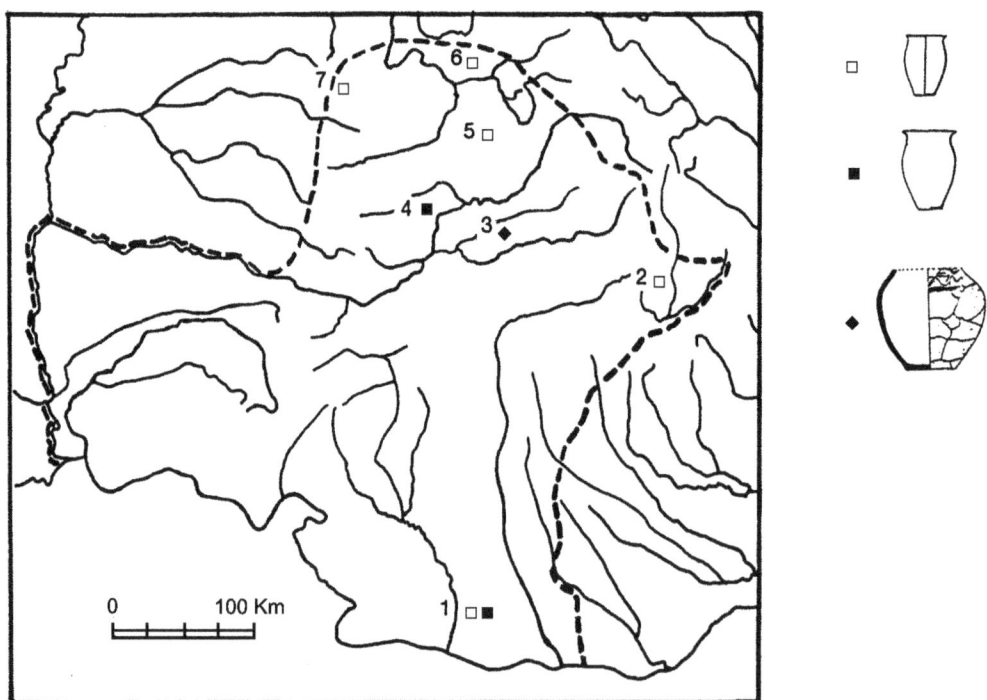

Figure 4. Hand-made pear-shaped and globular jars: 1. Locusteni; 2. Olteni; 3. Obreja; 4. Aiud; 5. Soporu de Câmpie; 6. Ilişua; 7. Buciumi.

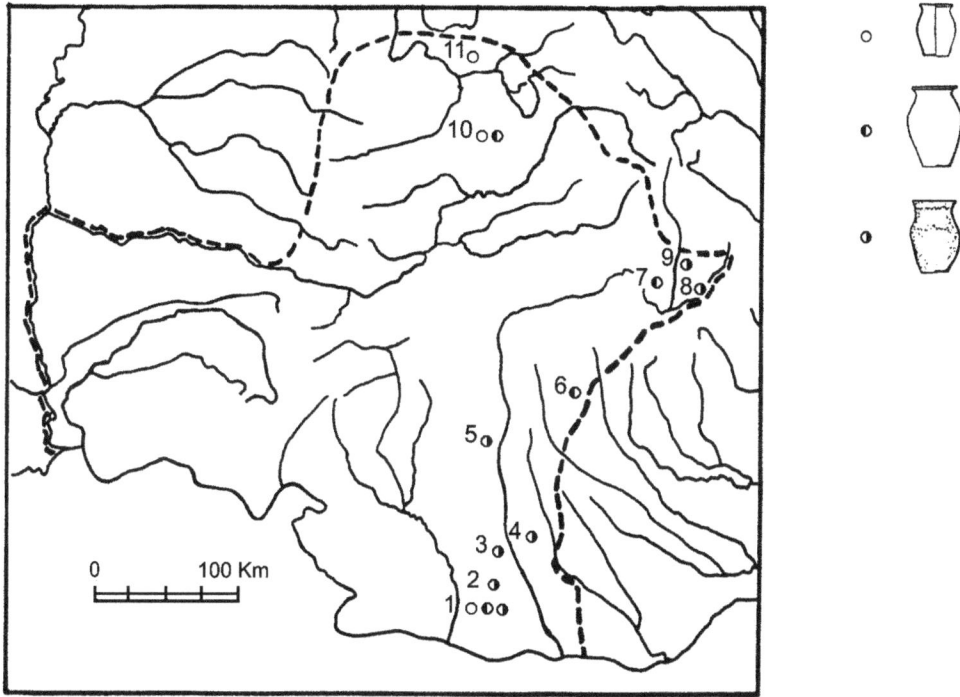

Figure 5. Hand-made pots: 1. Locusteni; 2. Leu; 3. Enoşeşti-*Acidava*; 4. Scorniceşti; 5. Stolniceni-*Buridava*; 6. Râşnov; 7. Olteni; 8. Boroşneul Mare; 9. Filiaşi; 10. Soporu de Câmpie; 11. Ilişua.

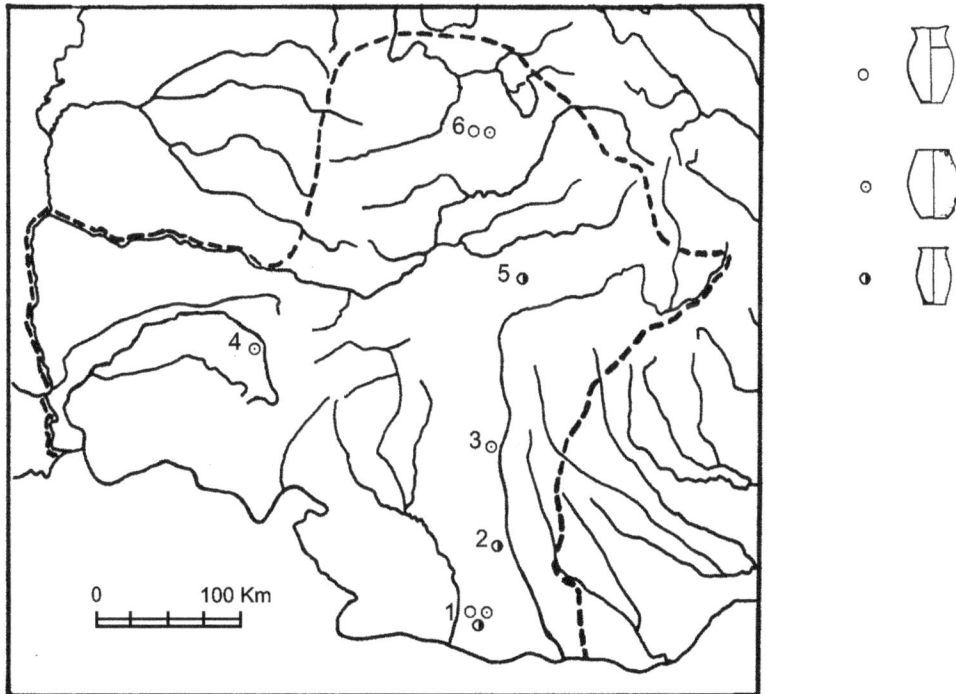

Figure 6. Hand-made ovoid jars: 1. Locusteni; 2. Enoşeşti-*Acidava*; 3. Soporu de Câmpie.

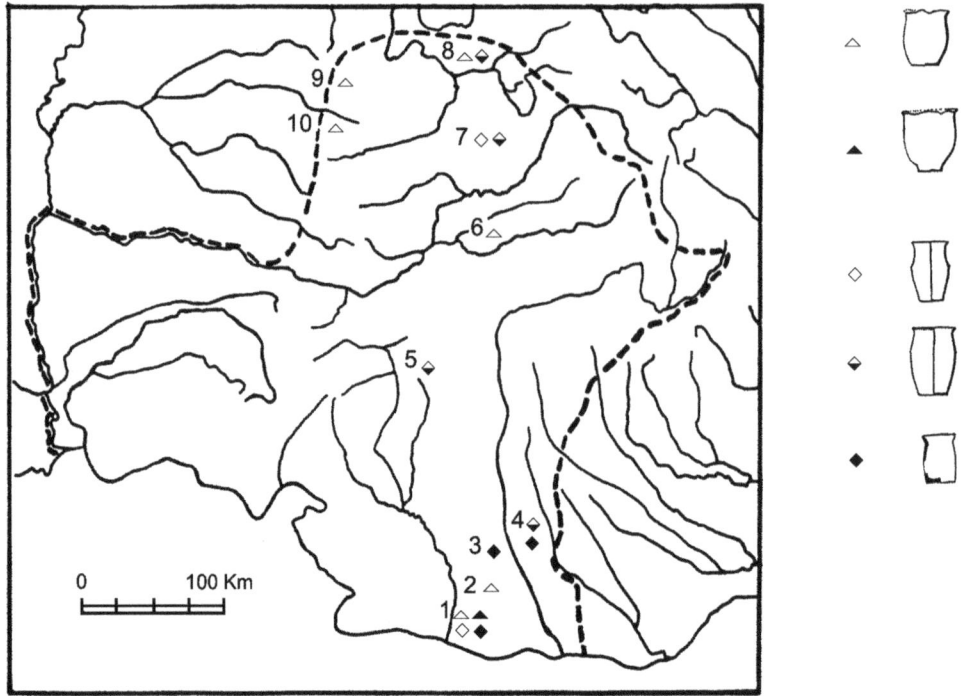

Figure 7. Hand-made cylindrical jars: 1. Locusteni; 2. Leu; 3. Enoşeşti-*Acidava*; 4. Scorniceşti; 5. Stolniceni-*Buridava*; 6. Olteni; 7. Breţcu; 8. *Drobeta*; 9. Buciumi; 10. Bologa.

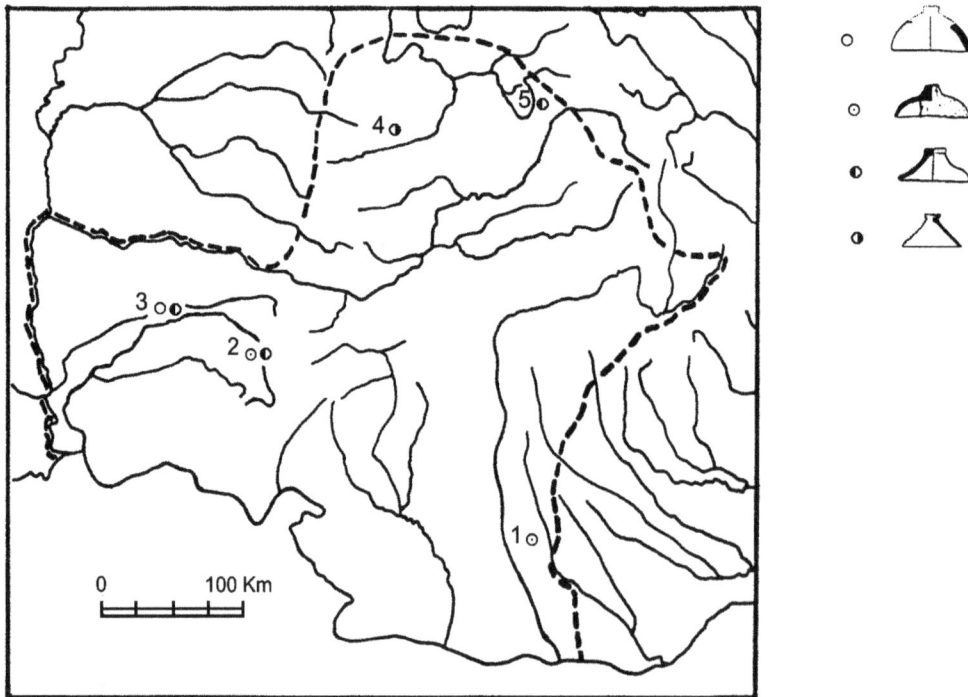

Figure 8. Hand-made lids: 1. Scorniceşti; 2. *Tibiscum*; 3. Timişoara-Freidorf; 4. Gilău; 5. Dedrad.

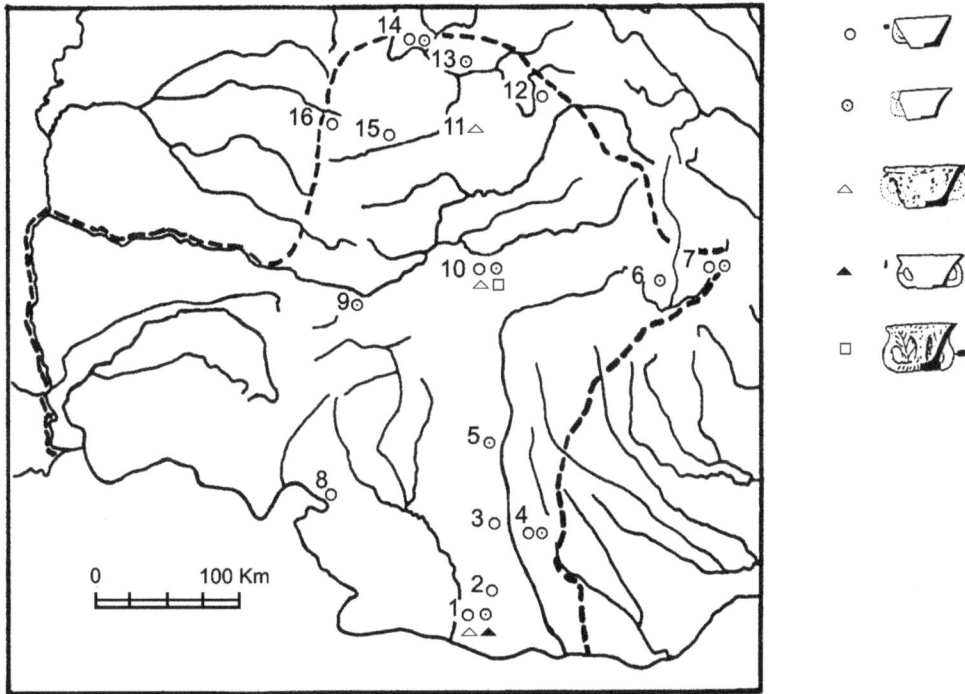

Figure 9. Hand-made Dacian cups: 1. Locusteni; 2. Leu; 3. Enoşeşti-*Acidava*; 4. Scorniceşti;
5. Stolniceni-*Buridava*; 6. Olteni; 7. Breţcu; 8. *Drobeta*; 9. *Micia*; 10. Obreja; 11. Soporu de Câmpie;
12. Orheiul Bistriţei; 13. Ilişua; 14. *Porolissum*; 15. Gilău; 16. Bologa.

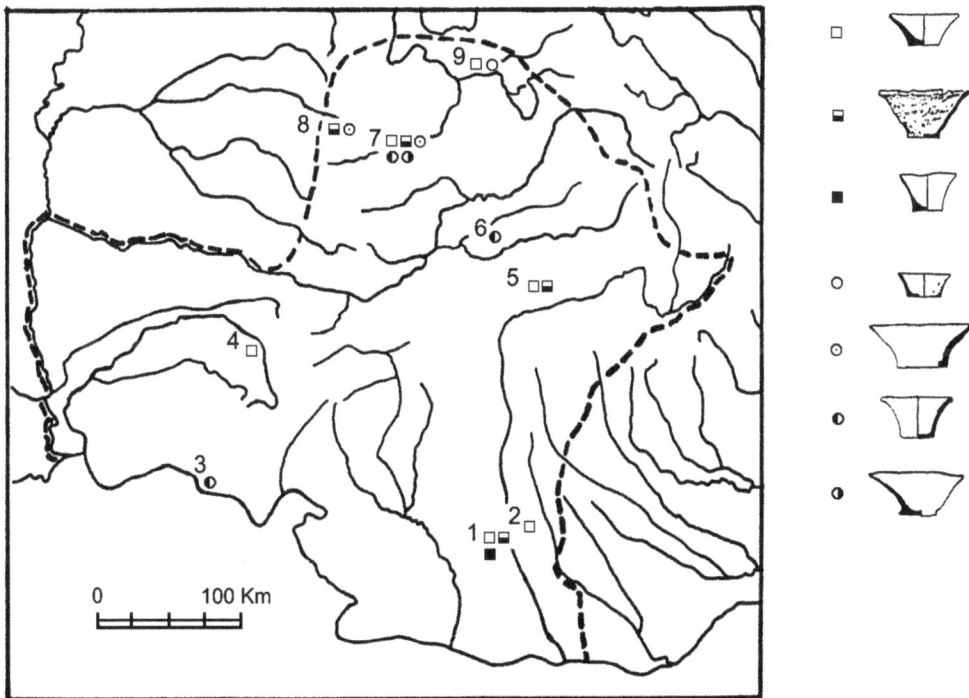

Figure 10. Hand-made conical vessels: 1. Enoşeşti-*Acidava*; 2. Scorniceşti; 3. Pojejena; 4. *Tibiscum*;
5. Slimnic; 6. Obreja; 7. Gilău; 8. Bologa; 9. Ilişua.

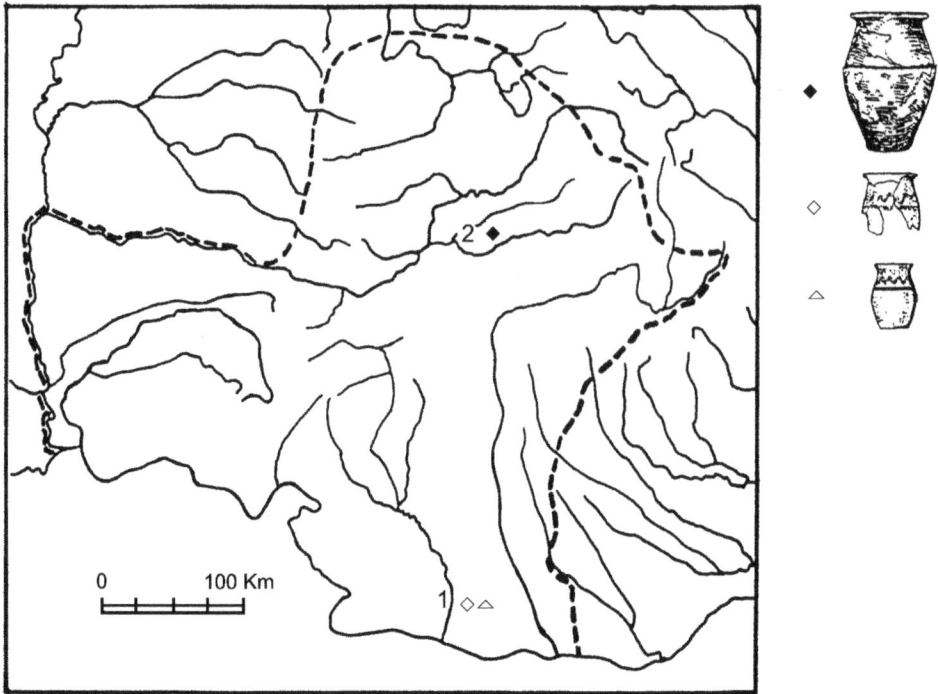

Figure 11. Wheel-made ovoid jars and pot: 1. Locusteni; 2. Obreja.

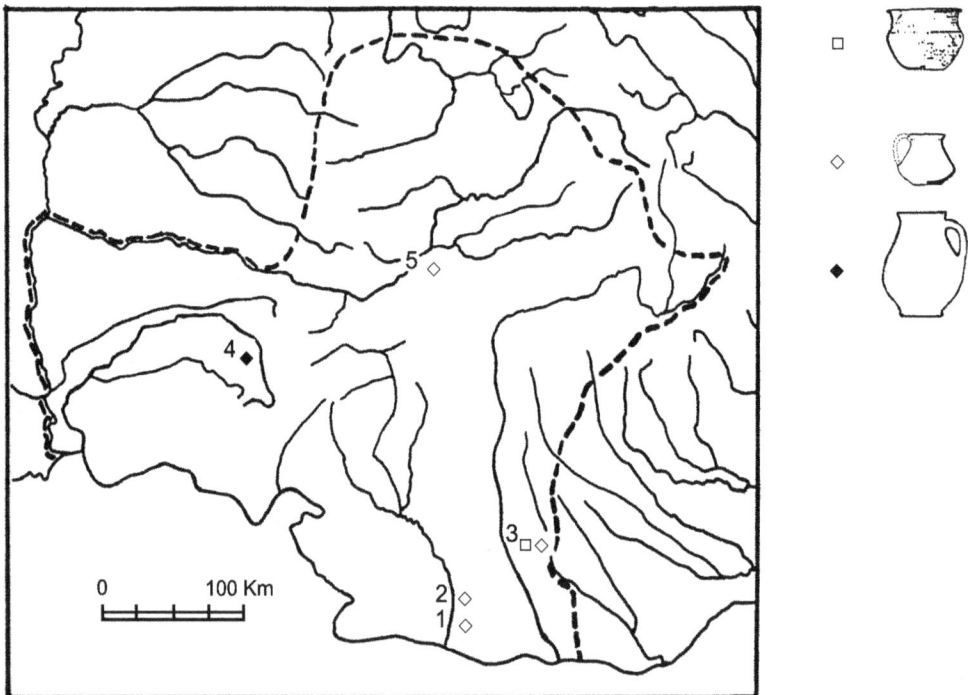

Figure 12. Wheel-made strainers and jugs: 1. Daneți; 2. Locusteni; 3. Scorniceşti; 4. *Tibiscum*.

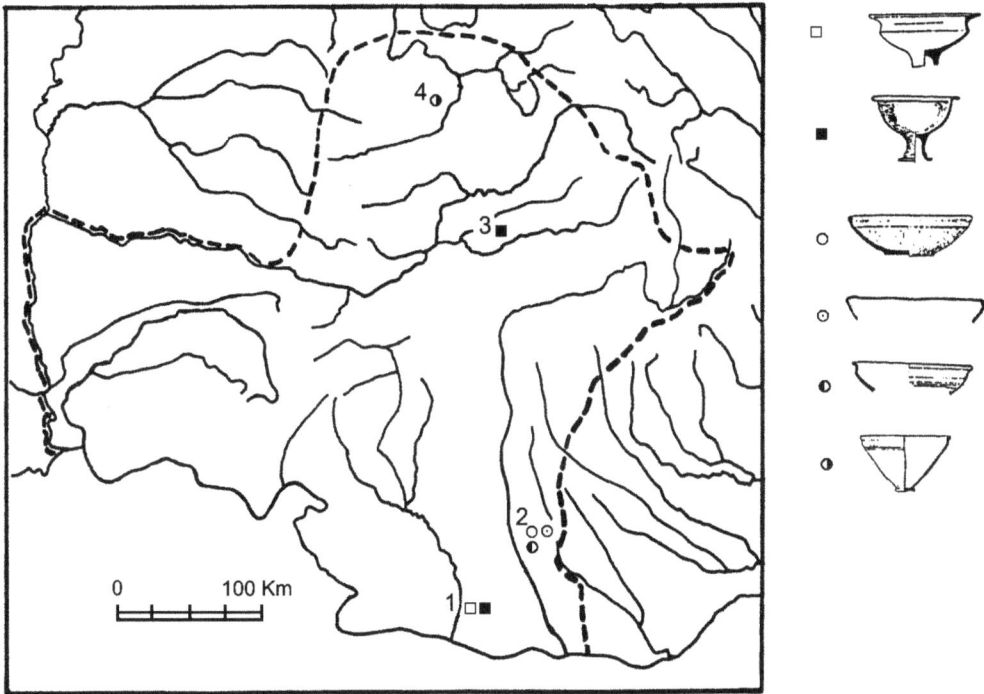

Figure 13. Wheel-made fruit-bowls and dishes: 1. Locusteni; 2. Scorniceşti; 3. Obreja; 4. Buza.

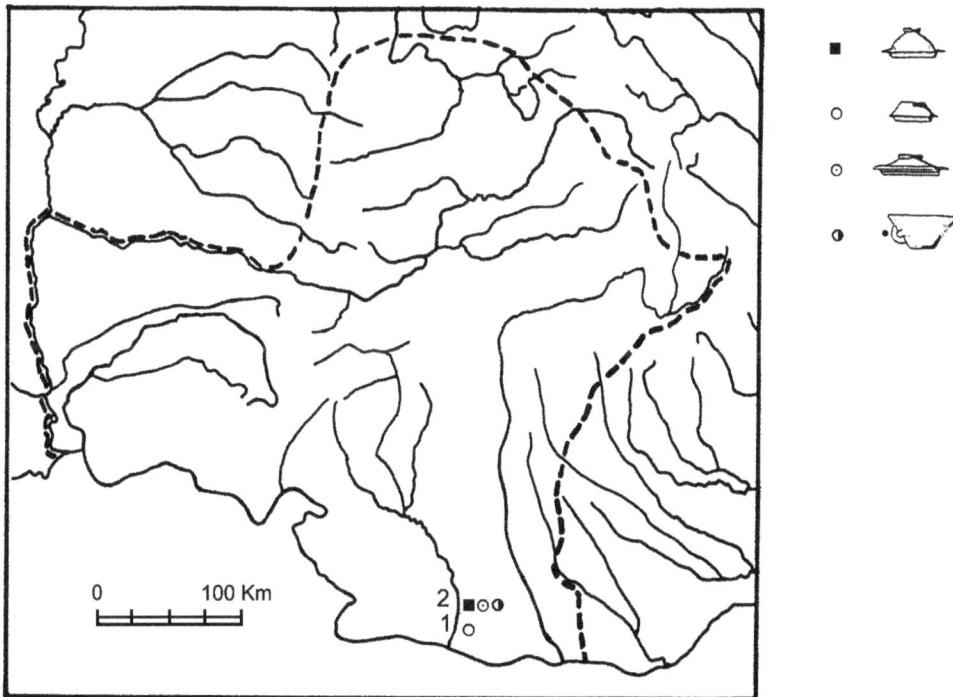

Figure 14. Wheel-made lids and Dacian cup: 1. Daneţi; 2. Locusteni.

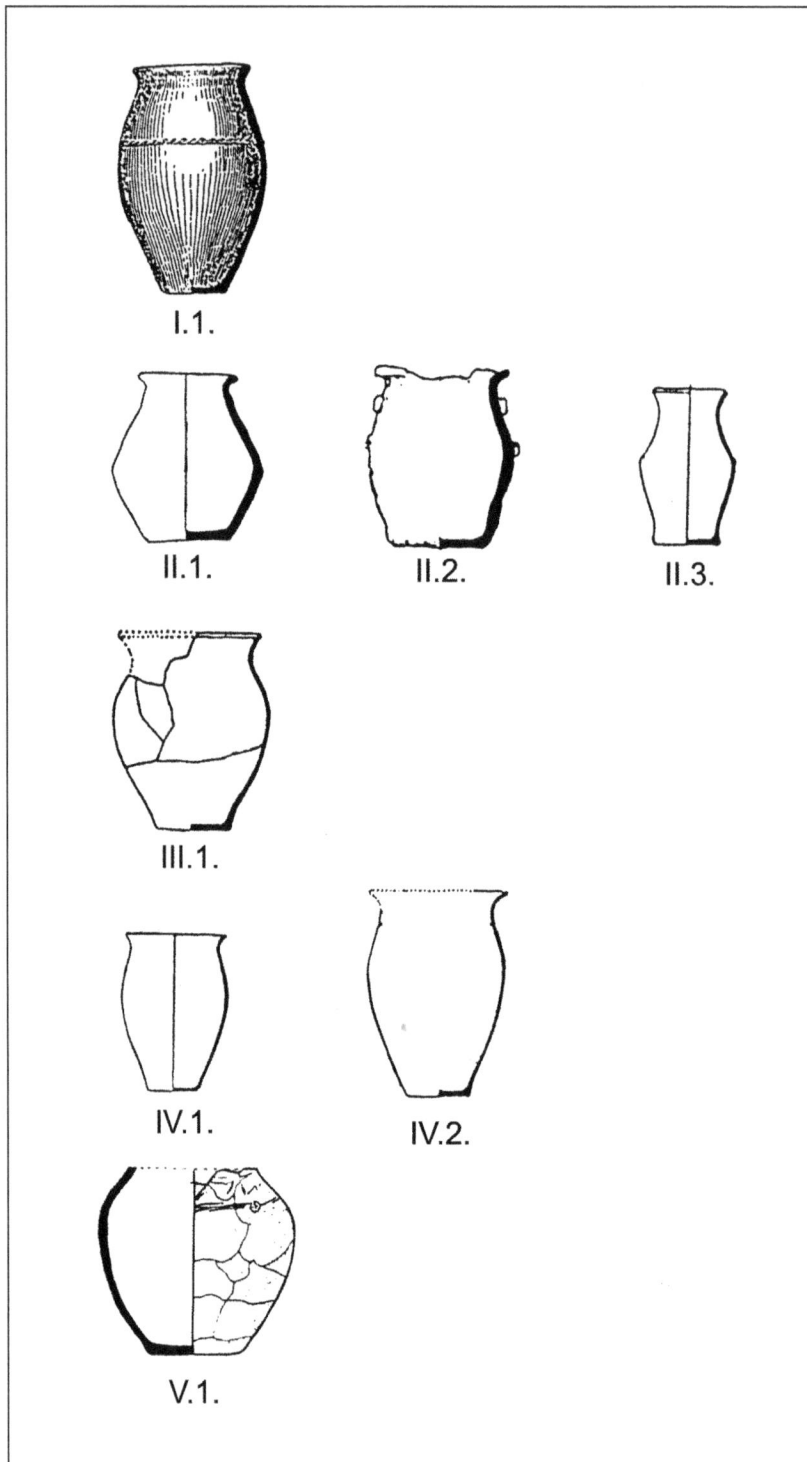

Figure 15. Hand-made pottery. Vessel categories and types.

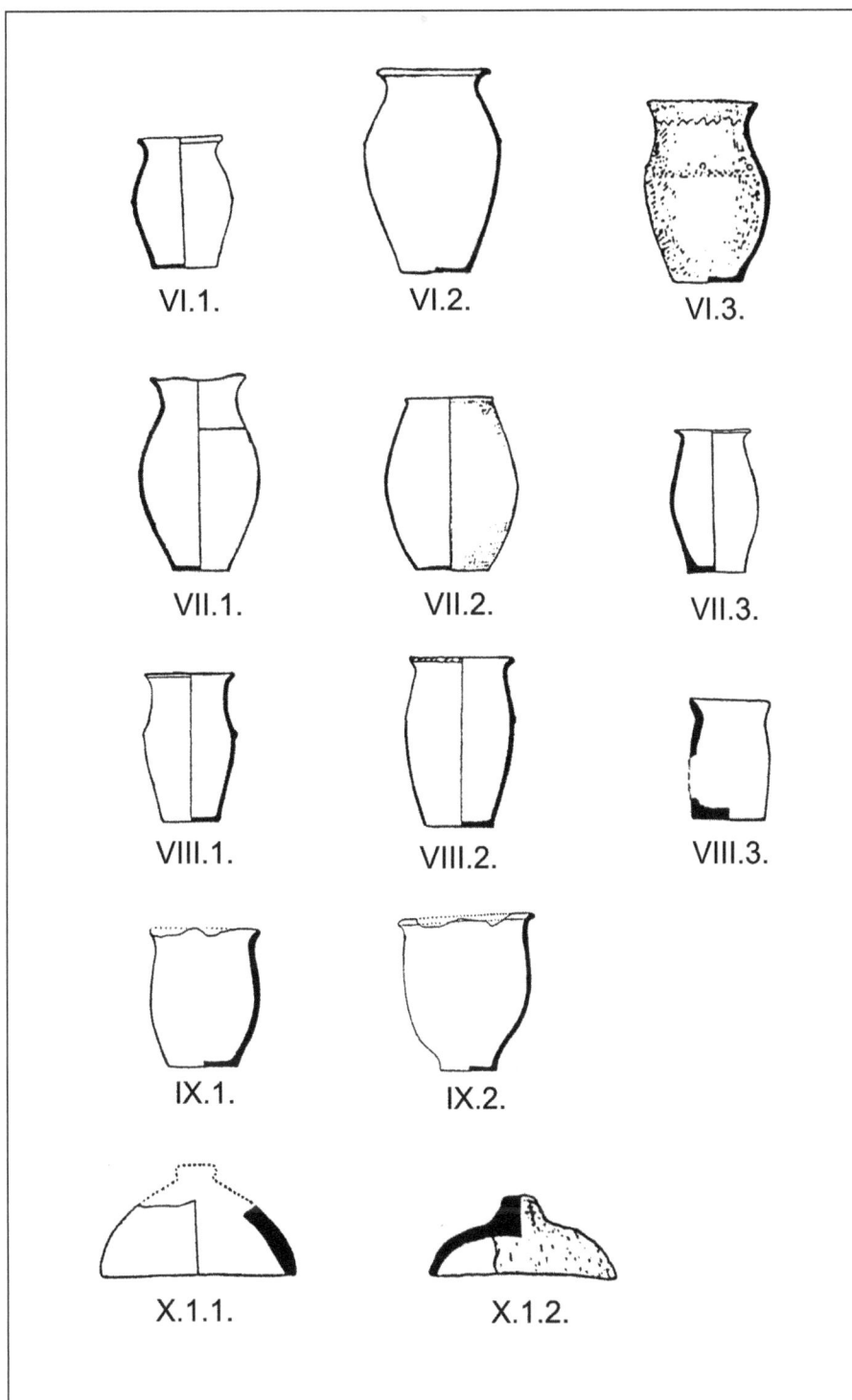

Figure 16. Hand-made pottery. Vessel categories and types.

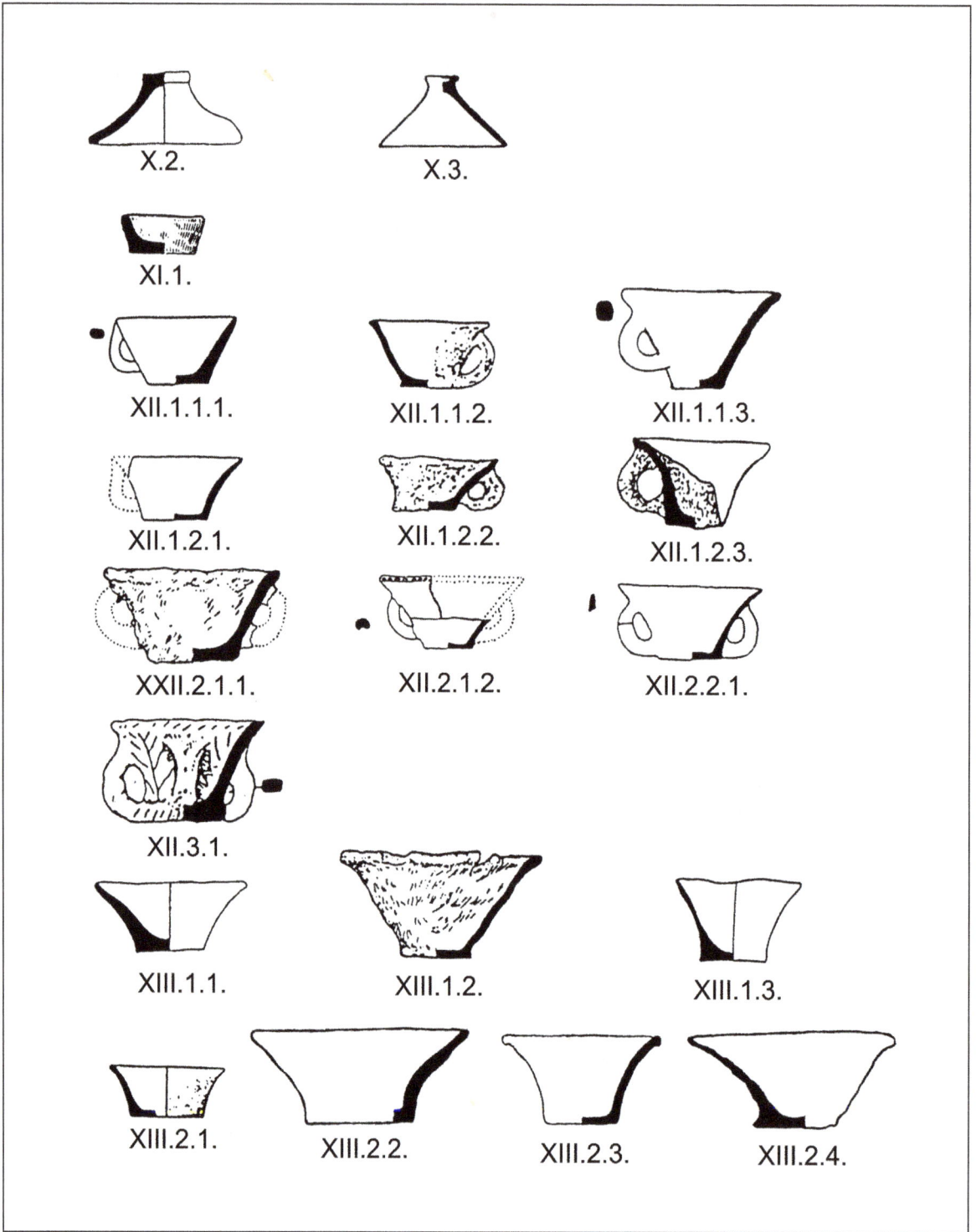

Figure 17. Hand-made pottery. Vessel categories and types.

A.1.

A.2.

B.1.

C.1.

D.1.

E.1.

E.2.

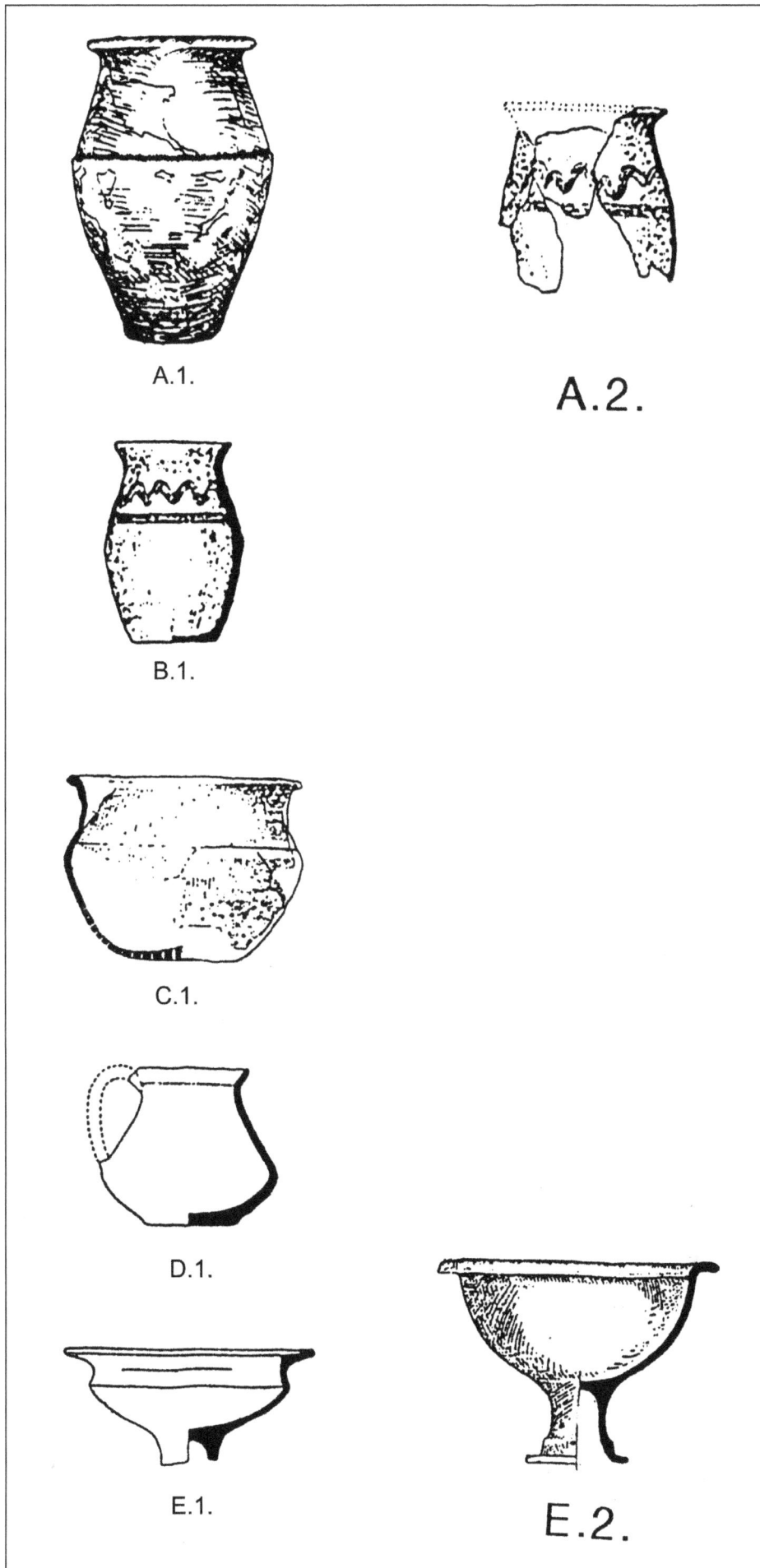

Figure 18. Hand-made pottery. Vessel categories and types.

F.1.1.1.

F.1.2.1.

F.1.2.2.

F.1.2.3.

G.1.1.

G.2.1.

G.2.2.

H.1.

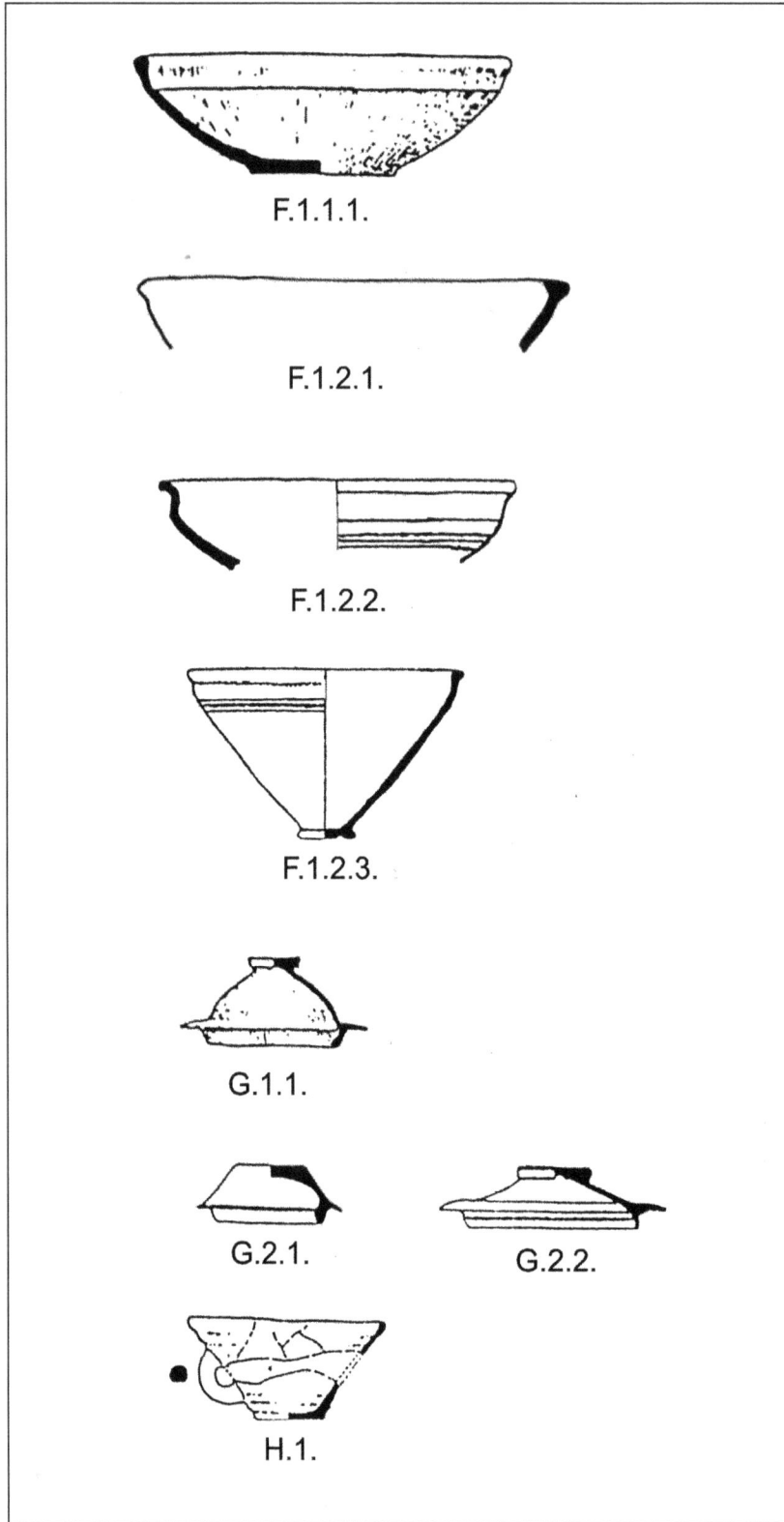

Figure 19. Wheel-made pottery. Vessel categories and types.

1.1.1.

1.1.2.

1.1.3.

1.1.4.

1.2.1

1.2.2.

1.2.3

1.3.

1.4.1.1.

1.4.1.2.

1.4.1.3.

1.4.2.

1.4.3.

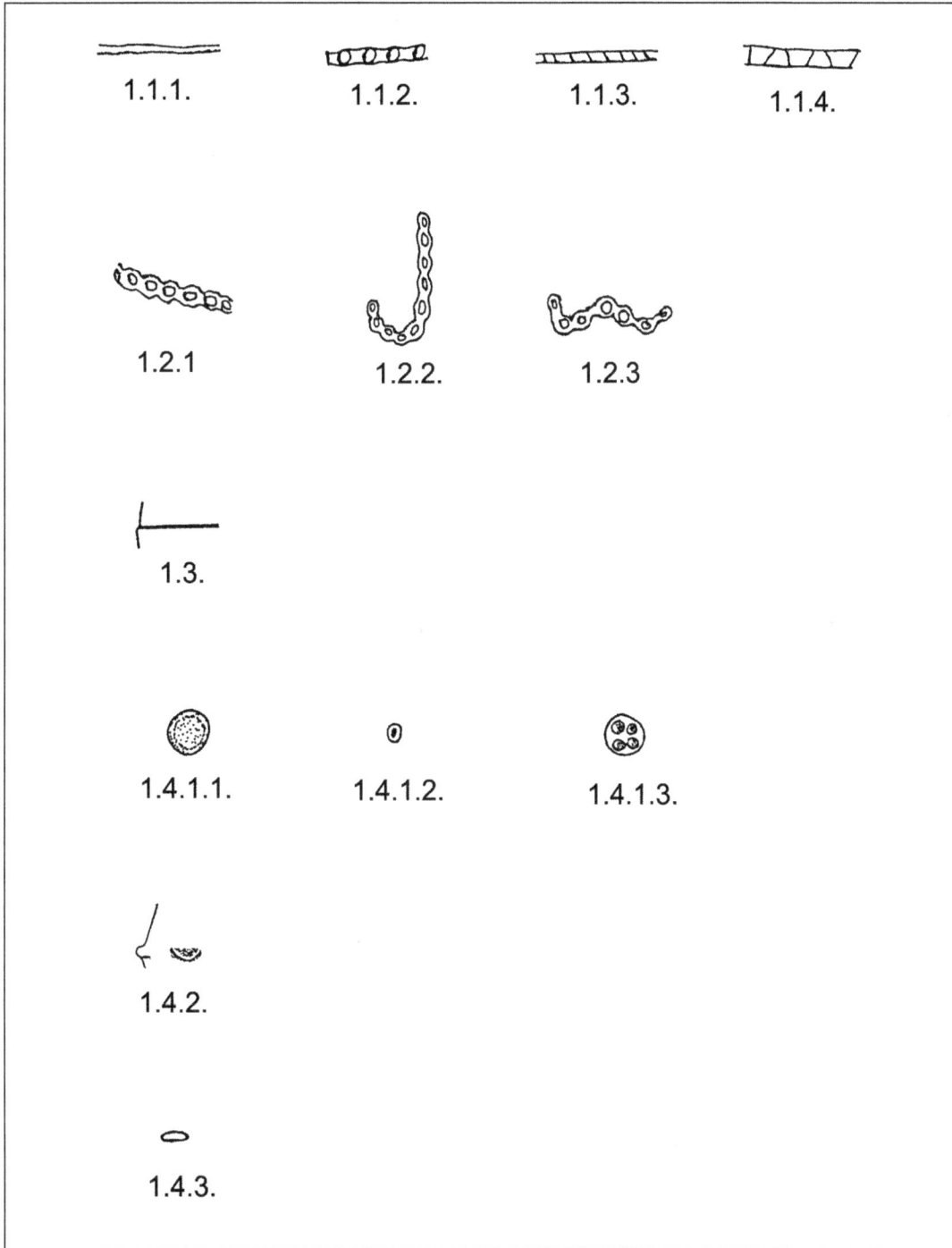

Figure 20. Hand-made pottery. Decorative motifs.

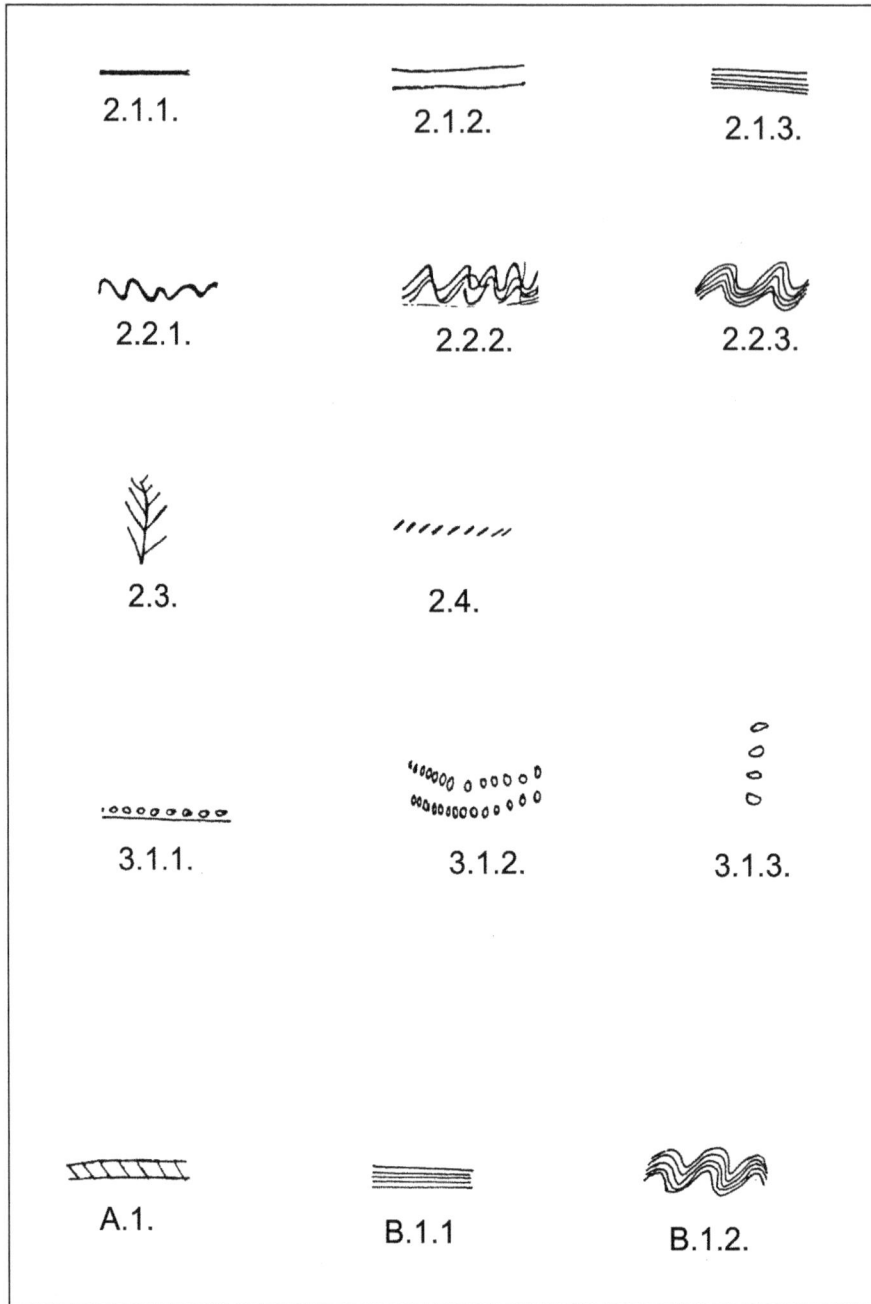

Figure 21. Hand-made and wheel-made pottery. Decorative motifs.

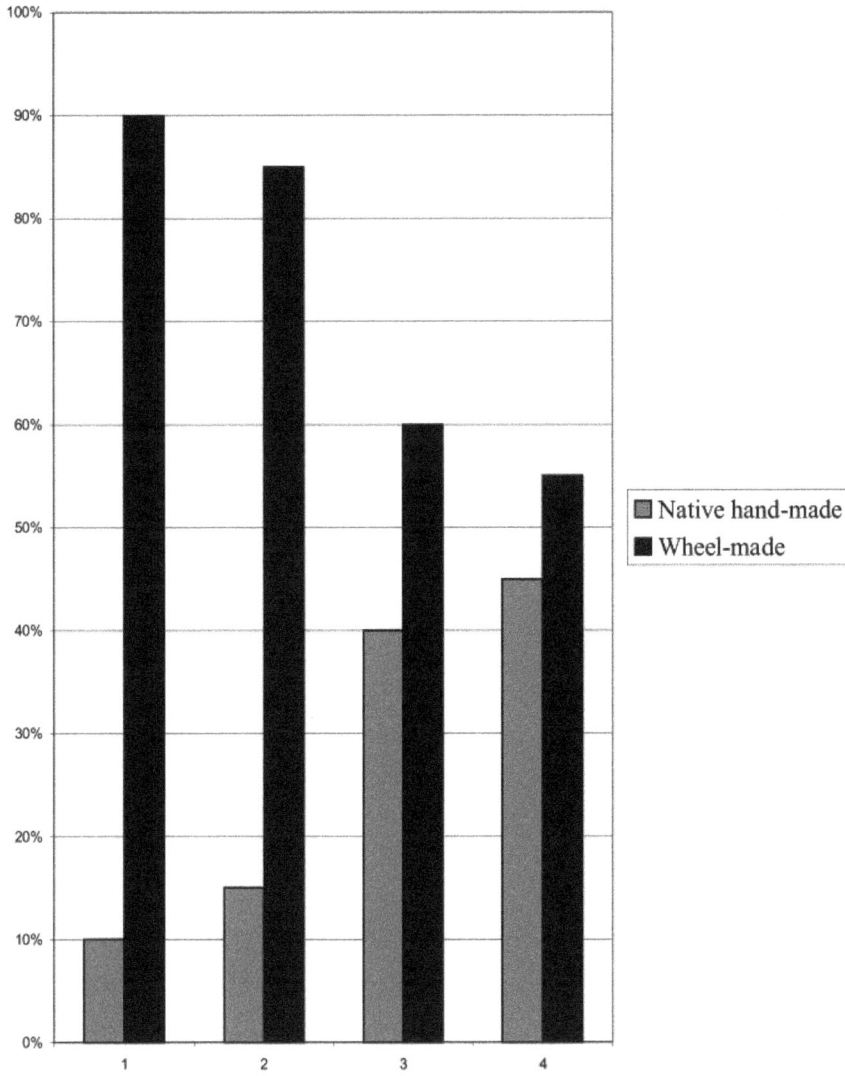

Figure 22. Native hand-made and wheel-made pottery discovered in some rural settlements from Roman Dacia.

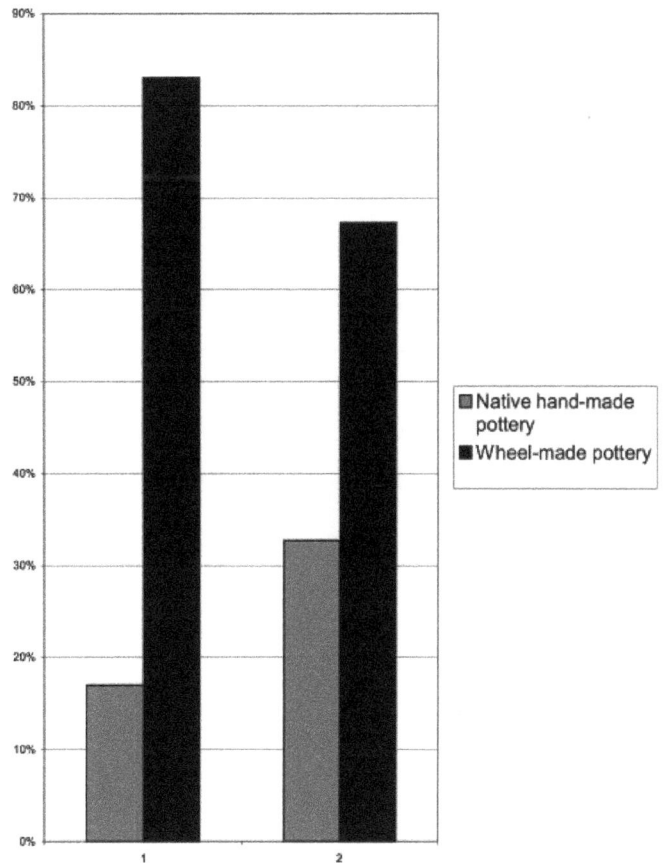

Figure 23. Native hand-made pottery discovered in the Locusteni and Soporu de Câmpie cemeteries.

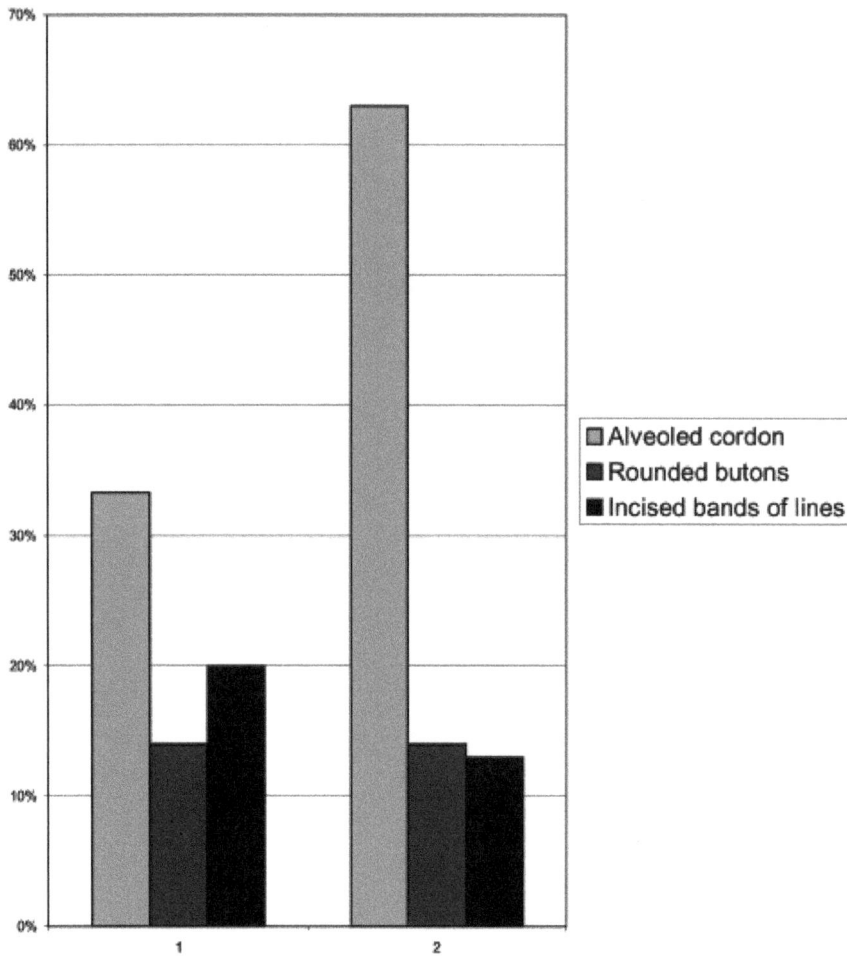

Figure 24. Decoration on the native hand-made pottery discovered in the Locusteni and Soporu de Câmpie cemeteries.

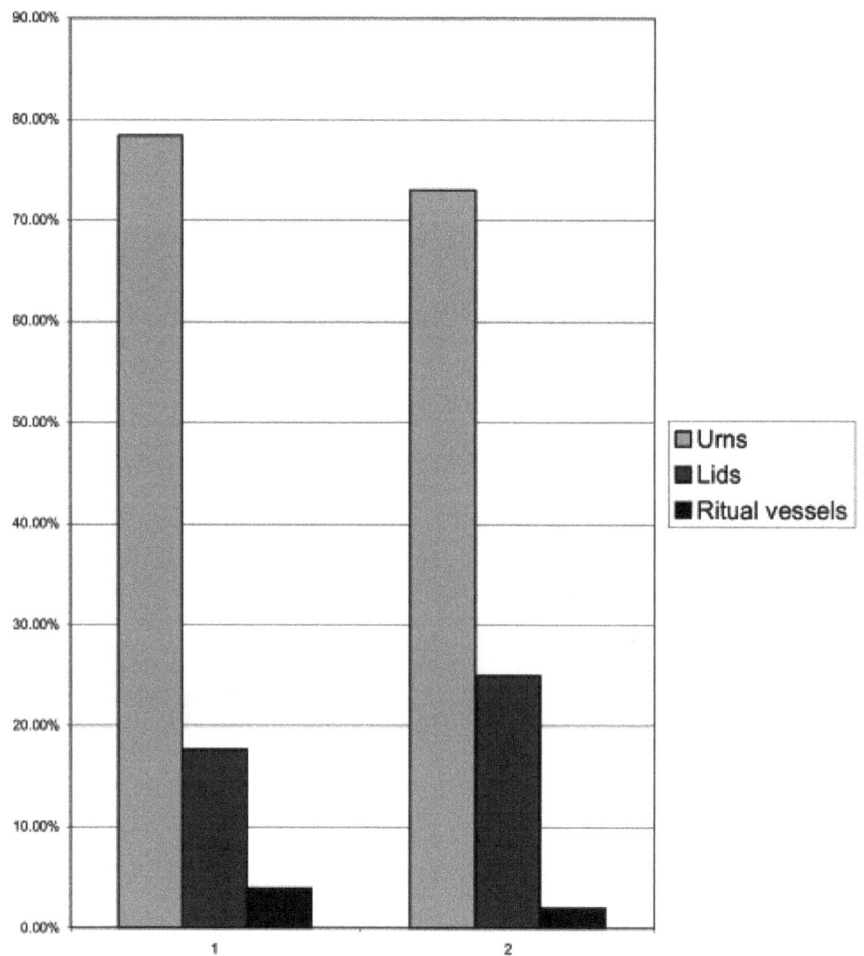

Figure 25. Decorative techniques on the native hand-made pottery discovered in the Locusteni and Soporu de Câmpie cemeteries.

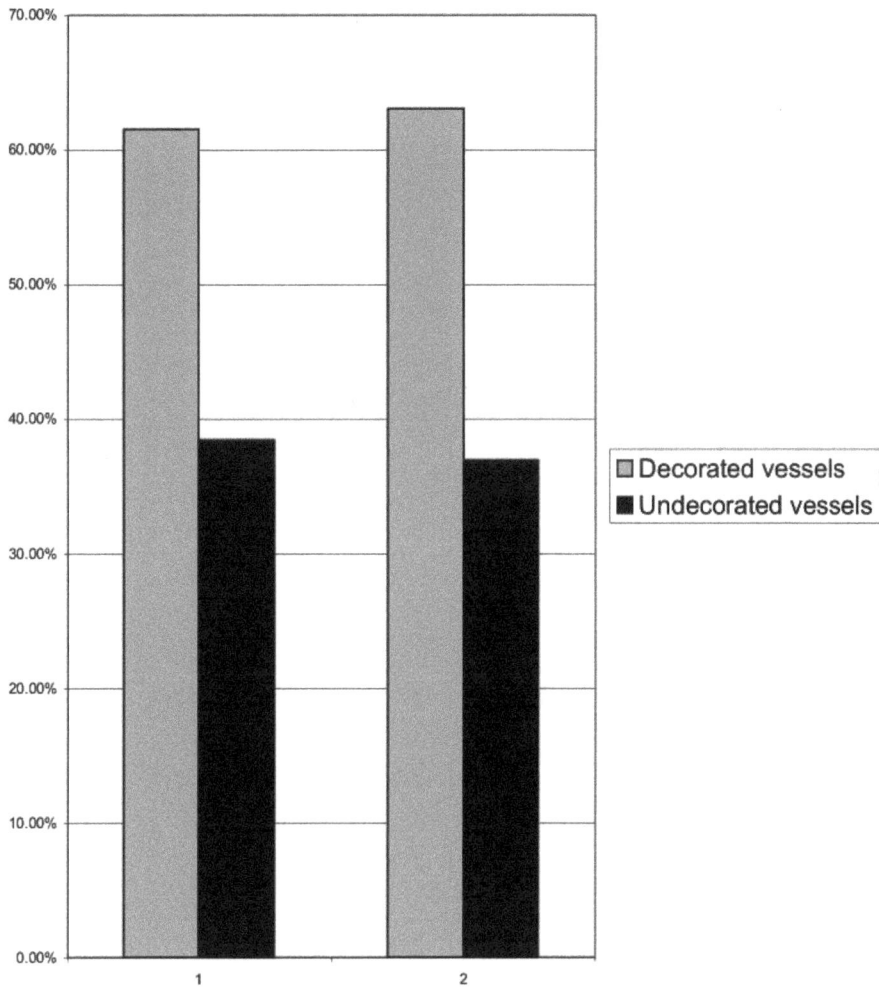

Figure 26. The functions of the native hand-made pottery discovered
in the Locusteni and Soporu de Câmpie cemeteries.

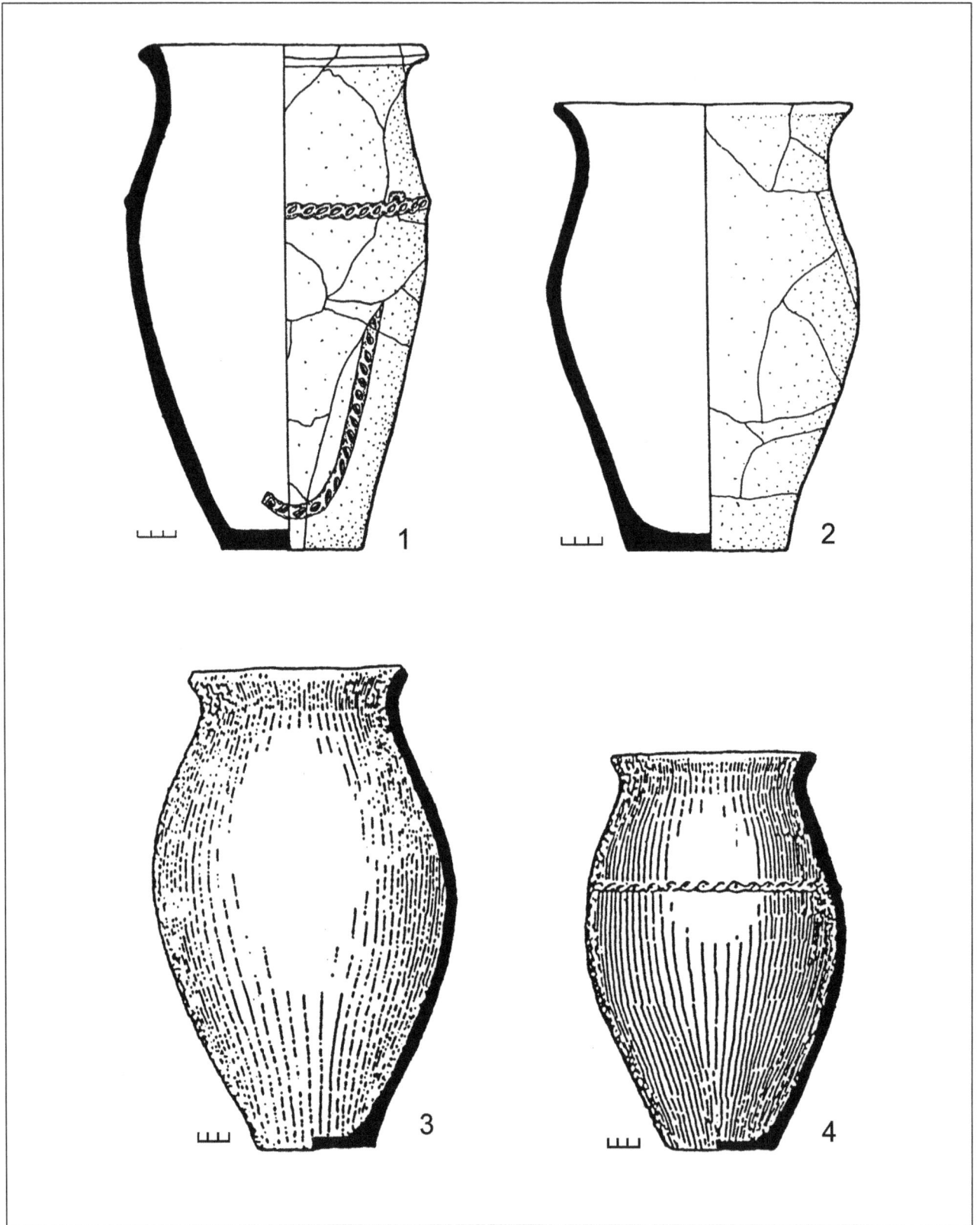

Plate 1. Ovoid jars: type 1 (1-4).

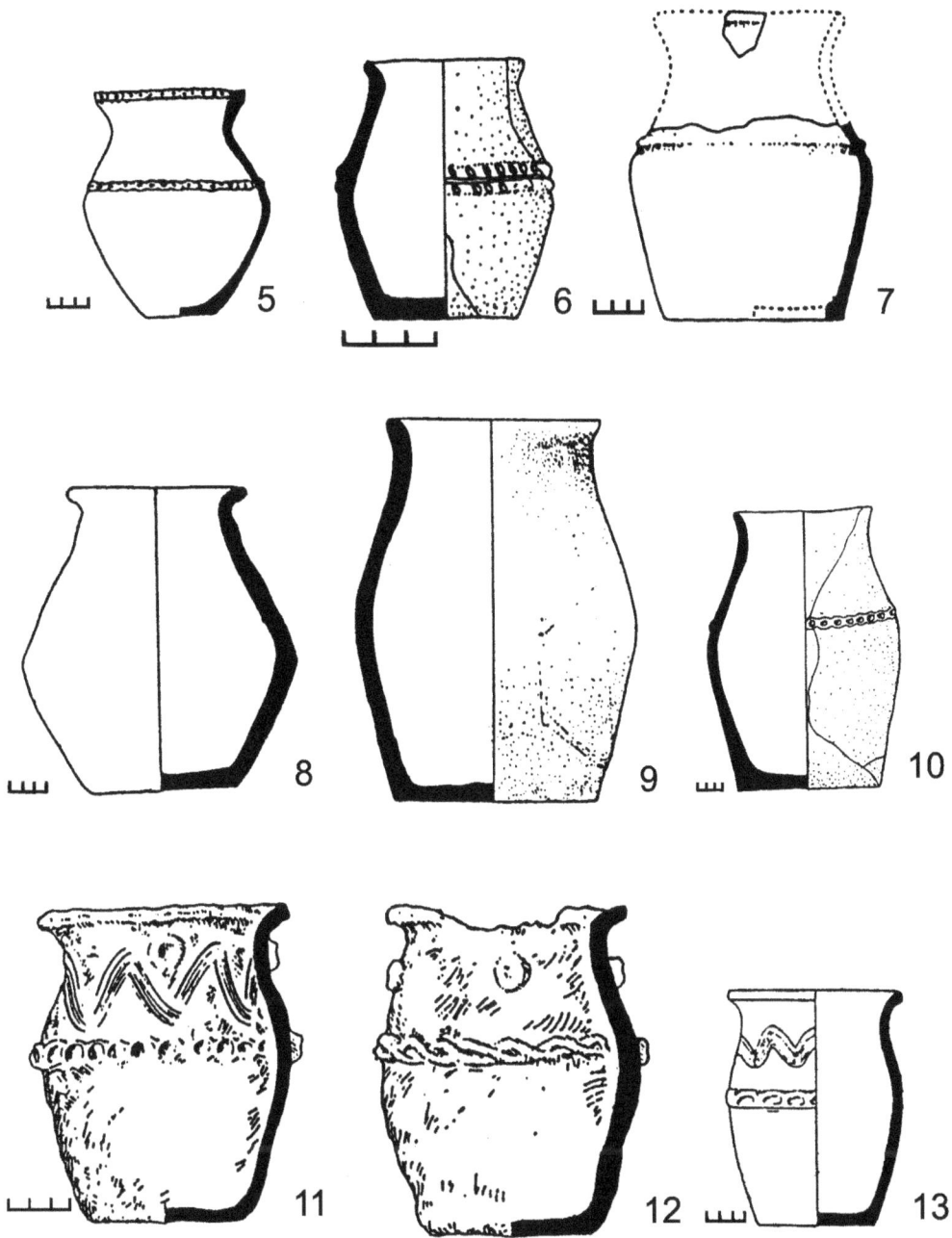

Plate 2. Ovoid jars: type 1 (5-10); type 2 (11-13).

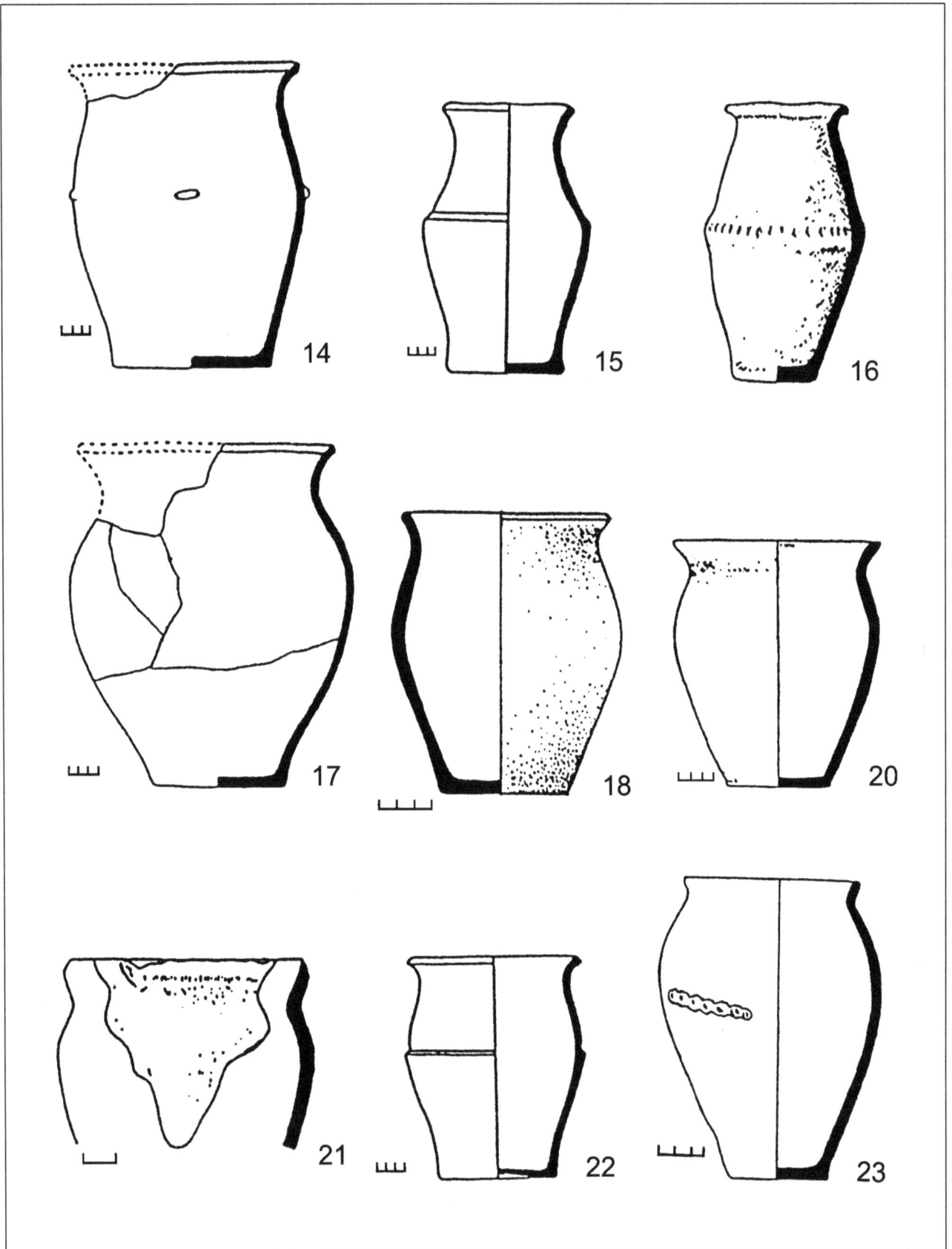

Plate 3. Biconical jars: type 1 (14); type 2 (15, 16); bell-shaped jars: type 1 (17, 18, 20-22); pear-shaped jars: type 1 (23).

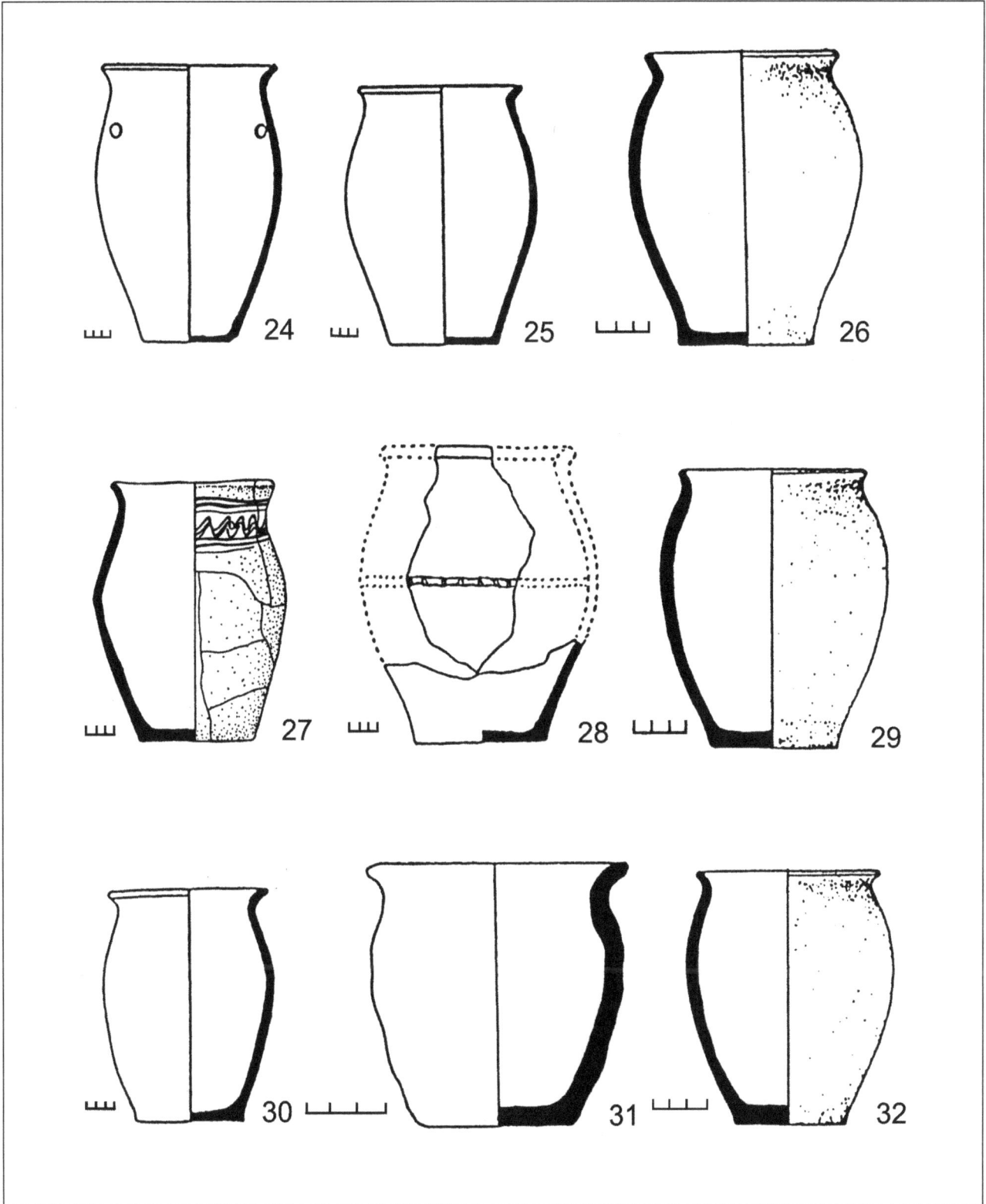

Plate 4. Pear-shaped jars: type 1 (24-32).

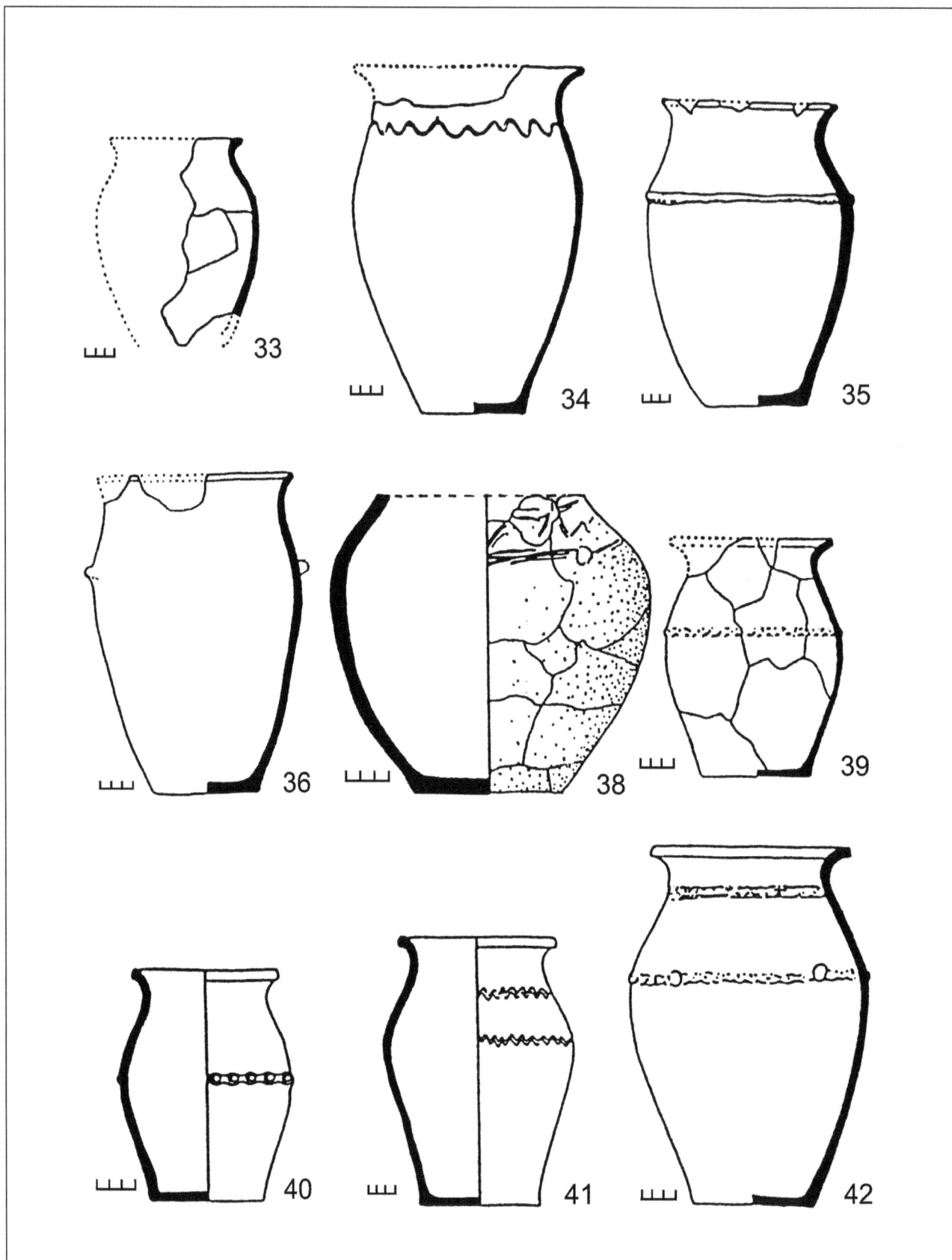

Plate 5. Pear-shaped jars: type 2 (33-36); globular jar (38); pots: type 1 (39, 40); type 2 (41, 42).

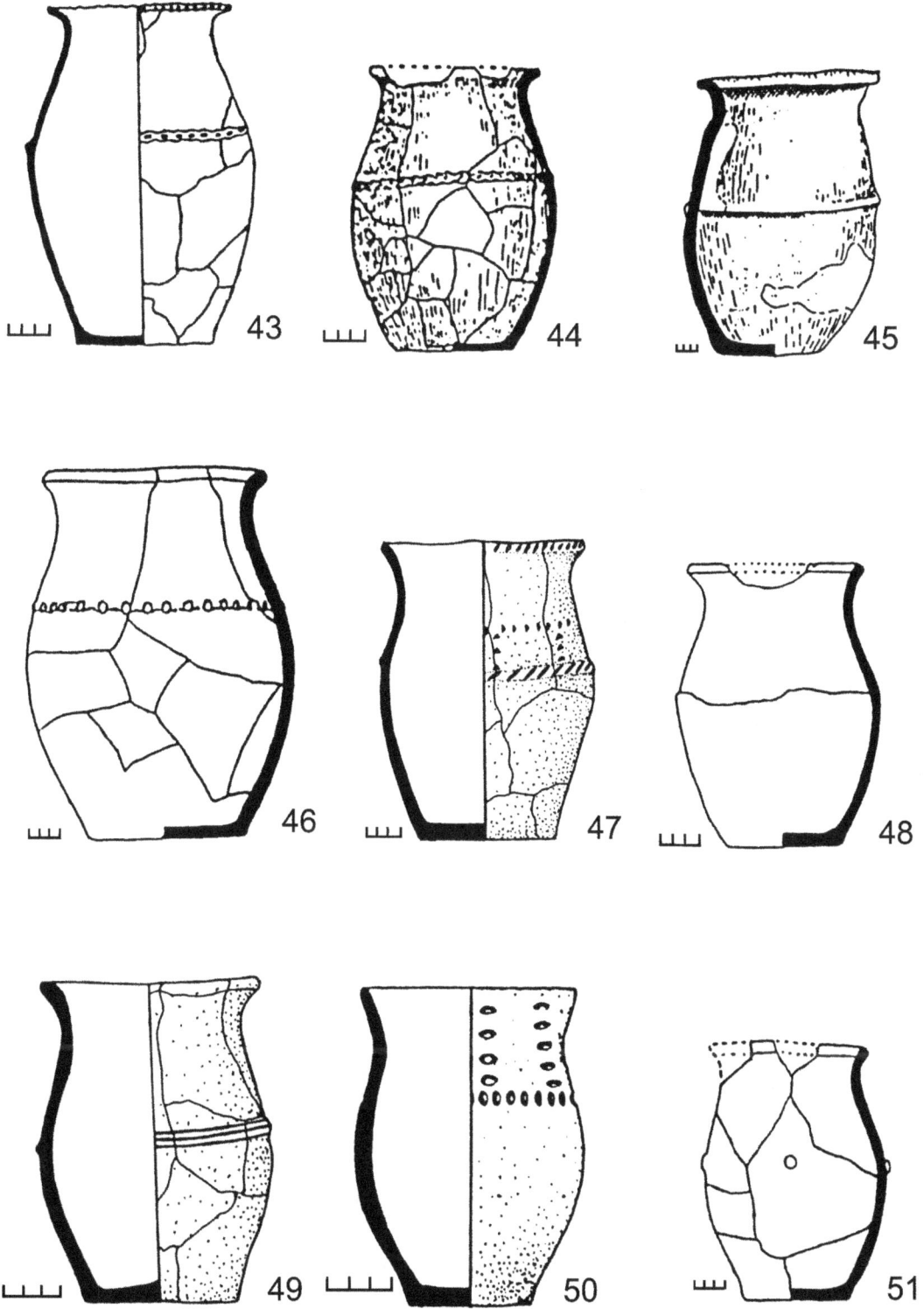

Plate 6. Pots: type 3 (43-51).

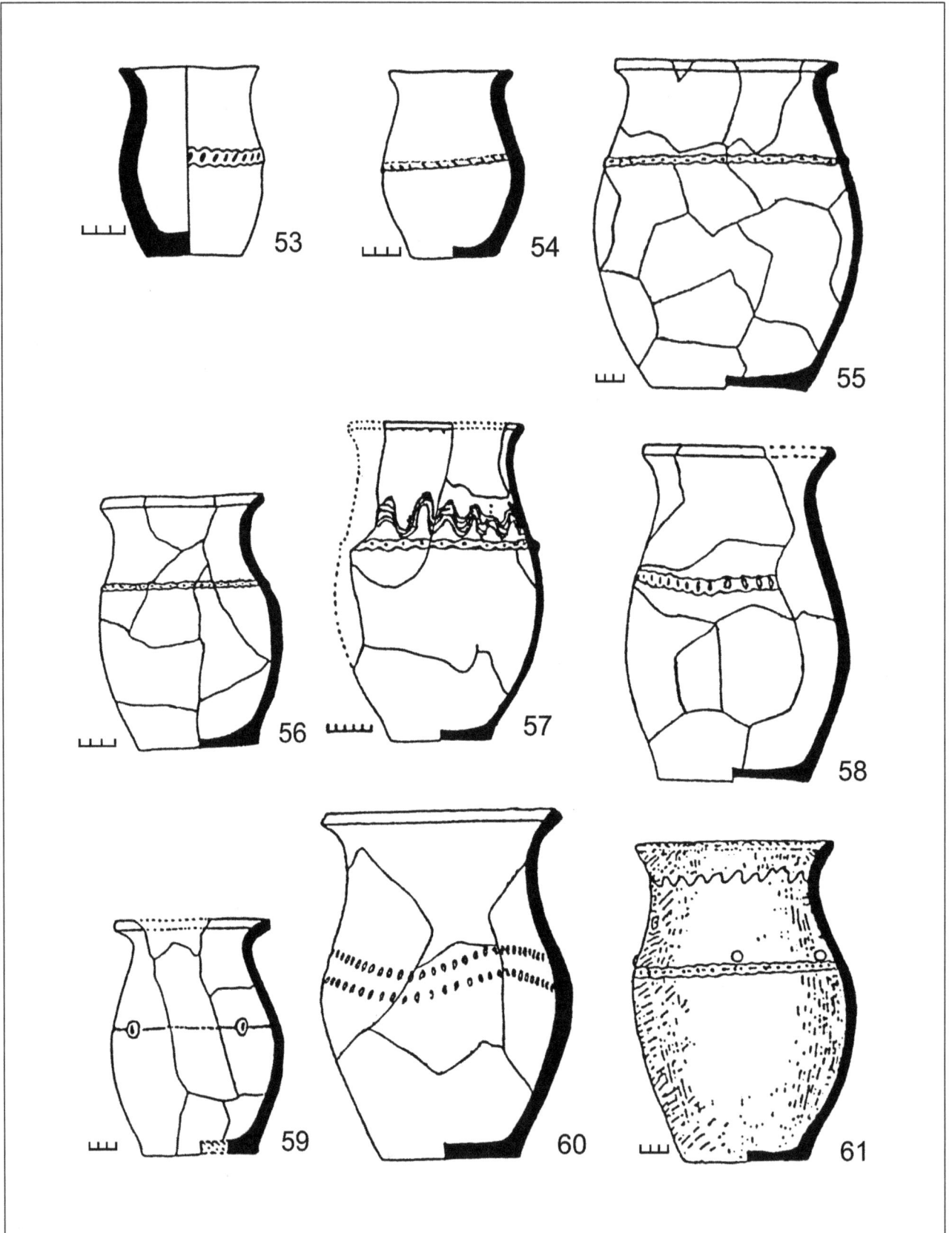

Plate 7. Pots: type 3 (52-61).

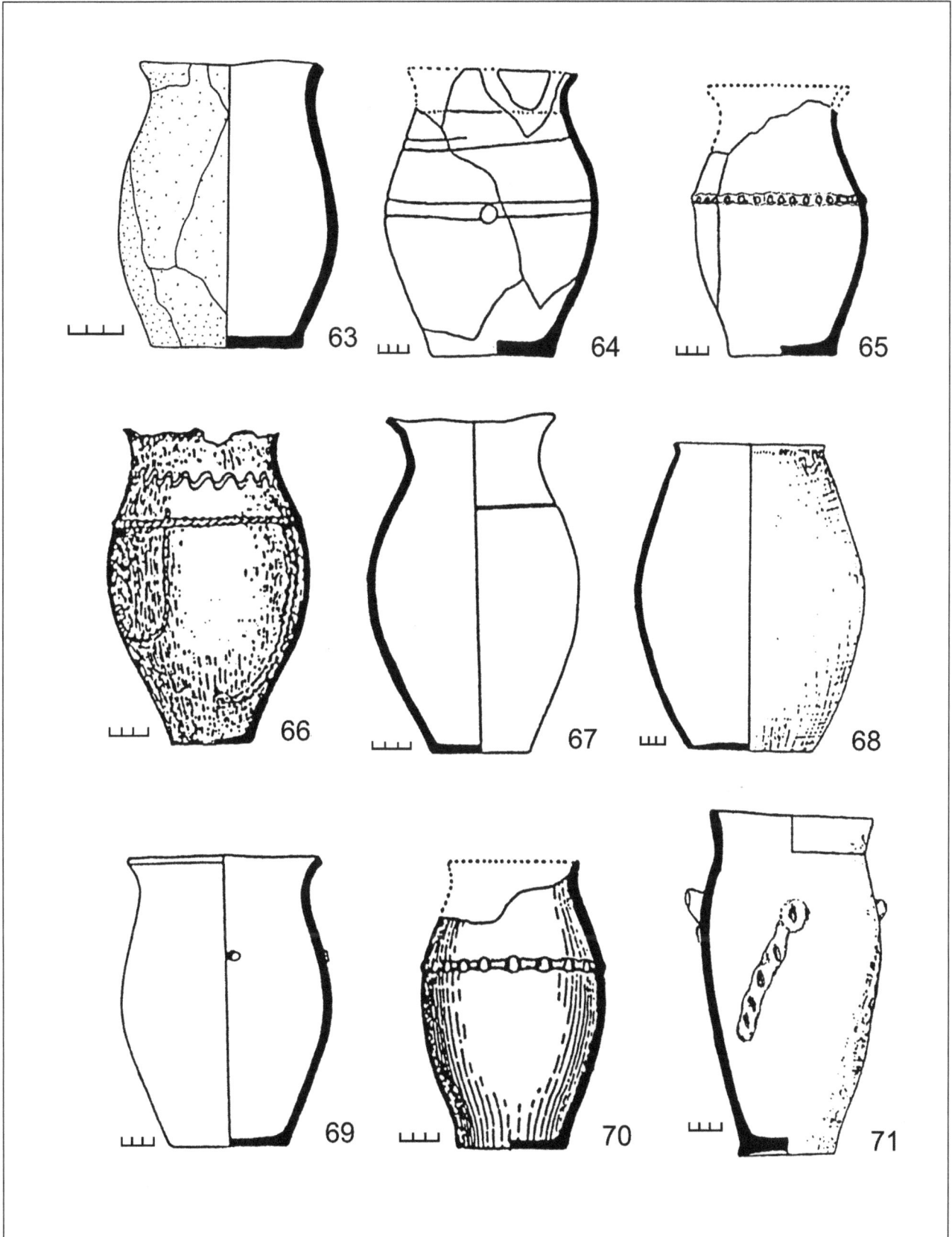

Plate 8. Pots: type 3 (63-65); ovoid jars: type 1 (66, 67); type 2 (68-70); type 3 (71).

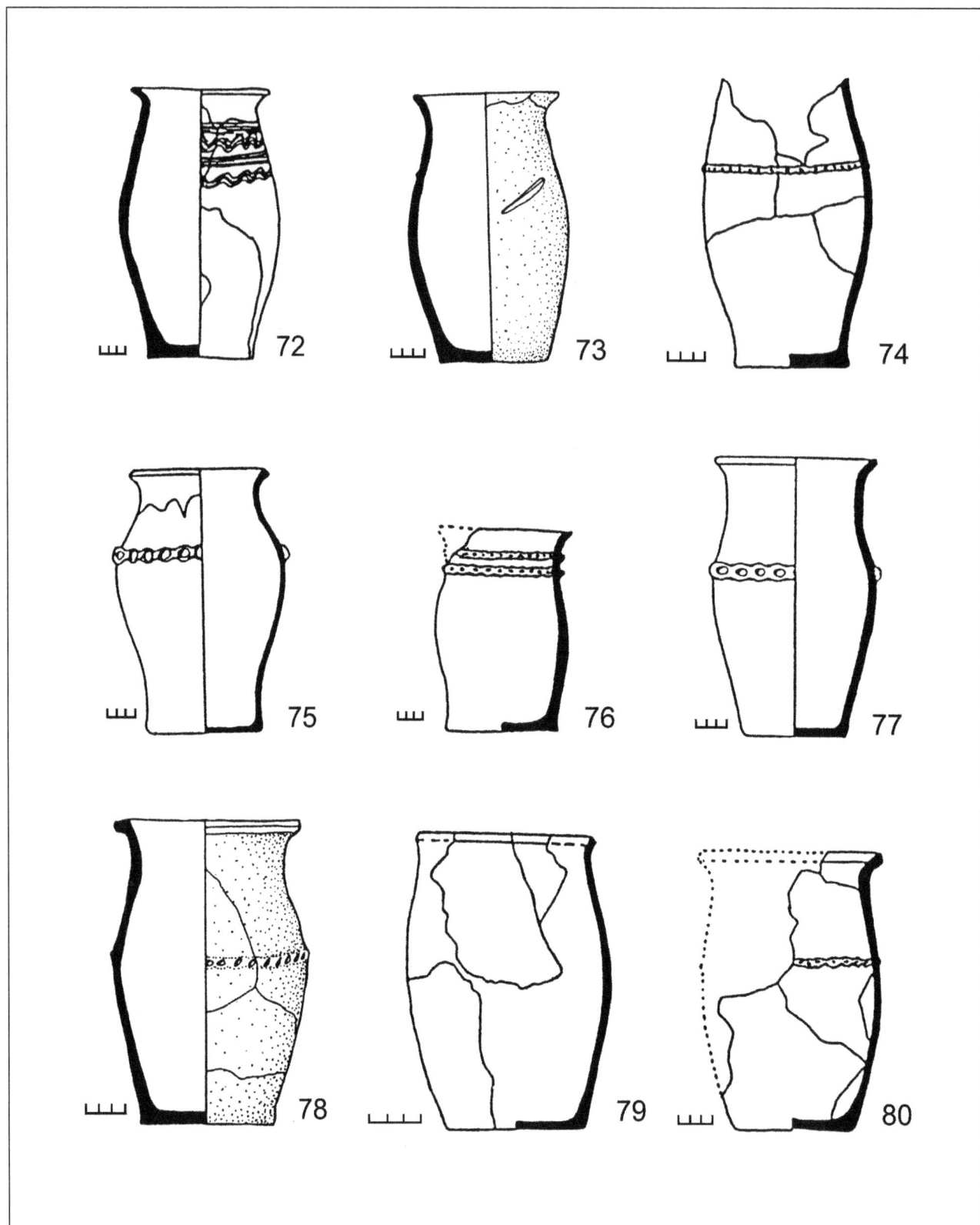

Plate 9. Ovoid jars: type 3 (72-74); tall cylindrical jars: type 1 (75-78); type 2 (79-80).

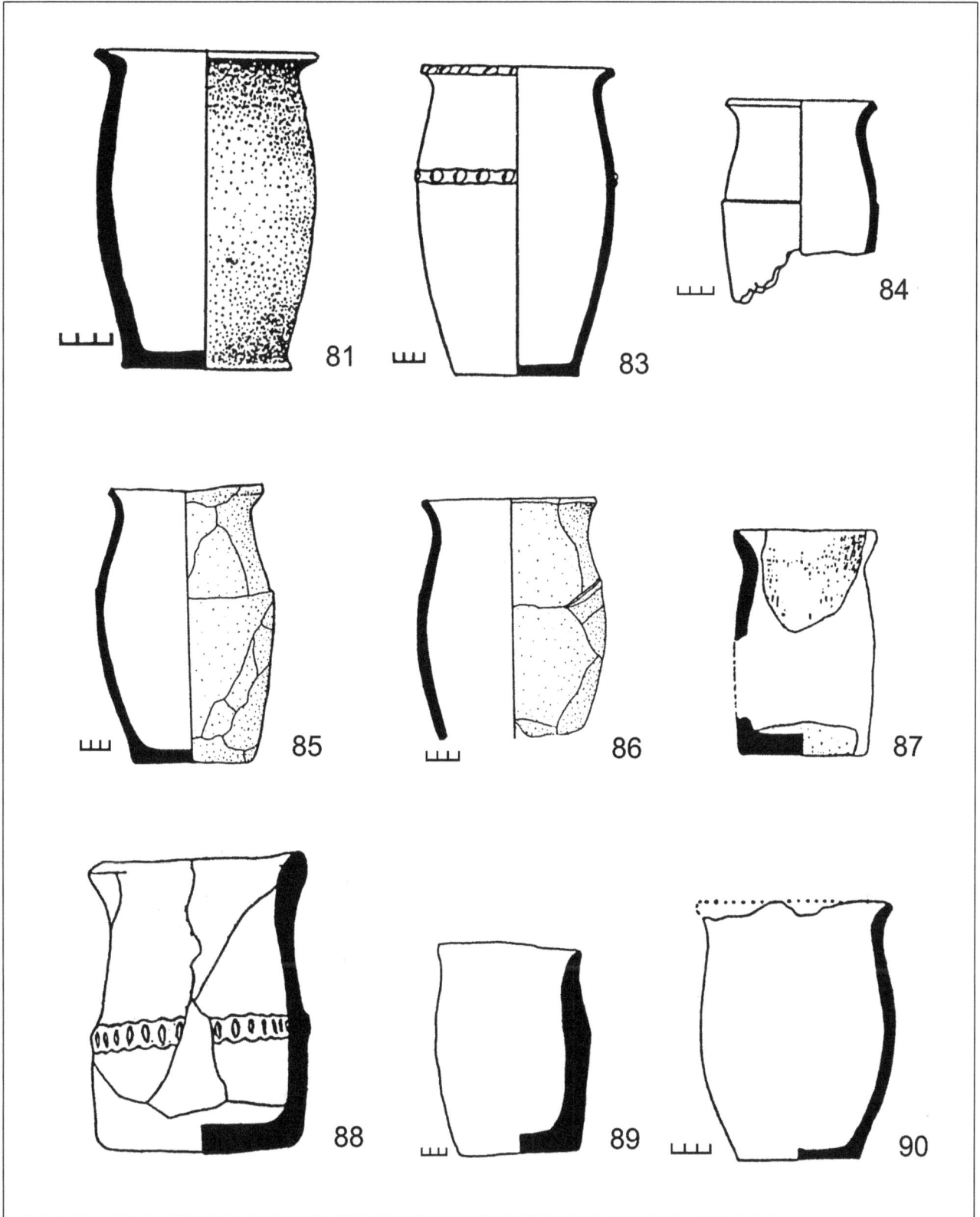

Plate 10. Tall cylindrical jars: type 2 (81; 83-86); type 3 (87, 88); large cylindrical jars: type 1 (89, 90).

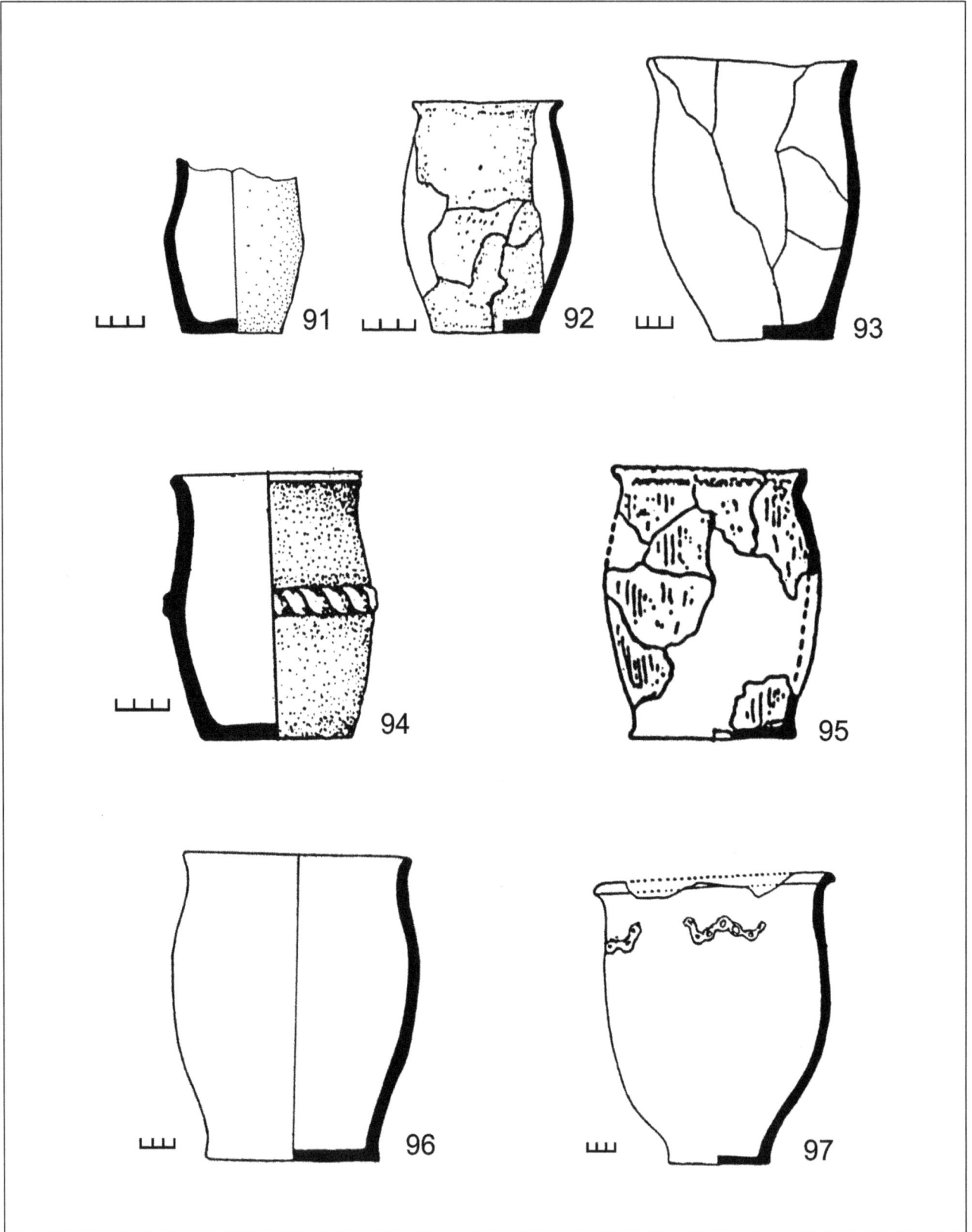

Plate 11. Large cylindrical jars: type 1 (91-96); type 2 (97).

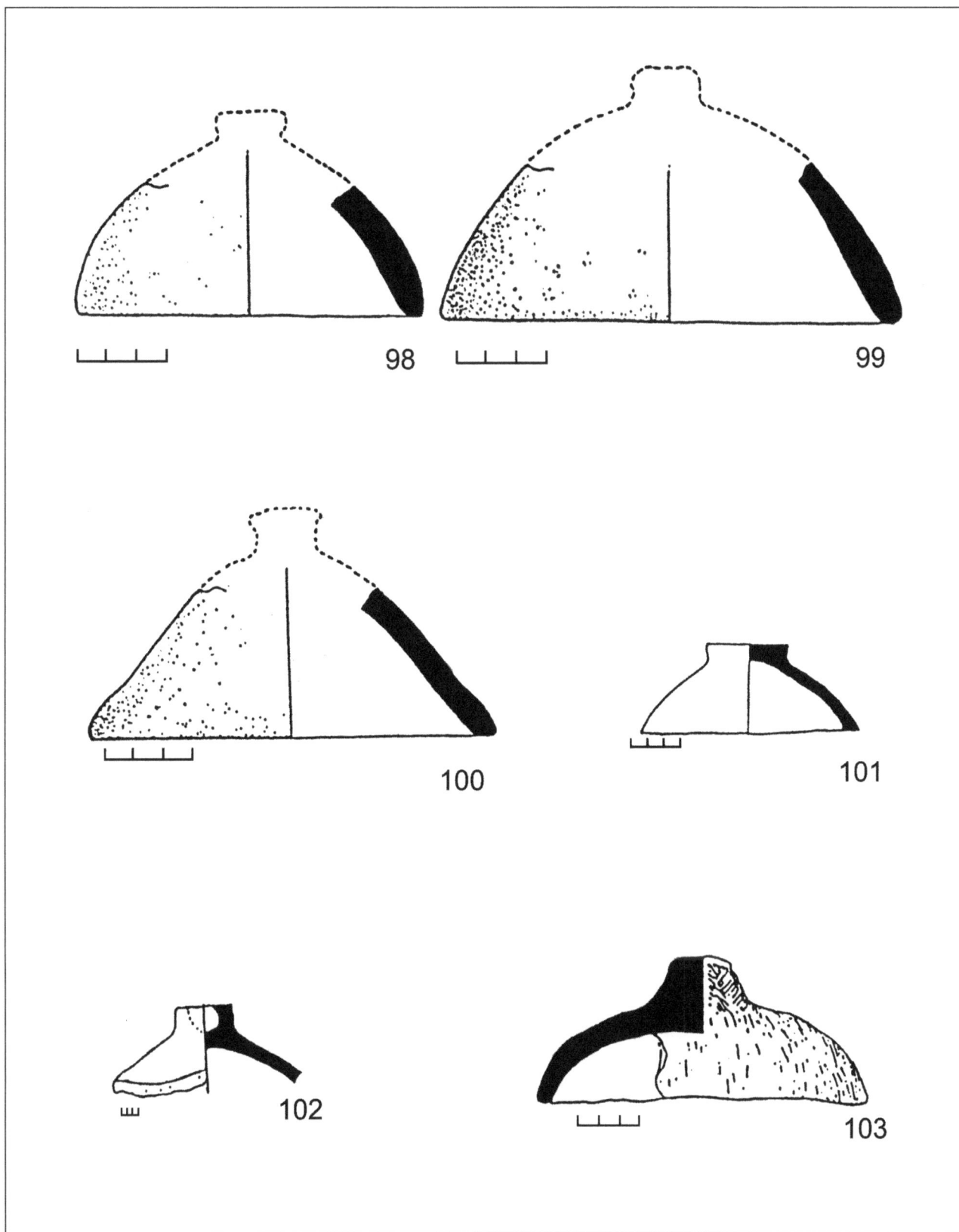

Plate 12. Hemispherical lids: type 1 (98-100); type 2 (101-103).

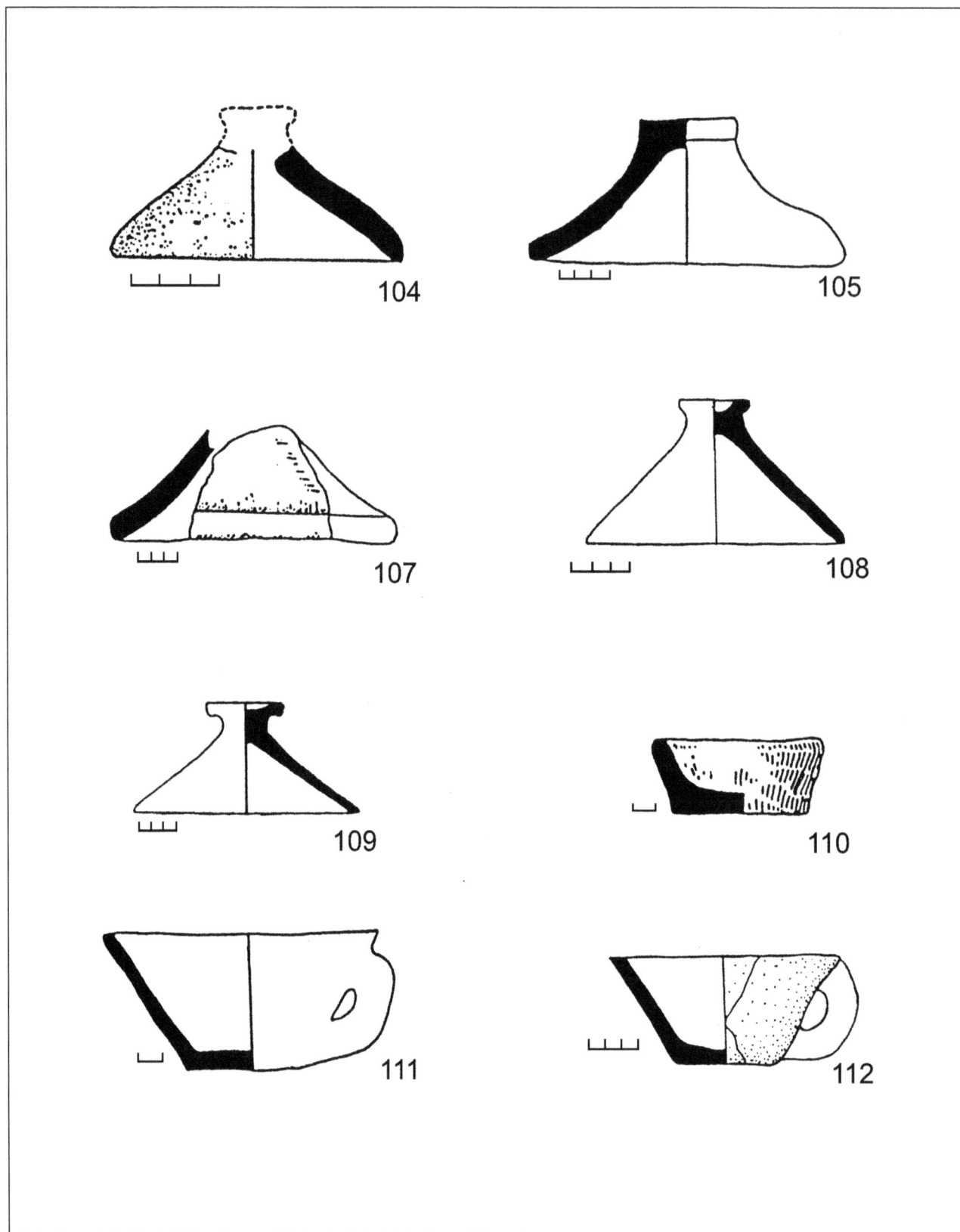

Plate 13. Conical lids: type 1 (104-107); type 2 (108, 109); trays (110); Dacian cups with handle: type 1 (111, 112)

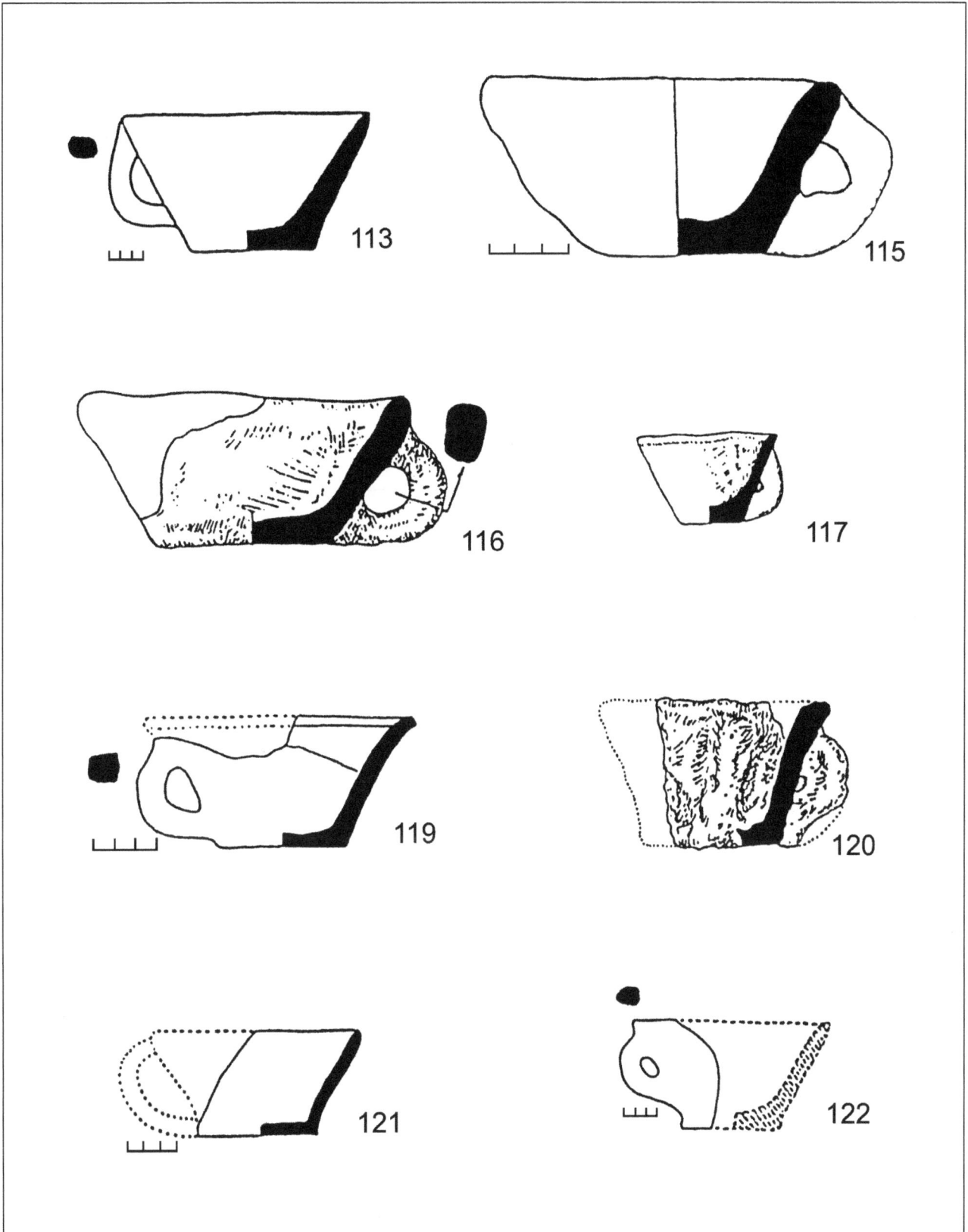

Plate 14. Dacian cups with handle: type 1 (113, 115-117, 119-122).

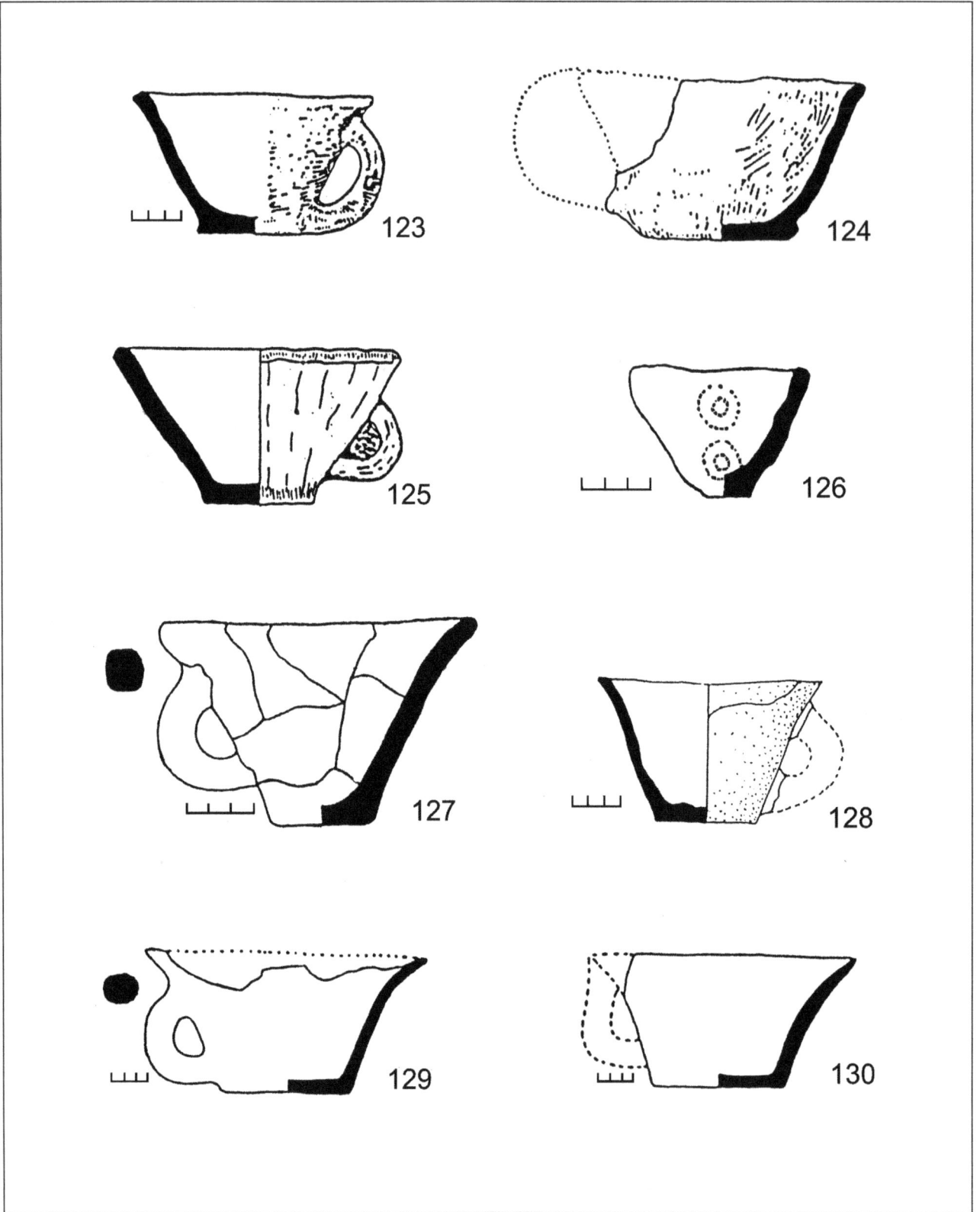

Plate 15. Dacian cups with handle: type 1 (123-128); type 2 (129, 130).

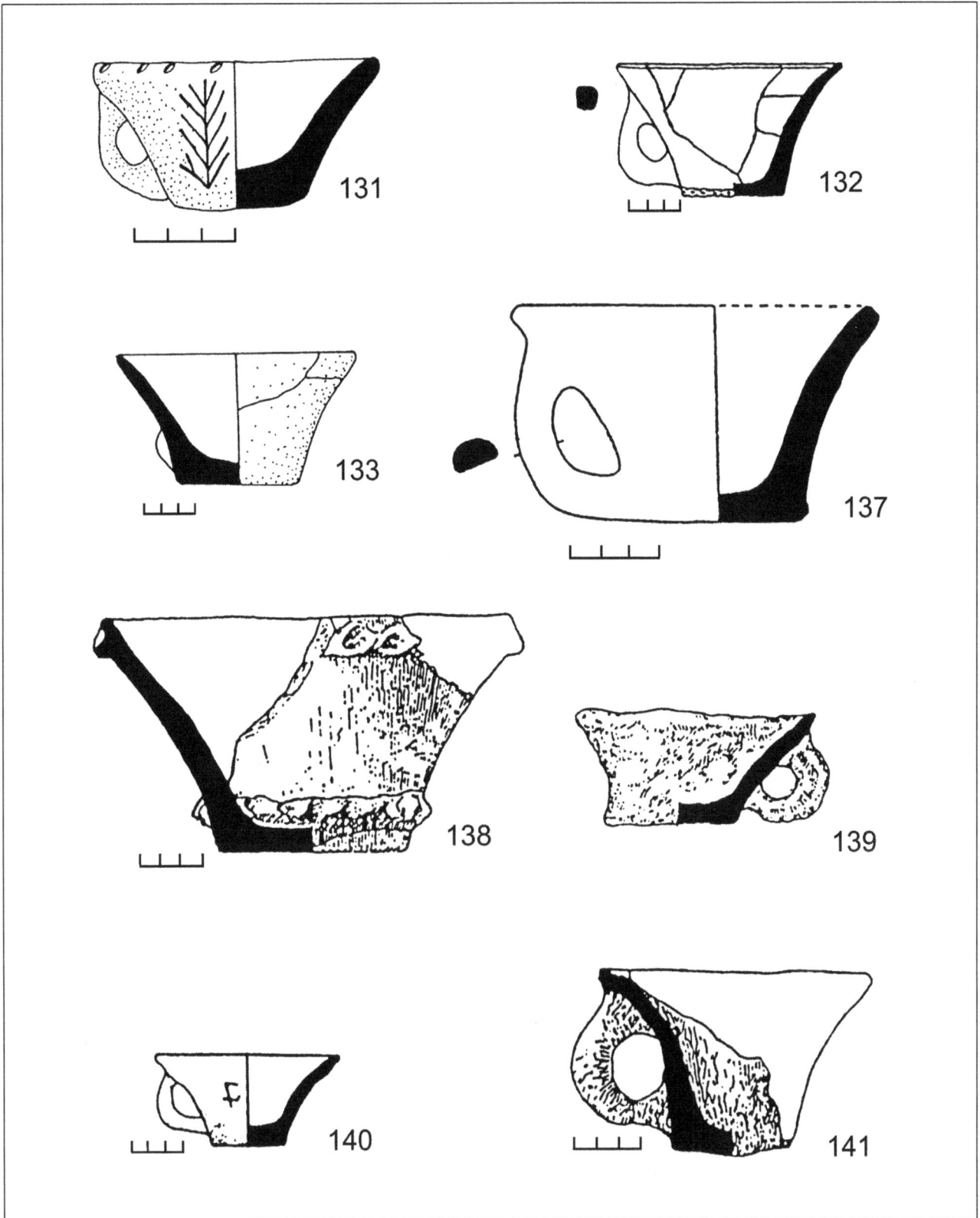

Plate 16. Dacian cups with handle: type 2 (131-133, 136-141).

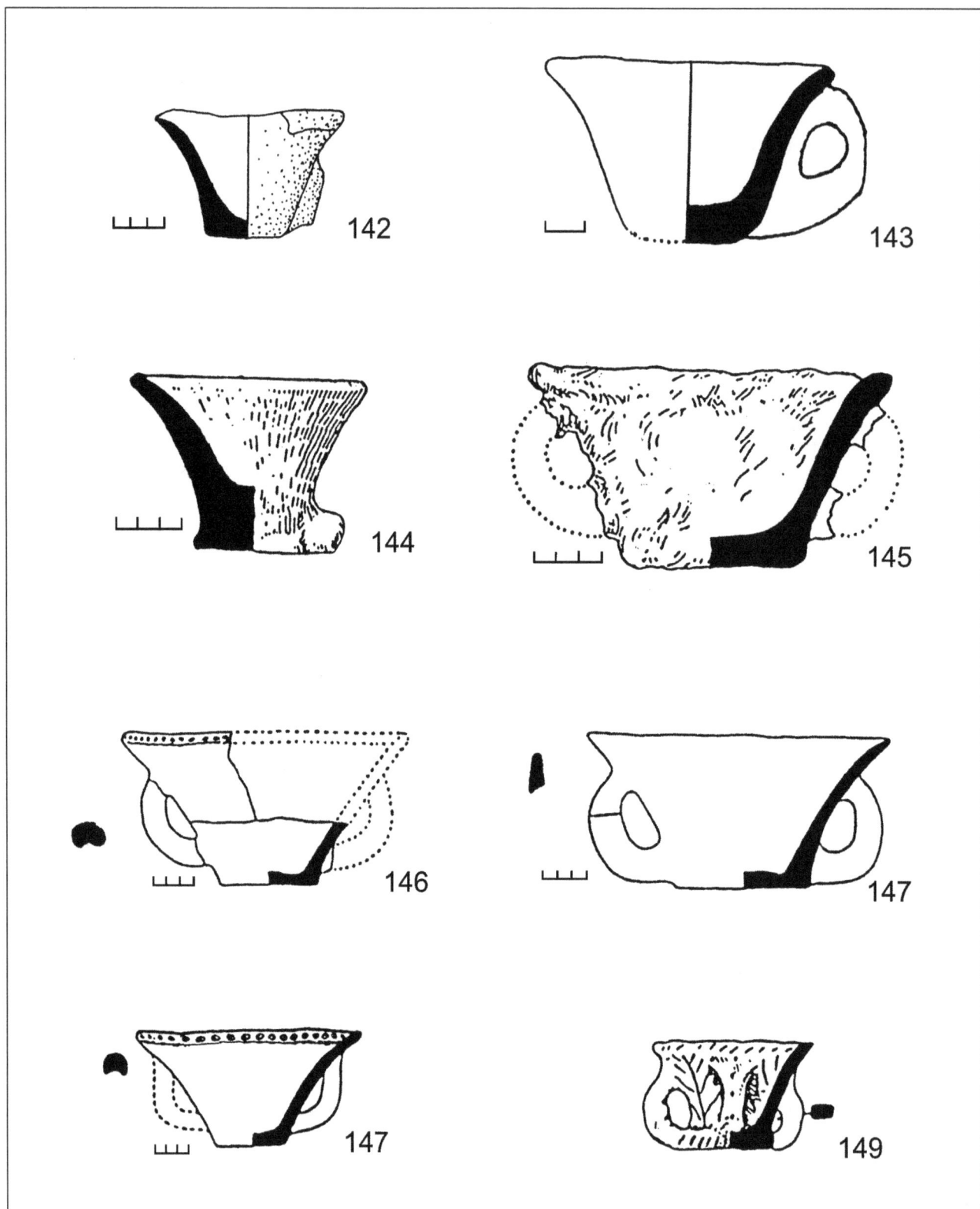

Plate 17. Dacian cups with handle: type 2 (142-144); Dacian cups with two handles: type 1 (145-147); type 2 (148, 149); Dacian cup with three handles (150).

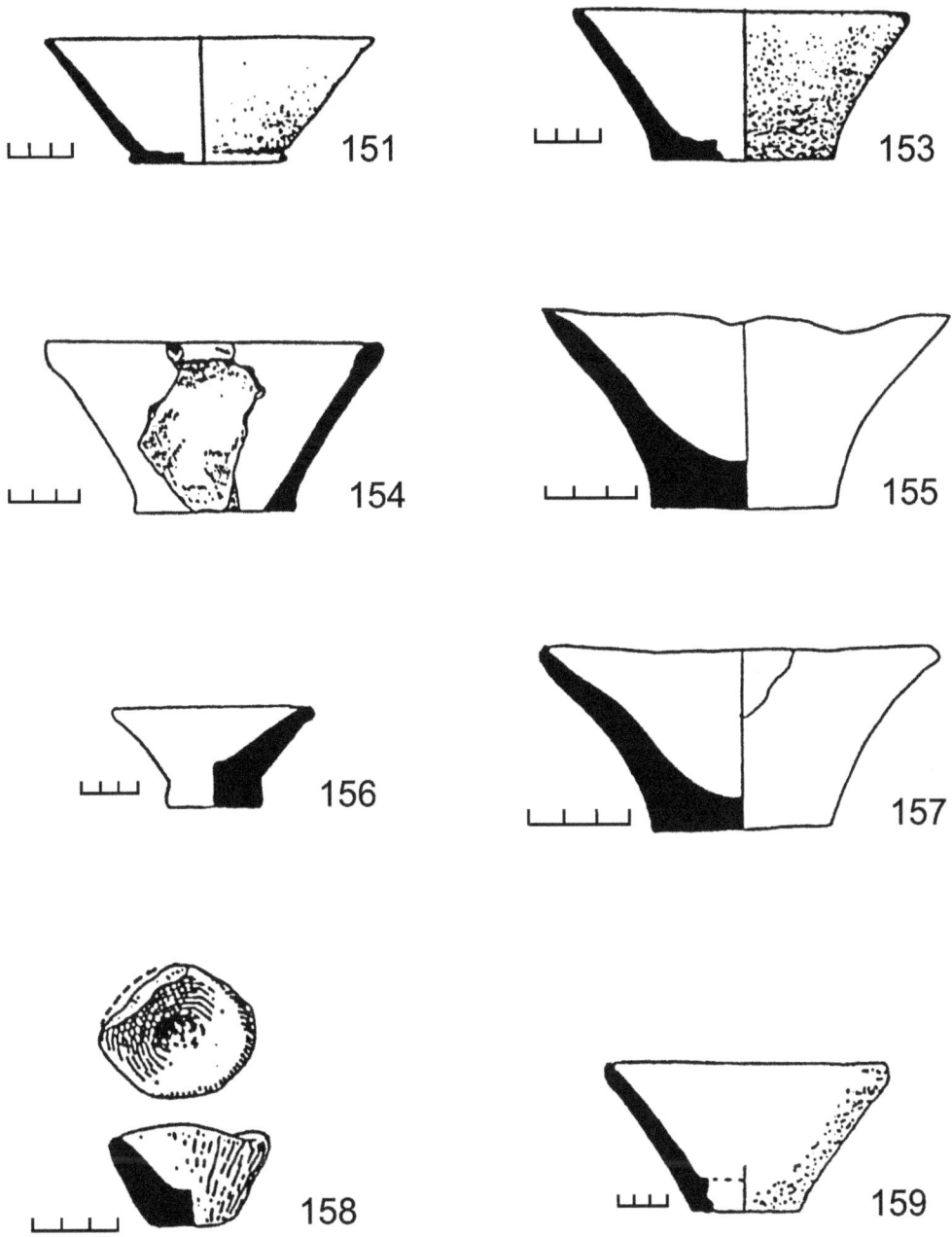

Plate 18. Conical vessels: type 1 (151, 153-159).

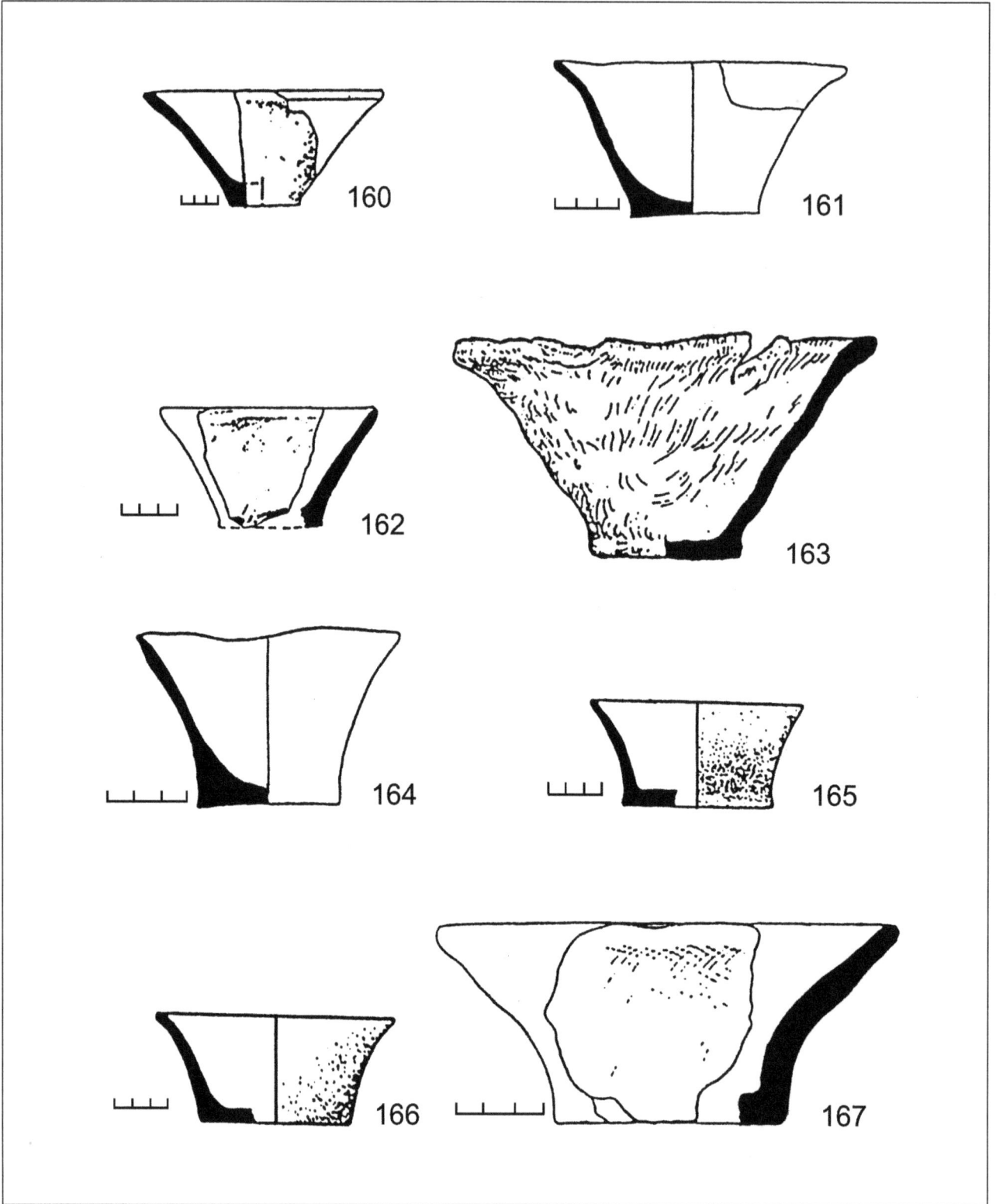

Plate 19. Conical vessels: type 2 (160-167).

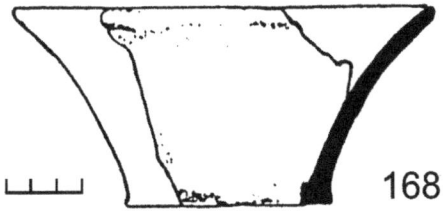

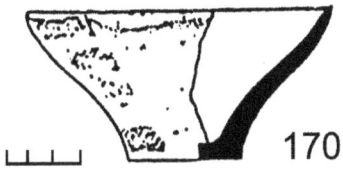

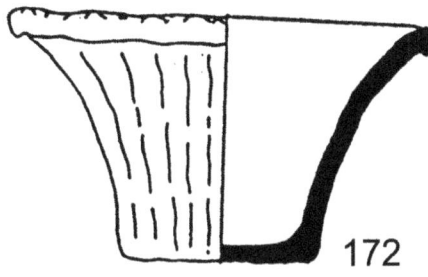

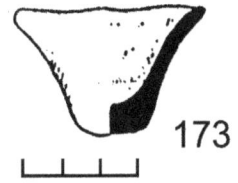

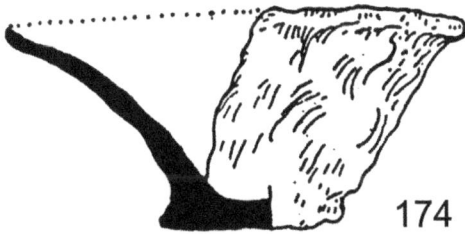

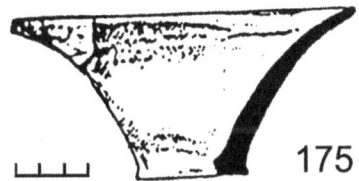

Plate 20. Conical vessels: type 2 (168-175).

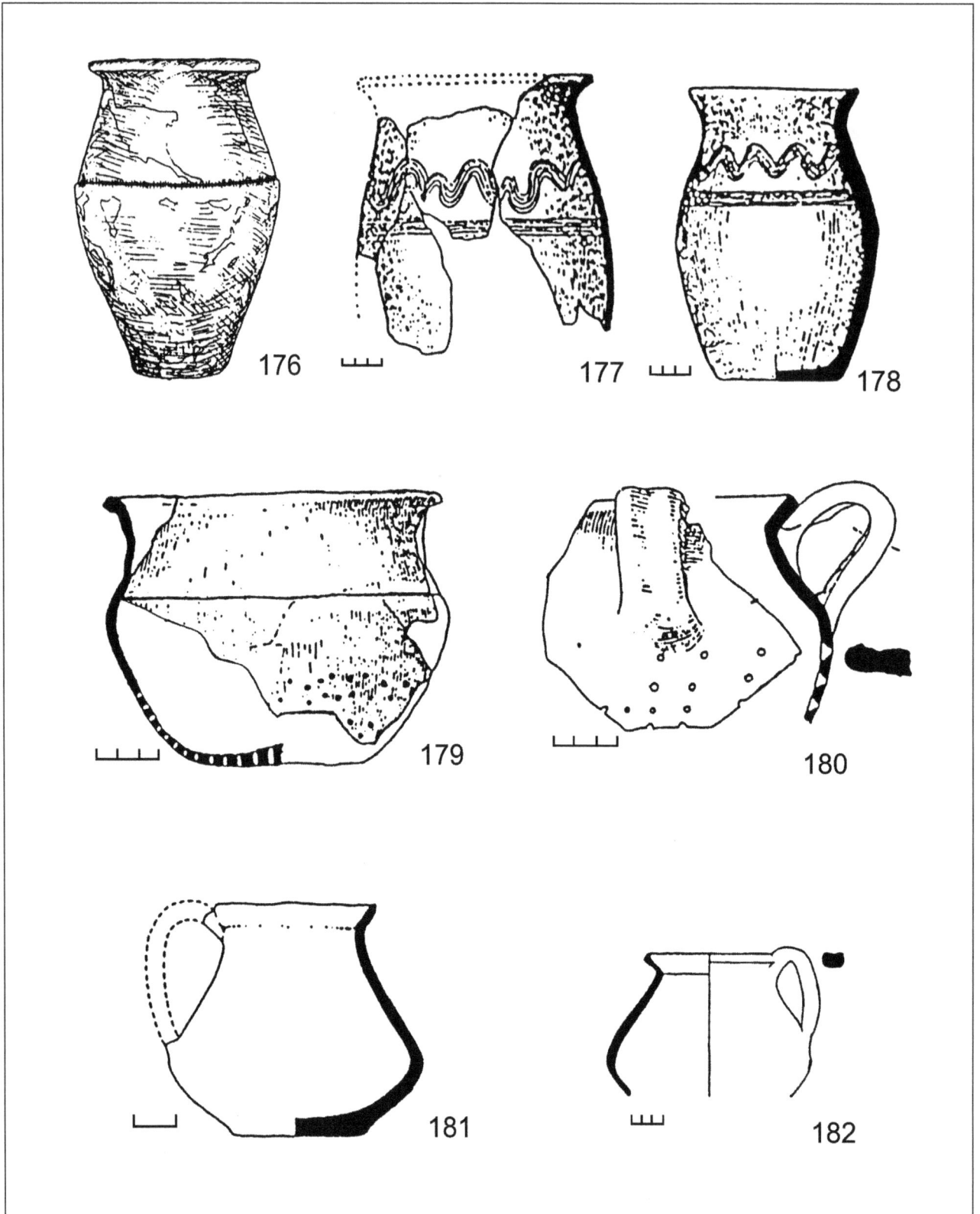

Plate 21. Wheel-made pottery. Ovoid vessels: type 1 (176); type 2 (177); pot: type 1 (179); strainers: type 1 (180); jugs: type 1 (181, 182).

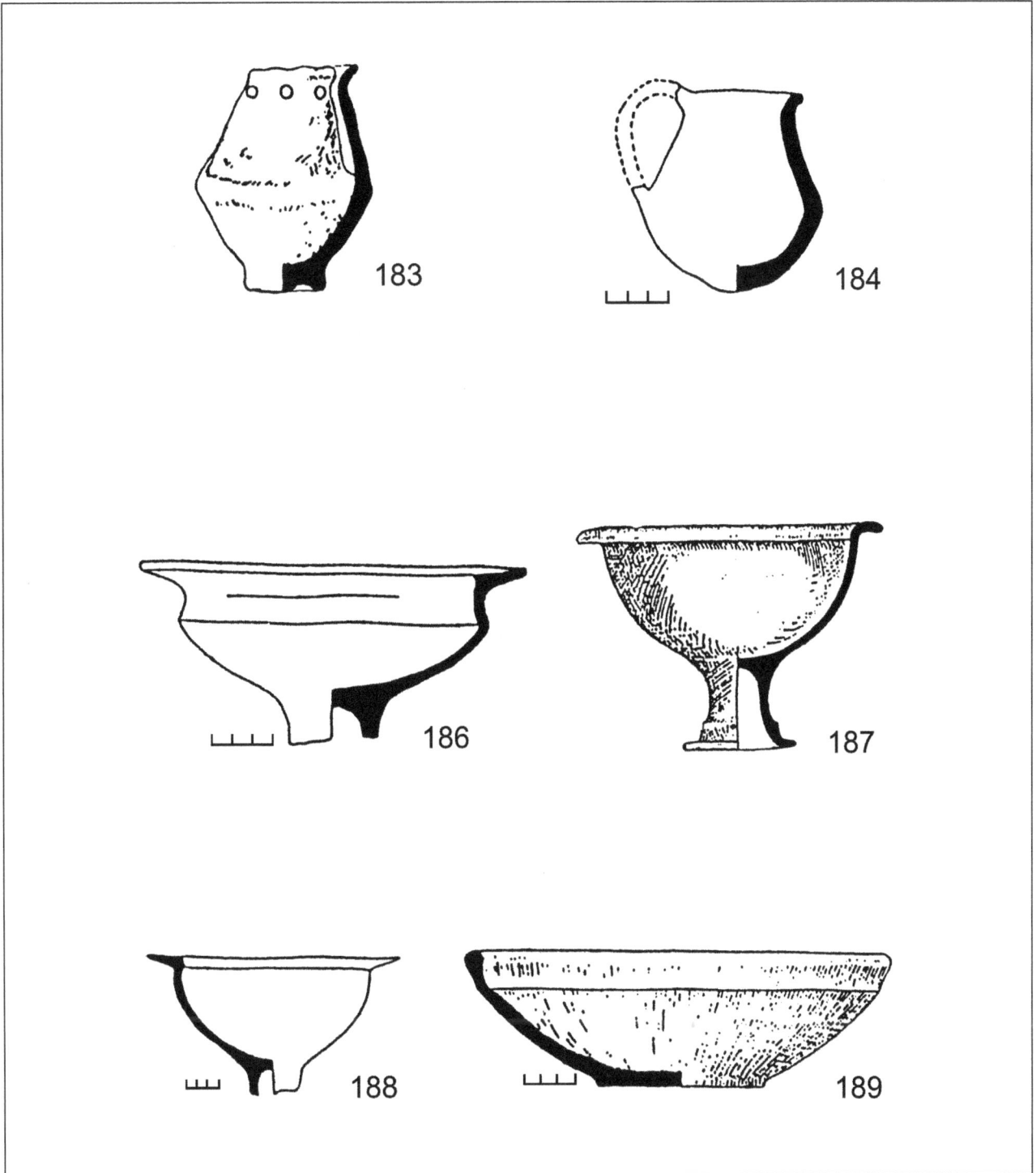

Plate 22. Wheel-made pottery. Jugs: type 1 (183, 184); fruit-bowls: type 1 (186); type 2 (1887-188); dish: type 1 (189).

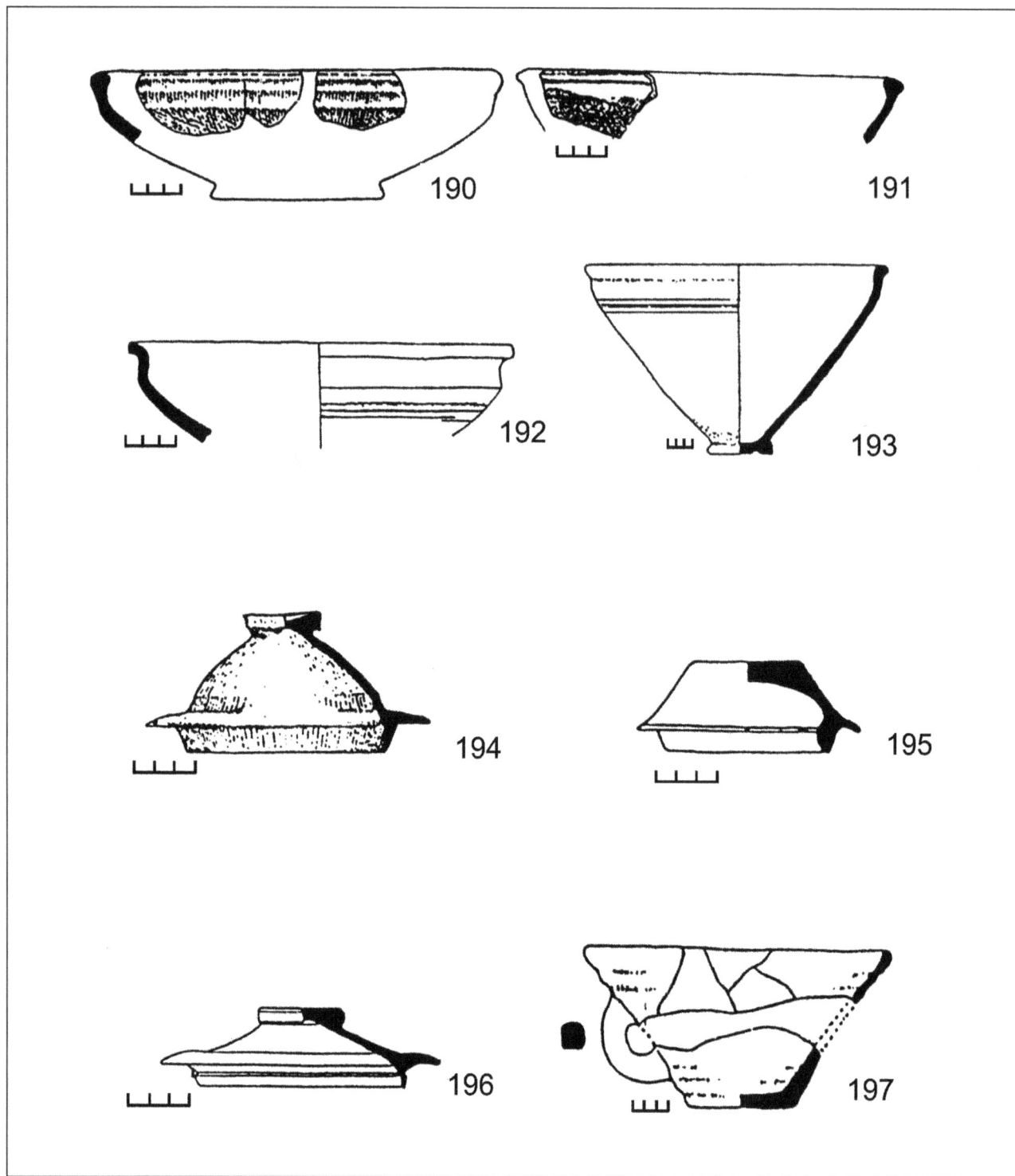

Plate 23. Wheel-made pottery. Dishes: type 1 (190-192); type 2 (193); lids: type 1 (194-195); type 2 (196); Dacian cup (197).

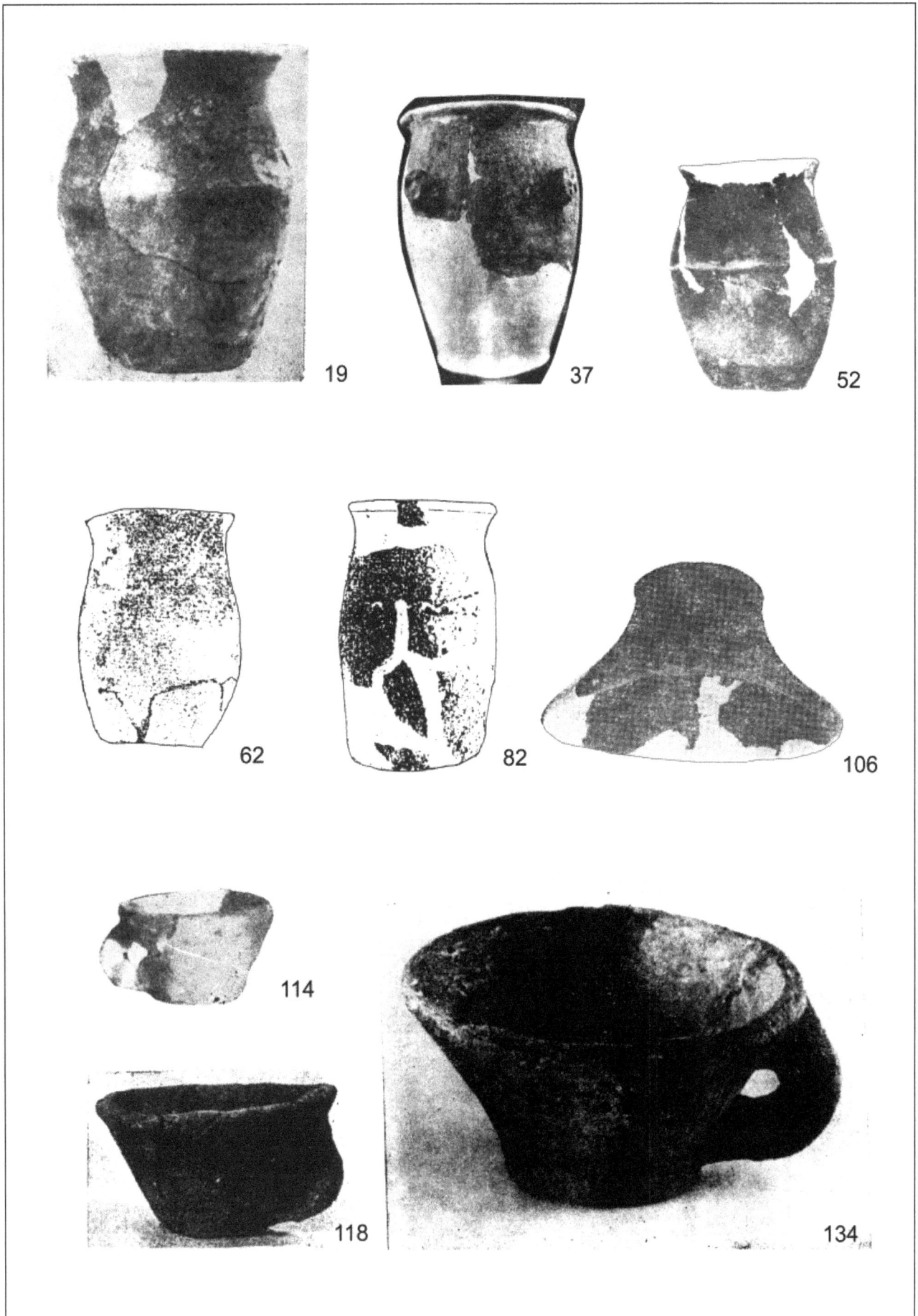

Plate 24. Hand-made pottery. Photographs (19, 37, 52, 62, 82, 106, 114, 118, 134).

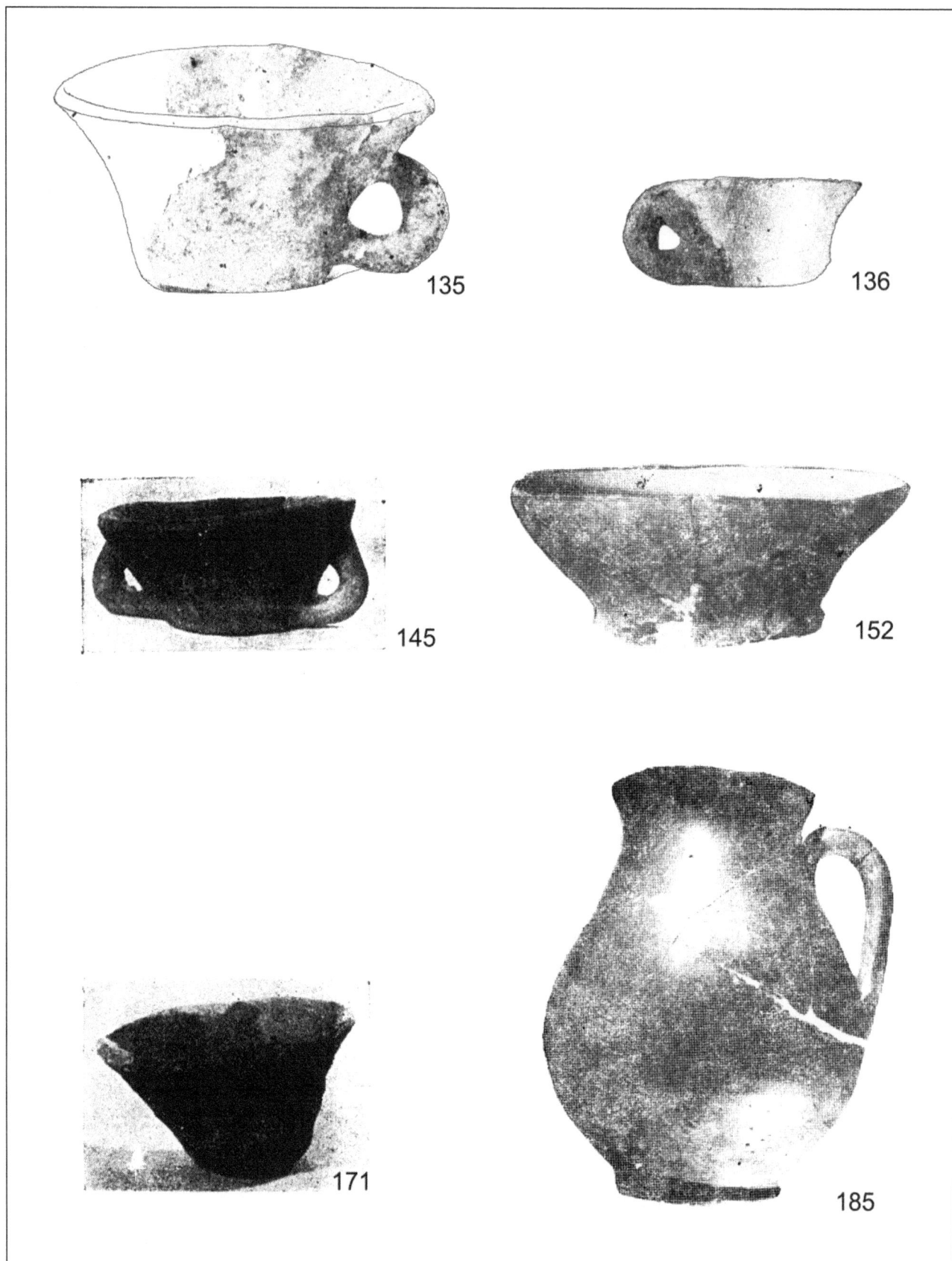

Plate 25. Hand-made and wheel-made pottery. Photographs (135-136, 145, 152, 171, 185).

www.ingramcontent.com/pod-product-compliance
Lightning Source LLC
Chambersburg PA
CBHW061006030426
42334CB00033B/3384